A Passion for the Possible

John D. Caputo, *series editor*

PERSPECTIVES IN
CONTINENTAL
PHILOSOPHY

Edited by BRIAN TREANOR
and HENRY ISAAC VENEMA

A Passion for the Possible

Thinking with Paul Ricoeur

FORDHAM UNIVERSITY PRESS
New York ▪ 2010

Library of Congress Cataloging-in-Publication Data

A passion for the possible : thinking with Paul Ricoeur / edited by Brian Treanor and Henry Isaac Venema.—1st ed.
p. cm.— (Perspectives in Continental philosophy)
Includes bibliographical references and index.
ISBN 978-0-8232-3292-5 (cloth : alk. paper)—ISBN 978-0-8232-3293-2 (pbk. : alk. paper)—ISBN 978-0-8232-3294-9 (ebook)
1. Ricoeur, Paul. 2. Christianity—Philosophy. I. Treanor, Brian. II. Venema, Henry Isaac, 1958–
B2430.R554P36 2010
194—dc22

2010011756

Printed in the United States of America
12 11 10 5 4 3 2 1
First edition

Contents

Acknowledgments

As is the case with any edited work, this collection is the result of a collaborative effort by many people. The contributors, of course, all deserve our thanks for having written such fine essays, for their willingness to answer our questions, and for their efforts to accommodate our deadlines. Their patience over the long labor of bringing this collection to press is much appreciated.

Boyd Blundell deserves special mention for not only contributing a chapter to this collection but, in addition, translating two of the other chapters. His facility with French and his close familiarity with Ricoeur's work made him a natural choice for this important task, and the editors are very grateful for his careful and conscientious work. Catherine Goldenstein and the Comité Éditorial du Fonds Ricoeur were instrumental in getting this project off the ground. We deeply appreciate being given access to Professor Ricoeur's work. David Pellauer and Richard Kearney have been enthusiastic supporters of this project since its inception during a spirited lunch at the 2005 meeting of the Society for Phenomenology and Existential Philosophy. Gitty Amini and Whitney Chelgren helped with proofreading and editing various chapters. Both have a keen editor's eye, and their helpful comments and insight improved several chapters. The editorial staff at Fordham University Press has been a pleasure to work with, patiently helping us through the process of bringing these essays to press.

The editors would like to thank the various journals and publishers that have graciously allowed us to reprint articles or parts of articles in the collection. Paul Ricoeur's "Religious Belief: The Difficult Path of the Religious" is a translation, by Boyd Blundell, of "La croyance religieuse: Le difficile chemin du religieux," which appeared in *Qu'est-ce que la culture?* edited by Yves Michaud, *Université de tous les saviors,* vol. 6 (Paris: Odile Jacob, 2001), 461–73, © Odile Jacob, 2001. David Pellauer's "Remembering Paul Ricoeur" appeared in *Philosophy Today* 51, SPEP Supplement 2007, 8–13. "Preserving the Eidetic Moment: Reflections on the Work of Paul Ricoeur" by David Rasmussen appeared in *Research in Phenomenology*, 37 no. 2 (2007): 195–202 and appears here by permission of Koninklijke BRILL NV. "Asserting Personal Capacities and Pleading for Mutual Recognition" was Paul Ricoeur's acceptance speech for the 2004 Kluge Prize in the Humanities, a transcript of which appears on the website of the Library of Congress. "Toward Which Recognition?" is a translation, by Boyd Blundell, of "Vers quelle reconnaissance?" by Jean Greisch, which appeared in the *Revue de Metaphysique et de Morale*, no. 50 (2006, issue 2), 149–71, © PUF, 2006. Some parts of Brian Treanor's "Emplotting Virtue: Narrative and the Good Life" are based on work that appeared as "*Phronesis* without a *Phronimos*: Narrative Environmental Virtue Ethics" in *Environmental Ethics* 30, no. 4 (2008): 361–79. An alternative and shorter version of Henry Venema's "The Source of Ricoeur's Double Allegiance" appears as "Twice Double Forgiveness" in *Paul Ricoeur (1913–2005): Remembering a Life, Continuing the Work*, edited by Farhang Erfani (Lanham, Md.: Lexington Books, 2009).

A Passion for the Possible

Introduction

How Much More Than the Possible?

BRIAN TREANOR AND
HENRY ISAAC VENEMA

The death of Paul Ricoeur brings to a close the brilliant career of one of the best and most important philosophers of the twentieth century. His books and essays have informed and inspired untold numbers of scholars, teachers, and intellectuals around the world, and will continue to do so for generations to come. As Ricoeur wrote, however, in memory of Emmanuel Mounier,

> One of the cruelties of death is to alter profoundly the meaning of a literary work in progress. Not only does the work no longer involve a continuation since it is finished in every sense of the word, but it is also torn away from the dialogue of questions and answers which situated its author among the living. It will forever remain a *written* work and that is all. The break with its author is final; henceforth it enters into the only history which is possible for it—that of its readers and the men whom it will inspire. In a sense, a work attains the truth of its literary existence when its author is dead: every publication and every edition begins the inexorable relationship of living men with the book of a man who is virtually dead.[1]

The "canon" is now closed, and as David Pellauer tells us, "we are able to see how much of what came later was already implicit in, if not already signaled in, [Ricoeur's] early work. . . . It is now possible, in other words, to trace lines of development in his thought because we know where they end."[2] In this sense the story is complete, Ricoeur's life has ended; but his books and essays remain open to productive interpretations.

Ricoeur has often been referred to as an occasional thinker for lack of any overall system that holds his thought together, and his oeuvre is complex and hard to assess without oversimplification. How does one remember sixty years of work, comprising thirty books and hundreds of articles?[3] While Ricoeur has written overviews of his work,[4] it remains a challenge for any reader to summarize his lifelong intellectual project. Since Ricoeur states, however, that "my life is my work, I mean, my books and my articles,"[5] and in *Time and Narrative,* but more specifically in *Oneself as Another*, he argues that personal identity is best understood as a story, it seems reasonable to assume that Ricoeur's work can be read as a story. Therefore, if we look at the path that Ricoeur's work has taken, it is fair to say that his entire project narrates a "passion for the possible" expressed in the hope that "in spite of" death, closure, and sedimentation, life is opened by the *how much more than possible* of superabundance.[6]

This narrative of the more than possible is particularly evident in Ricoeur's philosophical anthropology and his religious thought. Readers of Ricoeur are well aware that he has tried to keep his religious and philosophical writings separate. In some of his most recent essays, however, these two lines of thought intersect in a remarkable way, allowing us, as Richard Kearney points out, to read Ricoeur's work as "a medial position between 'philosophical theology' and 'theological philosophy,'"[7] or as an "eschatology of 'restored capacity'"[8] that liberates selfhood with the affirmation that "you are better than your actions"[9]: grace is possible.

Rooted in the development of Ricoeur's philosophical anthropology, the passion for the more than possible can be understood as a forward movement of liberation and freedom, described by a phenomenology of human capacity, founded on an ontology of possibility, which gives way to a *Grund/Abgrund*, the groundless ground of human being, namely, God.[10] Alternatively, we can say that there is a narrative unity to Ricoeur's work that tells a story of *the capable man*, beginning with original goodness held captive by a "servile will,"[11] and ending with the possibility of liberation and regeneration of the heart. Such a story or configuration is of course an imaginary construction, a unity of themes pulled together in convenient manner for heuristic purposes. Nevertheless, the story of the capable man, set within a phenomenology of human capacity, is for Ricoeur "a philosophical anthropology on which I risk, as it were, the meaning of my existence."[12] And for Ricoeur such meaning is profoundly religious,[13] attesting to the gift of the "Christic symbol"[14] that makes possible the experience of "regenerative power" within "the most secret level of selfhood."[15] In *Memory, History, Forgetting,* Ricoeur gives greater specificity to this narrative of the human condition as "the enigma of a fault held to paralyze the power to act of the 'capable being' that we are; and it is, in reply, the enigma of the possible lifting of this existential incapacity, designated by the term 'forgiveness.'"[16] This is a story that tells of two kinds of possibility: 1) what is already possible, described by means of a phenomenology of human capacity, expectation of what is predictable, or what Derrida calls "the programmable"; and 2) the possibility for the "more than possible," the surplus that makes all things possible in hope and love, the arrival of something more than can be measured by expectation of what is possible. To put this more theologically, these two logics of possibility are understood by Ricoeur as: 1) the Cross, the in spite of, the what is already possible, the possibility of that which is here; and 2) the Resurrection, the how much more, the possibility for, the not yet. Hence, the relation between these two logics is eschatological, "the hope of things to come," for the "God who is coming [as] opposed to the religion of the God of present manifestation."[17]

For Ricoeur this is a religious story of decentered selfhood and nonmastery that folds into a phenomenology of capacity, and vice versa. Ricoeur offers us an open-ended, multivariate, and polysemic identification of selfhood by means of the Word spoken in many ways, and by means of descriptive phenomenological words or logos of capability. The unique singularity of the Word, or the Christic symbol, calls and liberates, whereas the universality of the logos describes the capability to receive and respond to the call.[18] This is "an identity at once singularized and universalized," called to selfhood, and a logos of self that is called.[19] Hence, the story of the capable man allows us to see how Ricoeur's longheld distinction between his philosophical agnosticism and his religious commitment[20] is now, by his own admission, an artificial and unnecessary one. In fact, at a conference at Trinity College, Dublin, Ricoeur confessed: "I am beyond that."[21] Referring to himself as "a Christian who expresses himself philosophically" rather than "a Christian philosopher,"[22] Ricoeur opens up his philosophical language of "excess," "surplus," and "height" to a second religious reading. This double reference is particularly evident in Ricoeur's essay "Religious Belief: The Difficult Path of the Religious," included in this volume, where he writes:

> At the very depth of my own conviction, of my own confession, I recognize that there is a ground, which I do not control. I discern in the ground of my adherence a source of inspiration, which, by its demand for thought, its strength of practical mobilization, its

emotional generosity, exceeds my capacity for reception and comprehension.[23]

Excess and generosity are synonymous with "the idea of a source of life that fragments according to the receptive capacity of its containers,"[24] a source that gives life and calls us to live the "good life with and for others, in just institutions."[25] This source is the "capable God" that calls the capable man to selfhood.[26]

The theme of the capable man has been Ricoeur's preoccupation since his earliest publications. In *Freedom and Nature*[27] Ricoeur gives us a phenomenology of volition by describing the essential structures of the capacity to will in relation to the involuntary features of human nature. In *Fallible Man,*[28] however, Ricoeur's exploration of the capacity for evil and/or fault sets the stage for the development of "the basic powers" or "typology of basic capacities"[29] central to his most recent formulations of human capacity, as detailed by David Kaplan in his essay "Paul Ricoeur and Development Ethics."[30]

Fallible Man sets out to understand the fragility of existence that "makes man *capable* of failing,"[31] without necessitating failure. Ricoeur writes: "To say that man is fallible is to say that the limitation peculiar to a being who does not coincide with himself is the primordial weakness from which evil arises. And yet evil *arises* from this weakness only because it is *posited.*"[32] Fallibility and fault are thus distinguished from each other as the difference between the innocence of a capacity that makes possible the evil act, and the action to which we can ascribe guilt. In other words, Ricoeur initiates an analysis of the structure of capacity for evil without losing the innocence of being. As Ricoeur explains, first "we sketched the neutral sphere of man's most fundamental possibilities, or as it were, the undifferentiated keyboard upon which the guilty and the innocent man might play. . . . For fault, we said, is not a feature of fundamental ontology similar to other factors discovered by pure description, e.g., motives, powers, conditions, and limits," or the typology of basic capacities.[33] Then what *Fallible Man* attempts to explain is the point of least resistance, or "the constitutional weakness which makes evil possible."[34] Although he understands the "keyboard" of human capacity to be "by nature fragile," making humanity "liable to err,"[35] Ricoeur places the capacity to fail, and thereby *capacity as such,* at the center of human existence: *capacity is fundamental.*

The story of capable man is thus one that starts with a phenomenology of the will set within an analysis of the fallible human capacity to act; and more than forty years later, in his acceptance speech for the Kluge Prize, when Ricoeur tells us that "I identify myself by my capacities, by what I can do,"[36] he is not far removed from these early formulations. Granted that *Fallible Man* is focused on the human capacity for evil, or what we shouldn't do, it nevertheless is referring to the same "personal capacity" to do. While Ricoeur's philosophical anthropology has been significantly expanded through an exploration of "a typology of basic capacities . . . the capacity to say, the capacity to act, the capacity to recount, to which I add, imputability and promising," the structure of analysis is similar. In his Kluge Prize acceptance speech Ricoeur says: "In this vast panorama of capacities affirmed and exercised by the human agent, the main accent shifts from what seems at first a morally neutral pole to an explicitly moral pole, where the capable subject attests to himself as a responsible subject."[37] There is a surprising continuity here over this forty-year span of thought. Capacity is the neutral keyboard that makes it possible for the agents to do what they should and shouldn't do. Therefore, the story of the capable man is not a movement from fallible man to capable man; it is the story of the fundamental capacity of a fallible existence that needs the "how much more" of superabundance in its struggle to liberate goodness from incapacity, dysfunction, error, fault, sin, and evil.

The continuity between Ricoeur's early and later development of his philosophical anthropology is striking, yet there is something missing from his later work that was essential to his understanding of fallibility. In his essays "Religion and Symbolic Violence" and "Religious Belief," Ricoeur engages the remarkable work of René Girard. Stating that "I am going to take the risk of a personal interpretation of the intimate relation between religion and violence,"[38] Ricoeur goes on to say that "I found [Girard's] interpretation not only to be complementary to my own, but its necessary complement . . . not simply within the context of my own conception but in terms of what is lacking in my interpretation."[39] Ricoeur insists, however, that before he can deal with Girard's theory of mimetic imitation to supplement what is missing from his own understanding of the capable man, he "would like to plead for the thesis . . . [of] the constitutive disproportion of my human being between my finite capacity of reception [possibility 1] and the excess of the source [possibility 2] of thought(s), action(s), and feeling(s)."[40] Here Ricoeur is repeating the thesis of *Fallible Man,* which also analyzes the capacity for fallibility by means of a disproportion found in thought, action, and feeling.

What has been missing, or left aside, from Ricoeur's philosophical anthropology is not the problem of human fallibility, but the "founding dialectic" or disproportion that is constitutive of the "power to fail . . . that makes man capable of failing."[41] This is the dialectic of my finite capacity and infinite excess, or what is possible and more than I think is possible. In *Fallible Man*, Ricoeur explains that

> the theory of fallibility represents a broadening of the anthropological perspective of the first work which was more closely centered on the structure of the will. The elaboration of the concept of fallibility has provided an opportunity for a much more extensive study of the structures of human reality. The duality of the voluntary and the involuntary is brought back into a much vaster dialectic dominated by the ideas of man's disproportion, the polarity within him of the finite and the infinite, and his activity of intermediation or mediation. Man's specific weakness and his essential fallibility are ultimately sought within this structure of mediation between the pole of his finitude and the pole of his infinitude.[42]

Here we see a key feature that seems to have slipped beyond the horizon of Ricoeur's later development of *homo capax*.[43] Capacity or human ability, in *Fallible Man*, is set within the *disproportion* between "originating affirmation" and "existential difference,"[44] which once again returns to center stage on an even grander scale in his essays "Religious Belief" and "Religion and Symbolic Violence," as the *disproportion* between infinite excess and the finite limitation of human capacity. Referring to Schelling, Ricoeur explains that

> dwelling in my finite capacity is something infinite, which I would call foundational. Schelling speaks of a *Grund*, a ground or foundation, which is at the same time an *Abgrund*, an abyss, therefore a groundless ground. Here the idea of a disproportion arises which is suffered and not simply acted upon, a disproportion between what I would call the excess of the foundation, the *Grund/Abgrund*, the groundless ground, and my finite capacity of reception, appropriation, and adaptation. . . . Now rightly or wrongly, *I take the problematic of capacity and excess, and therefore disproportion to be constitutive of human being.*[45]

This reaffirmation of human existence as disproportion allows Ricoeur to combine philosophical and religious interpretations of selfhood under the single heading or location of the capable man.

In "Religious Belief," Ricoeur tells us "it is in my desire to be, in my capacity to exist, that the arrow of the religious comes to hit me. . . . It is indeed to a specific incapacity that the religious offers an answer, a word: the incapacity to do the good oneself."[46] Whereas in *Fallible Man,* Ricoeur analyzes incapacity as such, or the incapacitation of human capacity, here Ricoeur focuses our attention on the religious liberation and restoration of the original affirmation of being or "predisposition to good."[47] Religion can liberate and call the capable man to do the good, because as radical as evil may be, it is never as original as the goodness of existence and/or capacity to do the good.[48] The "function" of the religious, is, according to Ricoeur,

> the deliverance of the core of goodness from the bonds that hold it captive. It is to this deliverance that the symbol, the belief, and the community of the church wish to contribute. . . . The religious problematic can be summarized as the extraordinary capacity to make the ordinary person capable of doing the good. It is in this sense that the capable man is . . . the recipient of the religious and the carrier of religious belief.[49]

The capable man holds goodness captive, or suffers to the degree that goodness cannot be released from his or her existence, yet the capable man can be released from this kind of incapacity by the "originary source of this powerful upsurge of benevolence," by an "extraordinary" capacity or "superabundance" of love that calls us to selfhood with others in just institutions.

Referring once again to the work of Girard, Ricoeur employs Girard's theory of mimetic rivalry to indicate the way communities of faith become mimetic rivals and fall prey to the worst forms of religious violence. Rather than "any desirable object" becoming the scandal or stumbling block between rival individuals or groups, Ricoeur makes it clear that in the case of the religious, not just any object is suitable for explaining religious violence. Taking Girard's thesis to heart, Ricoeur explains:

> My suggestion is that the creative source of the process of the release of goodness, the way that Kant named—that is, by means of the great foundational symbols, the traditions of belief, and the community mediations of an ecclesial nature—that the originary source of this powerful upsurge of benevolence can be, as such, an object of mimetic rivalry, of scandal, of lynching, of the reconciliation of all against one, of the divinization of the guilty victim and the exoneration of the violent.[50]

It is in the process of naming or identifying this creative source, however, that violence erupts. The groundless ground, or "the foundation that is abyss," is for Ricoeur "the very source of life that all receive, but which one cannot encompass." Mimetic rivalry between religions tries to capture the source. "The source overflows, but the container would like to collect it all. It would like to lock it up."[51] Here, in this "dialectic of overflow and finitude," we find the heart of the religious, which is capable of liberating goodness but is also capable of violent exclusion and vain attempts to own and control the source.

This foundational dialectic, or disproportion of overflow and finitude, is for Ricoeur the key to a fluid movement between his philosophic anthropology and his religious thought. He explains that the metaphor of overflow

> easily allows interpretation in the language . . . which expresses well the conceptual thread of all my recent work: the language of capacity. There is with regard to the source of life a finite capacity of reception. It is this capacity that shapes the receptacle with the partitions that fear and hatred reinforce. It is this finite capacity that is put to the test in any religious experience, of whatever confession. One could still add to the metaphor of the source and the container, with the idea of Pascalian tonality of disproportion. The foundation, the groundless ground, is too much for our finite capacities of reception. It is through this excess, which I call *foundational excess*, that violence will slip into the Girardian model of mimetic rivalry. Another metaphorical equivalence of disproportion is that of superabundance.[52]

Here we see how the language of capacity, set within the disproportion of excess and reception, allows Ricoeur to name the source a second time as superabundance, a term synonymous with his understanding of *agape* love.[53] Superabundance thus opens the problematic of disproportion to love as gift,[54] to a "donation that precedes any collecting, transforming the donation into a threat,"[55] to an abundance of giving in the overflow of excess understood as God. Ricoeur links the naming of this excess, however, to the Babel myth of dispersion and multiplicity of speech, and therefore the naming of the source, or the naming of God,[56] shares the same polysemic structure as his philosophical anthropology, which takes "the merely analogical unity between the multiple uses of the term acting," or capacity, as the thematic unity of selfhood.[57]

In "The Self in the Mirror of the Scriptures" and "The Summoned Subject," two essays Ricoeur delivered as Gifford Lectures but excluded when the Lectures were published as part of *Oneself as Another*, he shows us how "the experience of the biblical human person," or "the believing self," is fragmented by the multiple possible responses to the multiplicity of the names of God. "This kind of polysemy, which is complementary to the typological unity of the bible, will be reflected in an equally polysemic production of the figures of the responsive self. . . . The unity of the naming [of God] is what first carried over into the secret and silence of the fact that none of the literary genres taken one at a time fully captures this Name."[58] The naming of God in the Scriptures takes place through multiple genres; therefore the "referent God is intended by convergence of all these partial discourses," but "the referent God is also the sign of the incompleteness of all the discourses of faith marked as they are by the finitude of human understanding."[59] The structure of the believing self follows from this referred/deferred unity of the "unnamable Name" of God understood as the source of excess and superabundance of love.

The capable self can now be understood as constituted by a fragmented disproportion between self and God, that polysemantically identifies God as the One who calls the "summoned subject" to respond. "What corresponds and conforms to the unity of God in the withdrawal of his name on the side of the self is the disappearance of the ego, the letting go of the self: who seeks to save his life shall lose it and who loses it will keep it. As for the quest for a personal center, it can only reflect the always deferred 'imaginative unity' conveyed by the withdrawal of the name."[60] Here we see Ricoeur's understanding of decentered selfhood, carefully developed in *Oneself as Another,* taken up into the vast "founding dialectic" of the call and withdrawal of God.

Human existence is indeed a disproportionate existence between finite capacity and the infinite excess. Such a disproportion is not, however, a barren desert space or oppositional power difference;[61] rather, as Kearney tells us, "*l'homme capable* and *le dieu capable* respond to each other in an act of daring complicity and co-creation."[62] The excess of the source is the original giving or affirmation that constitutes the space of disproportion as a loving gift, as the good gift of life more primordial than any evil act or fault; but this infinite excess is also named as the one who calls for and solicits our response in loving co-creativity that enables the release of goodness held captive by the servile will.

All the figures of the self proposed by Ricoeur in "The Summoned Subject"[63] are decentered by the Word that calls and sends, that instructs us through reading and interpretation of Scriptures, but also instructs the testimony of conscience as the word of wisdom within the most secret level of selfhood. Here within the heart of selfhood the wisdom of universal logos and the singularity of the Word speak together as one, forming "the hinge connecting historical singularity and universality."[64] To put this in theological terms, Ricoeur is proposing an intimate connection between the creative Word, the Word that calls us to selfhood, and Word made flesh.

> It can be said that wisdom is at once timeless and daily. As immemorial, wisdom joins the beginning celebrated in the creation stories, and through them joins the creative word. This is the meaning of Proverbs 8, where wisdom personified speaks in the first person and declares itself older than creation itself. . . . "With wisdom, Israel rejoiced in being universal, but it is still Israel." This declaration could not be without an echo among the Christian gentiles: its ecclesiology is invited to assume the new singularity from which it proceeds, the Christic singularity, but by relocating it within the horizon of the new universality expressed in the terms of the Greek Logos.[65]

Selfhood is at its very core a self that has the capacity to respond to the other, in particular, to respond to the source that has been given as the Word/gift of the goodness of existence, and the Word/call releasing us from what was hidden in the heart all along, namely the good gift of life understood as fallible goodness. While we have the capacity to fail, human capacity is first and foremost our capacity to hear the call that has gifted life and to receive the goodness of the overflow of the excess, gift, and generosity that comes from a groundless ground that the believing heart names as God, and calls upon in the intimacy of prayer.

The multiple figures of the summoned self are part of an expanded understanding of Ricoeur's philosophical anthropology of disproportionate capacity. Starting with *Fallible Man* as disproportion of thought, action, and the affective fragility of our desire to be, Ricoeur opens this dialectic of human capacity to a groundless ground as overflow and excess, and wagers that it is the source of divine superabundance expressed through the Christic symbol. Fragmented by the polysemy of the names of God, the fragmented self is nevertheless unified by the response to the call of God to engage in acts of forgiveness, generosity, and love. Believers are

> invited to identify themselves with the book that itself stems from the metaphorical identification between the Word of God and the person of Christ. Through this second-degree identification, readers are equally invited to "repeat"—in the Kierkegaardian sense of "repetition"—the pulsation between the withdrawal of the name and the quest for the center.[66]

The believing self is thus one that identifies with the Word of God, and at the same time finds its identity, as St. Paul says, "hid in Christ," hidden in a source that "exceeds my capacity for reception and comprehension."[67] Therefore, the summoned self repeats the "pulsation" of the decentered-center of the God who gives and calls, by letting go of the ego for the sake of the one who calls the subject to selfhood, or as Ricoeur has so often said, "the exchange of the *me, master* of itself, for the *self, disciple* of the [other]."[68]

The philosophy of the capable man describes the possibilities of human capacity; but such description is incomplete without the extraordinary capacity of superabundance. This is why Ricoeur's understanding of the capable man is inescapably hermeneutical. To understand selfhood is to understand oneself as capable of responding to the call. To hear the call is to receive the immemorial gift daily. To respond to the call is to live the gift of life. Hence, the gift of the possibilities of human capacity [possibility 1], and the call of "the how much more than possible" [possibility 2], offer an interesting story or narrative account of Ricoeur's work.[69] If this story rings true, then perhaps we need to understand Ricoeur's oeuvre not simply as a phenomenology of capacity, but as a hermeneutic of a *"historically incarnated religious consciousness"*[70] capable of responding as gift to the call of the other, and incarnating a Word that can make the desert bloom.

The remarkable feature in this reading of Ricoeur's work is fluidity of movement between phenomenological and religious interpretation of the capable self. If *Oneself as Another* is Ricoeur's best description of these various anthropological capacities, it must be remembered that all these abilities are intersubjectively structured, or constitutionally open to others, otherness, and the divine Other. Human capacities are place markers of self location only in relation to various forms of otherness that together constitute the space of selfhood as oneself as another and another as oneself. The self is therefore marked at all levels of existence by receptivity to that which is more than the simple repetition of same [possibility 1], and by an excess of my finite capacity to know, apprehend, and understand [possibility 2]. While Ricoeur has reintroduced the category of disproportion by way of the religious description of finite capacity and infinite excess, we can now see how this disproportion of possibility is already inscribed within each individual human capacity.[71] Hence any level of capacity can be enlarged or contracted, moving from a single capacity to the source of all capacity, and at each stage of analysis disproportionate capacity can be expressed in either philosophical or religious discourse. In fact, we would argue that Ricoeur is simply acknowledging that if the capable man can be spoken of in many ways, as can the ontology of capacity, as well as the names of God, so too can disproportion itself be spoken in many ways. The hermeneutic circle can be drawn tightly and focused on a single capacity, or it can be expanded to include the height of height itself. Either approach finds the description of human capacity structurally open to the more than possible, and open to multiple interpretations, such as those included in this volume.

When Paul Ricoeur passed away, French Prime Minister Jean-Pierre Raffarin said, "We lose today more than a philosopher. . . . The entire European humanist tradition is mourning one of its most talented spokesmen." In 1994, Ricoeur's humanism was recognized when he was awarded (along with co-recipient Jaroslav Pelikan) the Kluge Prize in the Humanities. This prestigious award, given by the Library of Congress, is often referred to informally as the "Nobel Prize in the Humanities." Ricoeur was awarded the prize for his lifetime of philosophical inquiry, which "draws on the entire tradition of western philosophy to explore and explain common problems."

In his acceptance speech for the Kluge Prize, "Asserting Personal Capacities and Pleading for Mutual Recognition," Ricoeur probes the sources of his humanism.

He begins by characterizing personal identity in terms of capacities that only find their full expression in intersubjective encounters with others. These capacities—and the vulnerabilities that are their ineluctable counterpart—constitute the primary foundation of being human: the capacity to say; the capacity to act; the capacity to recount; and the capacity to impute and to promise. Each of these capacities, however, demands recognition from others. "What is missing, however, in this listing of how others are implied in the private certainty of the capacity to act, is reciprocity, mutuality, which alone allow us to speak of recognition in the strong sense." Although the demand for mutuality is not without struggle, Ricoeur takes pains to distinguish his approach from a Hobbesian struggle of all against all. Reciprocity, he insists, and the moral character of the social bond, are irreducible. We experience actual recognition in peaceful modes as well, as in the ceremonial exchanges of gifts in traditional societies, which are noneconomic and follow a logic of reciprocity that creates mutuality. The same phenomenon persists in our own society in, for example, holidays and celebrations with family and friends. Where does this obligation come from? Ricoeur does not hesitate: "I prefer to follow those who see in the exchange of gifts a recognition of each by the other, a recognition unaware of itself as such, and symbolized in the thing exchanged, which becomes its pledge. This indirect recognition would be the peaceful counterpart to the struggle for recognition. In it, the mutuality of the social bond would find its expression."

Ricoeur's second contribution to this volume, "Religious Belief: The Difficult Path of the Religious," is an excellent example of his treatment of many of the themes we have highlighted in this introduction: a blurring of the division between Ricoeur's philosophical thinking and his theological thinking; his anthropology of the capable man; the groundless ground (*Grund/Abgrund*); and the priority of goodness over evil. He begins the essay by asking the question, "who is the bearer of religious belief?" Ricoeur finds the answer in his analysis of the capable man, the acting and suffering subject who he describes in terms of the capacities and incapacities associated with speaking, doing, telling, and imputing responsibility. Following Kant, Ricoeur adds the religious problematic to this description through a meditation on evil, claiming that religion offers an answer to a specific incapacity in man: the incapacity to do good oneself. Like Kant, he emphasizes the priority of our "predisposition to good" over our "propensity to evil." Religion functions as a sort of "deliverance of the core of goodness from the bonds that hold it captive," the "extraordinary capacity to make the ordinary person capable of doing the good."

Nevertheless, as the title of the essay suggests, the path of the religious is beset with significant difficulties, most notably charges of intolerance and violence. Here Ricoeur follows for a time René Girard's famous account of *mimetic rivalry*; he ultimately finds Girard's account unfulfilling, however, because of a "missing link" concerning mimetic rivalry in the case of the religious: "the pretension to monopolize the source." Religions are, like languages and cultures, subject to dispersion and confusion (as related in the Hebraic myth of Babel). The radical fragmentation of religion, combined with the inevitable overflow of the "source" of goodness when placed in the finite "receptacle" of any concrete religious community, leads to the violence of exclusion and forced inclusion. Against this tendency to intolerance and violence, Ricoeur deploys religious "resources of self-criticism mobilized by the intelligence of faith." Building on his work on the capable man, Ricoeur points to our finite capacity of reception, which puts to the test any and all religious experience. Ultimately, we are called to a higher form of tolerance, in which "I recognize that there is a ground which I do not control . . . [which] exceeds my capacity for reception and comprehension."

In "Remembering Paul Ricoeur," David Pellauer gives us a call to action. This essay, first delivered at the 2006 meeting of the Society for Phenomenology and Existential Philosophy, asks us to move beyond grief at Ricoeur's passing and to focus on his work. Ricoeur, Pellauer says, "never wanted or encouraged a school" and would be dismayed by a Ricoeur Society (though inevitably, and appropriately, one now exists). Pellauer can imagine Ricoeur urging us, "Talk about my philosophy, about philosophy, not about me."

Nevertheless, Ricoeur's passing has fundamentally altered our relationship to his work. The canon has closed. We can now see his work as a whole, we can trace the lines of development in his thought because we know where they end, and we know where those lines lead. In hindsight we can, for example, now see how much of his later work was implicit in or signaled by his earlier work. Ricoeur was an "occasional" and "piecemeal" thinker, however, a man who worked on the problems that interested him rather than following philosophical fads, although he was also attentive to the philosophical trends around him. Given the character of his thinking, what, Pellauer asks, would it mean for us "to take seriously the work" that Ricoeur produced?

He cautions us against turning our work into "a kind of Ricoeur-scholasticism, *exposés des textes* that do not take seriously that Ricoeur's thought was given to us as something to build on, not something just to repeat in a reverent voice." Although there are important questions internal to Ricoeur's work, Pellauer claims there is more to be gained by taking up Ricoeur's thought and building on it, something several of the essays in this volume attempt to do. Pellauer also reminds us that Ricoeur provided not only exceptional philosophical insights, lines of thought worth pursuing and developing, but also an exemplary model of how to *do* philosophy—one that sought truth not through polemics but by *thinking with* others in order to advance knowledge and understanding. Pellauer demonstrates his commitment to this spirit, ending his essay by pointing us toward some of the work to be done—clarifying Ricoeur's movement beyond the still-prevalent Cartesian model of the self—and offering us a compelling example of how to think with Paul Ricoeur.

In "Capable Man, Capable God," Richard Kearney argues that Ricoeur was, among other things, a philosopher of *possibility.* He suggests that, by remaining attentive to both human fallibility and human capability, Ricoeur charts a *via media* between extremes, wagering that "human existence [is], in all its frailty and finitude, *capable of meaningful being in spite of everything.*" Ricoeur's ontology of the possible is manifest throughout his work, but especially in the work that occupied his final years, including reflections on *l'homme capable* and its counterpart, *le dieu capable.* With respect to the former Kearney situates his teacher and friend between "traditional metaphysics, which thinks being in terms of presence or substance, and skeptical deconstruction, which often considers being a screen against the radical alterity of the other." Ricoeur's habit of detour and return engages possibility in Aristotle, Spinoza, Leibniz, Heidegger, and Merleau-Ponty, among others, and touches on epistemological, moral, and practical aspects of possibility. These aspects are, in turn, expressed personally and interpersonally. "One does not simply act for oneself; one acts for or against others." One area of particular concern is Ricoeur's analysis of justice and his associated concern with forgiveness. "*Dunamis* is never just an abstract metaphysical concept for Ricoeur. It *matters*, it *counts*, it *affects* the lives of really existing and suffering human beings." Forgiveness is difficult, but, *pace* Derrida, not impossible. In forgiving the other we restore her capacity to act, recognizing that she is capable of things other than her offenses and faults, telling her "you are better than your actions." Finally, Ricoeur's meditations on *l'homme capable* point toward his interest in the idea of a *dieu capable*. Greek ontology and biblical theology do not present us with an either/or—Athens or Jerusalem; rather, the crossing of these two traditions results in an enlargement of ontology, facilitating its encounter with an eschatology of the possible. The latter is articulated in terms of promise, a promise of living up to death.

Henry Isaac Venema addresses Ricoeur's "double allegiance" to philosophical and religious thought. Venema asks what we should make of these "two legs" that support Ricoeur's work. What is the point of intersection between the philosophical and the religious? Venema locates the key to addressing this question in Ricoeur's "Difficult Forgiveness," the epilogue to *Memory, History, Forgetting*. The challenge of forgiveness lies in the problematic relationship between action and agent. On the one hand, I am accountable for all my actions; they are imputed to me and I am bound to them. On the other hand, forgiveness is supposed to unbind an action from an agent so that she is no longer accountable for what was done. This supposed unbinding presents us, however, with a cluster of significant problems. How can we separate an action from an agent in such a way that the action is no longer ascribed to who one is? Assuming we can do so, would separating the action from the agent make forgiveness itself guilty of a kind of immorality? Finally, if an evil action is avowed by an agent who binds herself to her acts, we have an impossible condition for unconditional forgiveness. Venema argues that Ricoeur has a keen appreciation for both the vertical relation between the depth of fault and the height of forgiveness, which is not subject to calculation, and for the horizontal relation of calculated and reciprocal exchange, in which forgiveness is subject to calculation. The height of forgiveness, however, demands that we move beyond economic, symmetrical forgiveness, that we bridge the gap between the conditional and the unconditional. This, argues Venema, is what Ricoeur means by "difficult forgiveness." How is this possible? "Evil action can be unbound from the heart of selfhood because the heart is never completely incapable of beginning again." In spite of all the difficulties, there is forgiveness. No matter how radical evil is, it is not as primordial as goodness. Forgiveness says, "you are better than your actions." The resources for such unconditional forgiveness can only be expressed in the language of hope. According to Ricoeur such claims are perfectly in line with his philosophy of action, based on the philosophical anthropology of the capable man. Venema suggests, however, that Ricoeur can attest to the unconditionality of forgiveness because it is another name for the God of the Bible who forgives unconditionally.

Gaëlle Fiasse sheds light on the difficulties of interpretation concerning the Golden Rule in Ricoeur's ethics. She argues that Ricoeur belongs to the group of philosophers (Levinas, Derrida, et al.) concerned with otherness. However, while Ricoeur shares their concern with the other and with otherness, he does not share their allergy to reciprocity. Rather, he acknowledges the asymmetry necessary in ethical relationship, without ignoring the ethical place of reciprocity. Ricoeur's approach includes both a teleological, ethical aspect based on Aristotle and a deontological, moral aspect based on Kant. He sees these two aspects as complementary rather than competing, and his interpretation of the Golden Rule provides an example of the bridge connecting these apparently incommensurate approaches. The Golden Rule "serves as a transition from the solicitude of friendship to the formal rule of the Kantian imperative." While the Golden Rule illustrates the importance of reciprocity in Ricoeur's ethics, Fiasse argues that what Ricoeur means by "reciprocity" is central to understanding both his interpretation of the Golden Rule and his "little ethics."

The Golden Rule does not involve a logic of reciprocity in the sense of a reaction to the benevolence of the other. Indeed, we can act according to the Golden Rule prior to being in a reciprocal relationship. Nevertheless, in seeing the other as oneself, a "mutuality" is established, one that retains the dissymmetry necessary to preserve the otherness of the other. In addition, Ricoeur's logic of superabundance suggests that the Golden Rule is itself based on a deeper call to love or, better, the call *of* love (*le commandement de l'amour*). As God loves me, I love the other. "The gift calls for another gift, but gratuitousness prevails over any kind of obligation or calculation of returns."

The Golden Rule is also the key to understanding the theme of forgiveness. Ricoeur does not want to start, as does Derrida, with the idea of impossible forgiveness. Rather, he speaks of "difficult forgiveness." Despite all the challenges and potential corruptions, there is forgiveness; forgiveness, like love, remains. Hope, Fiasse argues, is the critical component of this account. In following the Golden Rule, we cannot expect or demand reciprocity; and in forgiving the other we know she may not acknowledge or recognize her fault. Nevertheless, we may hope for a response, and that hope helps to sustain our "limited ability to love absolutely."

In "Toward Which Recognition?" Jean Greisch argues that Ricoeur's last book, *The Course of Recognition*, offers us an "invitation to reread Ricoeur's philosophical path as the slow and patient beginning of an unfinished, and by definition unfinishable, work of recognition." Read in this way, Greisch suggests the addition of the dimension of "recognition-exploration" to the three conceptual foci of this final work: recognition-identification; self-recognition; and mutual recognition. He connects this concern with recognition to the rest of Ricoeur's oeuvre. Beginning with an examination of *Fallible Man* and *The Symbolism of Evil*, Greisch argues that Ricoeur's well-known claim that "the symbol which gives rise to thought" is, by definition, a form of recognition. Ricoeur's attempt, in *Oneself as Another*, to reconcile Aristotle's *phronesis*, Kant's *Moralitat*, and Hegel's *Sittlichkeit* is, says Greisch, the "first work of recognition." This work points the way toward a phenomenology of the capable human, a theme Ricoeur returns to in *The Course of Recognition*.

Greisch then traces the development of the course of recognition in Ricoeur's final work, paying close attention, in turn, to recognition as identification, the recognition of oneself, and mutual recognition, offering an illuminating analysis of each of these dimensions of recognition. Confronted with the challenges associated with struggles for recognition in the third moment—multiculturalism, the recognition of disadvantaged minorities—Ricoeur points to the "small miracles" of mutual recognition. He evaluates these instances in terms of *philia*, *eros*, and *agape*. His analysis of the latter concept, especially his defense of the possibility of bridging the gap between a poetics of *agape* and a prose of justice, lead Greisch to conclude that Ricoeur finds himself, "once again," *pontifex maximus* of contemporary philosophy.

In "Paul Ricoeur and Development Ethics," David M. Kaplan focuses on parallels between the philosophical project of Paul Ricoeur and the economic development ethics of Amartya Sen (as well as the philosophical work of Martha Nussbaum). Kaplan argues that there is a fundamental similarity between the projects of Ricoeur and Sen, insofar as both "take the notion of human capability as the central descriptive and normative feature of human existence." By developing the congruencies and incongruencies between these thinkers, Kaplan hopes to open a dialogue between theory and practice, between a hermeneutics of the self and development ethics. Ricoeur—whose *l'homme capable* is "both descriptive and normative"—is attracted to Sen's account of human capability, and both argue that human capabilities—seen as social capabilities related to social practices—"define our humanity as it is and as it should become." Kaplan argues, however, that Ricoeur's work makes several distinct contributions to the field of development ethics.

First, Ricoeur clarifies how the imagination "directs and affects capabilities," which has "tremendous relevance for the development of ethics." For example, Ricoeur's work argues that imagination affects action as well as meaning, augmenting an account such as Nussbaum's. Second, Ricoeur's approach ties capabilities to the vulnerabilities within which they are framed, suggesting that the capabilities approach of Sen and Nussbaum needs to be complemented by a "vulnerabilities approach." Finally, Ricoeur argues that political power is always paradoxical and, therefore, "However noble the call to expand the notion of capabilities might be, we should be wary of the authority that would enforce such an expanded notion of rights. . . . As more aspects of life are politicized, we become more susceptible to political abuses."

Ellen Herda, herself an anthropologist and development worker with the Mlabri people of Southeast Asia, offers a view from the field in her essay, "Narrative Matters among the Mlabri: Interpretive Anthropology in International Development." Herda argues that Ricoeur's work on narrative imagination and narrative identity can be especially useful for the development anthropologist. Traditional top-down development practices are ineffective because, in addition to reducing progress to economic growth, they depend on the imposition of an external model on those they intend to help. Bottom-up development, intending to redress the problems of the top-down model, has nevertheless relied on an inadequate model of the self. Ricoeur's anthropology of the capable man gives us a model that emphasizes the capacity of a self to inhabit a new world. The Mlabri initially had a sense of time that addressed the past and present, but not the future; the development response required introducing a space for expectation, the sense that the future could be different from the past. Herda's development work required helping the Mlabri to imagine, through narrative, an alternative future that would liberate them from their past (a way of life that was no longer possible) and their present (living in very challenging circumstances in what amounts to servitude under other ethnic groups in Thailand).

In "The Place of Remembrance: Reflections on Paul Ricoeur's Theory of Collective Memory," Jeffrey Andrew Barash calls our attention to Ricoeur's work on collective memory. Memory, according to Ricoeur, is itself a matter of "civic concern" through the theme of "just memory." Thus, remembering and forgetting have genuinely political manifestations. Barash affirms Ricoeur's desire to steer between the social atomism of Locke—where personal identity extends only so far as remembrance—and a theory of collective memory—like that of Halbwachs, which accounts for personal consciousness in terms of the social collective wherein "our social milieu expresses itself in us." Ricoeur, in contrast, seeks a way that will account for both the autonomy of personal experience and the extra-personal dimension of communal experience. Inspired by Husserl, he finds this third way in the extension of individual consciousness and memory to collective memory, expressed in the moral category of debt and the "obligation to remember," and in the "work of memory" inspired by psychoanalysis. Collective memory exists between the poles of 1) the multitude of perspectives retained by personal memories, and 2) the symbolic embodiment of memory constituting an identifiable locus. According to Barash, however, Ricoeur's emphasis on personal experience and memory comes at the cost of obscuring the symbolic aspects of collective memory, leading him to question whether or not Ricoeur's categories (e.g., the duty to remember, the work of memory) actually help to illuminate collective memory.

Ricoeur's philosophical project is characterized by the pattern of detour and return. In "Refiguring Virtue," Boyd Blundell uses Ricoeur's philosophical project as a detour for theologian James Keenan's work on virtue ethics. The resurgence of interest in virtue ethics has helped to shift ethical analysis away from the act and back toward the person, a movement eminently congenial to Ricoeur's work on personal identity. What should the moral agent look like? Virtues do not exist in a vacuum, which is problematic because contemporary anthropology has changed drastically from the anthropology of Aristotle or Aquinas. If Keenan hopes to reevaluate and update the cardinal virtues, the anthropology underlying those virtues needs to be reconsidered as well. Blundell finds in Ricoeur's work on personal identity, and ethics, a relational anthropology to fit Keenan's project.

Blundell sees "a striking number of similarities" between Keenan's proposed new cardinal virtues—fidelity, self-care, justice, and prudence—and Ricoeur's anthropology and analysis of the ethical perspective.

Ricoeur's account of self-esteem, solicitude, and justice map nicely, although not seamlessly, onto Keenan's self-care, fidelity, and justice. Prudence, however, cannot "survive this refiguring process unaltered." Indeed, the changes are so dramatic that Blundell recommends we bypass the Latin *prudentia* in translating *phronesis* in favor of translating *phronesis* as "practical wisdom." On Blundell's account, practical wisdom still aids us in hitting the golden mean; that mean is no longer represented, however, by a point on a line between two extremes, as in Aristotle. Rather, Blundell's new mean is planar, mediating between and balancing the three points of a triangle, representing the virtues of self-care, fidelity, and justice.

Like Blundell, Brian Treanor focuses on the virtue ethics component of Ricoeur's "little ethics," in which he finds rich resources for the development of virtue theory in light of Ricoeur's account of narrative identity. Treanor claims that virtue ethics—which, due to its nature, has always been general rather than specific, and flexible rather than dogmatic—faces serious challenges in the contemporary, postmodern context. Today the metanarratives that frame any picture of human flourishing—and, therefore, any virtue ethics in the Aristotelian, eudaimonistic tradition—come into contact with other, conflicting metanarratives as never before. The resulting incredulity toward metanarratives undermines confidence—not only confidence in individual metanarratives, but confidence in the very ideas of right and wrong, virtue and vice. The result is that the challenges associated with 1) identifying a model of flourishing and the virtues that constitute it, and 2) cultivating those virtues in oneself, are exacerbated by our postmodern condition.

Treanor argues, however, that Ricoeur's account of narrative identity, in particular his account of *mimesis*, contains resources that help us to confront these challenges. Indeed, he suggests that all virtue ethics are by nature narrative virtue ethics. Treanor contends that narratives can help us to distinguish between various models of flourishing, and can help us to identify good models and the virtues that constitute them. Moreover, basing his argument on Ricoeur's account of the way in which narratives change the identity of the reader, he maintains that narratives can, in some measure, help us to cultivate virtues in ourselves. Finally, by putting a face to ethical arguments, an emphasis on the narrative aspect of virtue ethics diminishes the appeal of exaggerated sorts of relativism, while preserving the flexibility of virtue ethics and the consequent aversion to rigid dogmatism.

In "Preserving the Eidetic Moment," David Rasmussen illustrates how, as Ricoeur's own work underwent a transition from eidetic phenomenology to hermeneutic phenomenology, Ricoeur developed a unique approach to the philosophy of language. Along the path from symbol and myth to metaphor and narrative, Ricoeur maintained a "passion for the nature of the self, the subject, personal identity—in phenomenological terms, subjectivity." He is the only philosopher of language who was able to maintain a sort of fidelity to phenomenology's early emphasis on subjectivity and individuality, retaining a "Husserlian preoccupation with subjectivity." This preoccupation was the result of Ricoeur's lifelong concern with the problem of the freedom of the will, the opposite of which is not limited to the bodily involuntary, but includes the hermeneutics of evil, "the self embroiled in its own inarticulate articulation expressed in the symbols of stain, sin, and guilt." Ricoeur's response, however, is not Nietzschean, but the "archaism of singular expression. . . . At the heart of language he would find something like subjectivity—the triumph of singular expression, the language of avowal." His theory of interlocution, based on *ipséité*, is able to overcome the problem of identity in the philosophy of language because he maintains the uniqueness of subjectivity while simultaneously affirming the continuity of identity as narrative identity. In doing so he provides us with a more compelling response to the problems that Husserl grappled with in his celebrated *Fifth Cartesian Meditation*. Ricoeur's work in this area contributes to philosophical work in other areas as well. When narrative identity is written into a theory of interlocution, it becomes "fraught with ethical obligation." Thus, Ricoeur's philosophy of narrative helps us to think through a variety of ethical problems, including the issue of global and cosmopolitan justice.

Together, the essays in this collection illustrate the remarkable fecundity of Ricoeur's thought. Our contributors have been inspired by both the diversity of his work—which can be seen in the "occasional" nature of his thinking pointed out by David Pellauer and in the pattern of "detour and return" that fascinates Boyd Blundell—and, paradoxically, by its persistent attention to the themes of subjectivity, identity, capability, evil, and forgiveness. The paradox of the unity and diversity of Ricoeur's work should not trouble readers of this volume. In his first major work, Ricoeur claims that "assurance of resolution is always the covert reason for paradox: in a certain way we are always confident of the unity of what we break up as we conceive of it."[72] Ricoeur himself is the source of the underlying unity that connects the various contributions to this collection, which represent diverse attempts to think with Paul Ricoeur and, in doing so, to remember and honor him.

Asserting Personal Capacities and Pleading for Mutual Recognition

PAUL RICOEUR

I

The prize with which I have been honored by the John W. Kluge Center at the Library of Congress, and for which I extend my sincere thanks, is motivated by the humanism attributed to my life's work by these generous benefactors. The reflections that follow are devoted to examining some of the bases of this humanism.

My title is twofold: it designates, on the one hand, the capacities that a human agent attributes to himself and, on the other, the recourse to others required to give to this personal certainty a social status. The stakes shared by both poles of this duality are those of personal identity. I identify myself by my capacities, by what I can do. The individual designates himself as a capable human being—and we must add, as a suffering human being—to underscore the vulnerability of the human condition.

Capacities can be observed from outside, but they are fundamentally felt, lived in the mode of certainty. The latter is not a belief, considered a lesser degree of knowledge. It is rather a confident assurance, akin to testimony. I am speaking here of attestation: attestation relates to the self as testimony relates to an event, a meeting, an accident.

It is possible to establish a typology of basic capacities, at the intersection of the innate and the acquired. These basic powers constitute the primary foundation of humanity, in the sense of the human as opposed to the nonhuman. Change, which is an aspect of identity—that of ideas and things—reveals a dramatic aspect on the human level, which is that of a personal history entangled in the innumerable histories of our companions in existence. Personal identity is marked by a temporality that can be called constitutive. The person is his or her history. In the typological outline I am proposing, I consider in turn the capacity to say, the capacity to act, and the capacity to recount, to which I add imputability and promising. In this vast panorama of capacities affirmed and exercised by the human agent, the main accent shifts from what seems at first a morally neutral pole to an explicitly moral pole, where the capable subject attests to himself as a responsible subject. A few words about each of these capacities: By *the power to say,* I mean a more specific capacity than the general gift of language expressed in the plurality of languages, each with its morphology, lexicon, syntax, and rhetoric. The power to say is the ability spontaneously to produce a reasoned discourse. In discourse someone says something to someone in accordance with common rules. "Saying something" is the sense; "about something" is the reference to the extralinguistic; "to someone" is the address, the basis of conversation. By the *power to act* I mean the capacity to produce events in society and in nature. This intervention transforms the notion of events, which are not only what occurs. It introduces human contingency, uncertainty, and unpredictability into the course of affairs.

The *power to recount* occupies a preeminent place among the capacities, inasmuch as events of every kind become discernable and intelligible only when recounted in stories; the age-old art of recounting stories, when applied to oneself, produces life narratives articulated in the works of historians. Emplotment marks a bifurcation in identity itself. Identity is no longer simply sameness. In self-identity, change is integrated as peripeteia. We can then speak of a narrative identity: it is that of the plot of a narrative that remains unfinished and open to the possibility of being recounted differently, and also of being recounted by others.

Imputability constitutes what is clearly a moral capacity. A human agent is held to be the genuine author of his acts, regardless of the force of organic and physical causes. Imputability, assumed by the agent, makes him responsible, capable of ascribing to himself his portion of the consequences. If harm is done to others, the way is opened to reparation and to final sanction.

Promising is possible on this basis. The subject commits himself by his word and says that he will do what he says. The promise limits the unpredictability of the future, at the risk of betrayal. The subject must keep his promise—or break it. He thereby engages the promise of the promise, that of keeping his word, of being faithful.

II

At first sight these basic capacities do not imply any demand for recognition on the part of others; the certainty of being able to do something is private. To be sure. Yet each of them requires a vis-à-vis. Discourse is addressed to someone capable of responding, questioning, entering into conversation and dialogue. Action occurs in conjunction with other agents, who can help or hinder. The narrative assembles multiple protagonists within a single plot. A life story is made up of a multitude of other life stories. As for imputability, frequently raised by accusation, I am responsible before others. More narrowly, imputability makes the powerful responsible for the weak and the vulnerable. Finally, promising calls for a witness who receives it and records it. What is more, its end is the good of others, when it is not aiming at wrongdoing and revenge. What is missing, however, in this listing of how others are implied in the private certainty of the capacity to act, is reciprocity, mutuality, which alone allow us to speak of recognition in the strong sense.

This mutuality is not given spontaneously; that is why it is demanded. And this demand is not without conflict or struggle. The idea of a struggle for recognition is at the heart of modern social relations. The myth of the state of nature accords to competition, to defiance, to the arrogant affirmation of solitary glory, the role of foundation and of origin. In this war of all against all, the fear of violent death would reign supreme. This pessimism concerning the ground of human nature goes hand-in-hand with praise of the absolute power of a sovereign who remains outside the contract of submission made by citizens delivered from fear. The denial of recognition is thus inscribed within the institution. An initial recourse to reciprocity can be found in a feature just as original as the war of all against all—in a natural right in which an equal respect would be recognized in all the parties to the social compact. The moral character of the social bond could then be held to be irreducible. What natural right does not recognize is the place of struggle in the conquest of equality and justice, the role of negative conduct in the motivation leading to struggle: lack of consideration, humiliation, disdain, to say nothing of violence in all its physical and psychological forms.

The struggle for recognition is pursued on several levels. It begins on the level of affective relations tied to the transmission of life, to sexuality, and to descendents. It is at its height in the intersection of the vertical relations of a genealogy and the horizontal relations of conjugality in the framework of the family.

This struggle for recognition is pursued on the juridical plane of the rights of civil society, centered on the ideas of liberty, justice, and solidarity. Rights cannot be claimed on my behalf unless they are recognized in the same way for others. This extension of individual capacities belonging to legal persons concerns not only the enumeration of their civic rights, but widens the sphere of application to new categories of individuals and powers previously scorned. This extension is the occasion for conflicts stemming from exclusions due to social inequalities, but also those arising from forms of discrimination inherited from the past that still afflict various minorities. Disdain and humiliation, however, infect the social bond at a level that surpasses rights; this concerns social esteem directed to personal value and to the capacity to pursue happiness in accordance with one's own conception of the good life. This struggle for esteem occurs in the context of different spheres of life: at work, the struggle to prevail, to protect one's rank in the hierarchy of authority; at home, relations of neighborhood and proximity, together with all the many encounters that make up daily life. It is always personal capacities that demand to be recognized by others.

III

The question then arises whether the social bond is constituted only in the struggle for recognition, or whether there is not also, at the origin, a sort of good will tied to the resemblance of one person to another in the great human family.

We have an inkling of this in the dissatisfaction that the practice of struggle leaves in us. The demand for recognition expressed in this struggle is insatiable: when will we receive sufficient recognition? This quest involves something like a bad infinity. Yet it is also a fact that we experience actual recognition in a peaceful mode. The model is found in the ceremonial exchange of gifts in traditional societies. This ritualized exchange is not to be confused with the market exchange consisting in buying and selling in the context of a contract of exchange. The logic of the exchange of gifts is a logic of reciprocity that creates mutuality; it consists in the call to give in return contained in the act of giving. Where does this obligation come from? Certain sociologists have sought in the item exchanged a magical force that makes the gift circulate and makes it return to its starting point. I prefer to follow those who see in the exchange of gifts a recognition of each by the other, a recognition unaware of itself as such, and symbolized in the thing exchanged, which becomes its pledge. This indirect recognition would be the peaceful counterpart to the struggle for recognition. In it, the mutuality of the social bond would find its expression. Not that the obligation to give back creates a dependence of the receiver with regard to the giver, but the gesture of giving would be the invitation to a similar generosity. This chain of acts of generosity is the model of a genuine experience of recognition without struggle that finds expression in all the truces of our struggles, in the armistices that, in particular, constitute the compromises issuing from negotiations between social partners.

In addition to this practice of compromise, the formation of the political bond that makes us citizens of a historical community perhaps does not stem solely from a concern with security and the defense of the particular interests of this community, but from something like a "political friendship," one that is essentially peaceful. A more visible trace of the ceremonial exchange of gifts remains in the practices of generosity that, in our societies, continue alongside market exchanges. Giving remains a common gesture that escapes the objection of calculated self-interest: it depends on the one who receives the gift to respond to the one who gives it by a similar gesture of generosity. This disinterestedness finds its public expression in holidays, in celebrations with family and friends. The festive in general is heir in our market societies to the ceremony of the gift, interrupting the market and tempering its brutality as it brings its peace into this sphere. This intertwining of struggle and celebration is perhaps the indication of an absolutely primitive relation at the source of the social bond linking the defiance of the war of all against all with the good will that arises from the encounter with the other, my fellow human being.

Religious Belief

The Difficult Path of the Religious

PAUL RICOEUR

Dear friends,

In agreeing to this title for my address to this prestigious group of conferences for 2000, I chose to add to it a more problematic subtitle: "the difficult path of the religious." I propose, under the aegis of this heading, to transform certain objections and accusations addressed to believers into intimate difficulties for their belief itself. It is in particular the threats of intolerance and violence contained in religious belief that I want to confront, by calling upon the resources of self-criticism that the intelligence inherent in such belief is able to mobilize.

Capable Man, Recipient of the Religious

To begin, I would like to answer the question that I take to be a precondition to the entire discussion. The question is as follows: what is the recipient of the religious message and thus the bearer of religious belief? In other words, in which area of my existence am I touched by the religious problematic? I answer this: it is in my desire to be, in my capacity to exist, that the arrow of the religious comes to hit me. I have adopted in my works on philosophical anthropology a condensed expression that serves as a heading for detailed analyses, the expression *capable man*. Under this expression I gather all the figures of power and impotence, as indicated by linguistic constructions using the auxiliary verb *can*. Power is the whole of what I can do; impotence, the sum of what I cannot. In the broad sense of the word, it is about an approach to the human phenomenon in terms of acting and suffering, of *praxis* and *pathos*. This is why I readily designate the human as an acting and suffering being. I will briefly point out the major divisions under which I place the examination of his capacities and incapacities. I will thus give an idea of the extent of the problems of the capable man. Four key headings deserve to be considered: a) the capacity for speech of a speaker who can say something about something to somebody; b) the capacity for action of an incarnated agent able to produce changes in the world, to bring events about; c) the capacity for recounting of a historical subject in search of identity in time; d) finally, the capacity for imputation of a moral subject responsible for the acts in which she recognizes herself as the true author. Under each of these headings there are incapacities, specific impotencies that correspond to the capacity to speak, to do, to tell, and to impute to oneself the responsibility for one's own acts. Of course it is such a being of power and impotence—such a capable man—who is the recipient of the religious message.

I propose to introduce the religious problematic as did Kant in *Religion within the Limits of Reason Alone*, starting from a meditation on evil. We will see in a moment that this is but one entry point into what one could call the negative facet of the religious phenomenon. But this approach has the advantage of making the religious appear at the heart of the problematic of the capable man. It is indeed to a specific incapacity that the religious offers an answer, a word: the incapacity to do the good oneself. That which is called bad will, captive free will, servant-will is about an easily identifiable experience: it is felt as an intimate binding of oneself by oneself. This experience that Pascal, before Kant, called "the misery of man" inscribes itself into all the other modalities of weakness, of vulnerability, that make the capable man a fragile being, and, thanks to a mysterious failing, a guilty man. That the religious problematic is moreover likely to reach us through experiences of abundance will readily be granted once the positive facet of the religious is brought to light. But the exaggeration engendered by a meditation on "radical evil" in the Kantian manner has the advantage of making the religious appear from the direction of a fault, of a defect, of a break, beyond which the happy continuity between the new capacities engendered by the religious and the more fundamental capacities constitutive of the human being could be restored.

In order to prevent any misunderstanding relating to this entry into the religious by way of the dark side of human existence, and to prepare the rediscovery of its lighter facets, I want to vigorously emphasize the distinction that Kant made from the start between what he called the "predisposition to good," which defines the basis of the human condition, and the "propensity to evil," which governs the empirical condition at the end of his treatise on the "radical evil" of humans. I insist on the difference in vocabulary between *disposition* and *propensity*; "predisposition to good" and "propensity to evil." Propensity to evil constitutes to some extent the existential condition of what Kant calls, in the language proper to him, particular morally bad maxims: those of murder, lying, theft, and so forth. But, as radical as this evil is, it will never be as originary as the destination of the good. This distinction between the originary and the radical will not cease to accompany us: it anticipates what will be later known as the luminous facet of the religious phenomenon. One can nonetheless say already that the religious will have a fundamentally dependent bond with the basis of originary goodness held captive and hidden—in a word, with the release of goodness.

That said, what then are the resources of the religious with respect to the prevalence of the propensity to evil in the history of individuals, communities, and nations? In the continuation of the treatise *Religion within the Limits of Reason Alone*, the Kantian analysis proposes a triple articulation of the religious phenomenon: first at the level of symbols, then at the level of belief, and finally at the level of communal existence, of living together. At the first level of the symbolic, the Jewish and Christian culture of the Occident was structured starting from a central symbol that can be called in broad terms the Christic symbol: that, said Kant, of the man pleasing to God who gives his life for his friends. It is not important for a philosophical approach within the limits of reason alone to resolve the question of the place of Jesus in the line of the prophets, nor whether the Jesus of history is identical to the Christ of the faith, nor even to know whether the Christ of the Christian confession exhausts the resources of meaning of the symbol of the Lamb of God, celebrated by the Second Isaiah in the "songs of the suffering servant." All that is important is the establishment in our imagination of this symbol that exceeds our capacity for invention. Its accession as founding event is so original or originary that from then on we find it at work in its capacity of iconographic production, in the broadest sense of the term.

At the level of belief—which is that of our favored title this evening, but which our analysis makes appear secondary—religious belief consists in an act of reception with regard to the prophets who announced the good news of the Christic symbol. To believe is first to believe in the words of these others who testify on behalf of the regenerative power of the Christic symbol. It is not initially to adhere to dogmatic formulations, which remain secondary, but to trust in the beneficent power exerted by the Christic symbol. Here, "to believe in . . ." means more than "to believe that . . ." This gap, between believing in and believing that, is where Kant's vigorous polemic against the dogmatists finds its place. But this polemic need not conceal Kant's positive apprehension of the core phenomenon of belief, beyond the interminable quarrels of the theologians over salvation by grace or by works, the external or intimate nature of grace, and so forth.

One the third level, that of the community, religious practice rests on a natural gathering that is essentially nonpolitical, which can be characterized in broad terms as mutual aid given one to the other, the listeners and interpreters of the foundational message contained in the symbol and the belief in the regenerative power of this symbol. That the *Ecclesia*, the Church, is not a political community centered on the central phenomenon of domination and equipped with the capacity for force—*there* is found the most delicate point of the religious problematic. This is also the moment when Kant's polemical tone reaches it highest degree of vehemence against "those priests." Yet this does not end up yielding to the temptation of opposing an invisible Church to the visible Churches but instead appeals for an analysis of the power of the visible Churches that would expose the only power of the symbol on the imagination, of belief on the intellect, of nonviolent fraternal action on the life of the city.

It is now possible to define what could be called the purpose of the religious. I do not believe it departs from the Kantian line followed thus far to say that the religious has as its function the deliverance of the core of goodness from the bonds that hold it captive. It is to this deliverance that the symbol, the belief, and the community of the church wish to contribute. To recall the initial vocabulary of this meditation, the religious problematic can be summarized as the extraordinary capacity to make the ordinary person capable of doing the good. It is in this sense that the capable man is, as noted above, the recipient of the religious and the carrier of religious belief.

As a transition between exposition of the religious problematic and examination of the difficulties of the religious, I would like to say a few things about the joining of the religious to the moral. Such reflection is essential insofar as, on the one hand, one defines the religious by the capacity to do good, while on the other hand, it is at this delicate junction that malevolent forces able to divert the religious from its fundamental vocation insert themselves.

"Delicate junction," I just said. In effect, it is important to articulate with precision the operative grounds of the religious and the moral. As the medievals did in characterizing ethical concepts as "common concepts" subject to a legitimate distinction, as Kant did in arguing for the autonomy of the moral subject, I will define moral experience as the primordial relationship between a freedom given and a rule addressed to a subject capable of imputation. It is at the level of the capacity of imputation that the position of the self and the imposition of a rule come together. We thus define moral experience in terms of autonomy—that is, the junction between oneself (auto-) and a rule (-nomy). The effective capacity to act according to a rule is then something else: Kant began his examination under the heading of the "motivations" of practical reason, but reduced these motivations to respect. Would one not have to open the sphere of moral "motivation," that is, the impulse to act according to a rule, to a larger field of motivations than respect? Unless one takes respect to be the generic term for an assortment of feelings such as shame, indignation, the sublime, admiration, veneration, and, most of all, the recognition of the dignity of man in his common humanity. It is, then, on the level of these motivations that we find the capacity to do good generated by religion according to the threefold frame of symbol, belief, and ritual community life. A thinker I admire, Paul Tillich, whom I succeeded at the University of Chicago, introduced in this context the concept of "courage to be." I see this courage operating at the axis of the religious and the moral, not on the level of normative content but on the level of the capacity to act according to the known good. To this courage to be I will connect the supra-ethical value of love, where the superabundance of the gift with respect to our capacity to receive is expressed. But love cannot replace justice; even less can it dispense with justice. Love requires more than justice; it asks that justice be at once even more universal and even more singular. Thus is the religious added to the moral: as courage to be and as love. The courage to be reaches the capable man in his private solitude, the love in his shared otherness.

Religious Difficulties

While starting I formed the wish to face the antireligious polemic and the charges of intolerance and violence very often addressed to religious people by unbelievers; I will do so by calling upon the resources of self-criticism mobilized by the intelligence of faith.

The testimony of history is undeniably overpowering: persecutions, inquisitions, wars of religion, coercion of hearts and sometimes of bodies, probing intrusion into the sphere of moral decision, private or public.

The indictment is incontestable. The question, then, is whether the religious as such comprises the occasion or, worse, the temptation to specific violence that would merit being referred to as *religious violence.* It is symbolic violence that I want to speak of as the source of eventual physical violence.

In ancient religions, most of the proven acts of violence revolve around sacrifice: the sacrifice of human beings, animals, plants and other vegetation, the destruction of consecrated objects. In turn, the sacrifice as behavior and ritual renews the heart of the sacred, so long as it takes place in a delimited sphere of existence separated from all other behaviors, which are referred to, in contrast, as profane. Sacrifice did not, however, disappear from the developed forms of the great historical religions. Freud, in *Moses and Monotheism,* showed its persistence. The Catholic mass, for example, is centered on the consecrated host, at once victim and offering, and the liturgy confers structure and rhythm on the offering and the sharing by the community of the broken body and shed blood. Since the time of the New Testament a sacrificial theology has circulated, in which the accent falls on the substitutionary aspect of the Paschal victim in response to the punitive requirement for retribution pronounced by a vengeful God. It is true that there are other lines of interpretation of the death of Christ, in which less stress is laid on the atonement in blood than on the pure offering of the victim, as I will have occasion to return to in a moment. One can nevertheless not avoid the topic of the link between violence and the sacred.

I propose, the problem having been set, to follow for awhile the clear and illuminating interpretation of René Girard in his famous work *Violence and the Sacred* (1972), then in *The Scapegoat* (1981) and his other works.

René Girard is not satisfied with the prevailing explanation of the instinct of aggressiveness considered common to all living things. He seeks and finds a source that is properly human in the competition between two similar desires relating to the same coveted object. He calls this spring of violence, which in fact contains the seed of murder, *mimetic rivalry.* It is important to emphasize from the outset the anthropological character—this is the vocabulary of Girard himself—of this initial analysis of the relationship between desire and hatred. In the exemplary cases of mimetic rivalry, one witnesses the mutual reinforcement of desire and its obstacles in what he calls *envy,* which the old translations of the Bible called the *stumbling block,* which today we call *scandal,* the obstacle on which one stumbles. The more one is wounded, the more one desires to be wounded. The peak is reached when one forgets the initial object of the mimetic rivalry and gets carried away, and the conflict is closed in on its cumulative effects. To escape this impasse, this rivalrous, chaotic crisis, societies would contrive a reconciliation at the expense of a third—namely, through the real and not simply metaphorical scenario of the collective expulsion of a victim, on the model of the scapegoat. On this basis Girard builds a complex theory from the occlusion and thus the ignorance of this process at work in religions and in political régimes, by means of institutions that are at bottom properly sacrificial. The illusion and lie would consist, then, in the divinization of the victim thus subjected to bloody expulsion in order to alleviate the mimetic rivalry. The violence of all against one: such would be the formula of the scapegoat. The camouflaging of this deadly process would then impose the task of unmasking the "representations" through which ignorance is imposed—the task of *revelation*, therefore, in the proper sense of *deciphering*. According to Girard, however, this conquest of the deafness of history can and must take support from the only exception to this religious violence, namely the evangelical proclamation of the pure victim, which, in spite of appearances about which the Christians themselves were mistaken, is not the product of lynching, but the expression of pure self-donation. From there, everything rides on the difference between the passion of Christ and a religious lynching. Girard reproaches historical Christianity, except for St. John, for not having drawn the difference between the divinization of the guilty victim, as in other religions, and the glorification of the persecutors, who are considered innocent. Girard interprets Easter, after the moment of the disciples' complicity in the collective lynching, as the proclamation of innocence that dissipates the collective illusion of the guilty victim. It is what Girard calls *resurrection*, resurrection of the religious content of the Gospels. It is there that we find what it is the believers believe. It is the object of their belief. At a recent conference that I attended under the auspices of the Geneva International Meetings in 1999, however, Girard declared this: "There is an evangelical (and biblical) revelation of the mythological illusion. This revelation is inseparable, undoubtedly, from the Resurrection of the religious content of the Gospels, but in its principle it is distinct. Its content is not religious but purely anthropological, scientific." By this Girard wants to say that the denunciation of the sacrificial myth is certainly dependent on the disciples' belief that Christ is sent by God, but that the operation of unmasking became an enormous cultural phenomenon centered on the innocence of the victim. This direction is found in modernity at the level of an increasing denunciation of collective violence. "This modern significance," continues Girard, "presupposes what I call the anthropological revolution of Christianity."

Whence comes Girard's benevolent tone with regard to modernity? Christianity can decline apace as a religious belief; its anthropological function of the revelation of the innocence of the wrongfully sacrificed victim remains unshakeable. It cannot help but develop in the line from the image of the lamb of God to that of the scapegoat.

I want to say now why Girard's idea does not satisfy me fully, or rather why it is not enough for me. And you will see, in a moment, how I once again take up the thread of the first, very Kantian, part of my address, concluding on the theme of originary goodness and religion as the release of the depth of goodness. Girard's thesis is of course very strongly expressed on the question of the obstacles that face the release of goodness—namely, that the very identity rivalry that opens the cycle of violence, starts the lynching, launches the process of reconciliation at the cost of the sacrificial victim, is to be completed in the divinization of the victim and the exculpation of the attackers. In this sense Girard's theory is strong concerning the moment of the display of religious violence. But there is a missing link concerning the specific object of the primary mimetic rivalry in the case of the religious. Over *what* is there mimetic rivalry in religion? Girard is perhaps so concerned to have his project be recognized as scientific that he calls the unmasking of the hidden violence of the generalized sacrificial system "anthropological." In the extreme, any desirable object can be the object of mimetic rivalry and be capable of causing "scandal," in the abovementioned sense of a stumbling block, in the revival of mimetic rivalry.

My suggestion is that the creative source of the process of release of goodness, in the ways that Kant named—that is, by means of the great foundational symbols, the traditions of belief, and the community mediations of an ecclesial nature—that the originary source of this powerful upsurge of benevolence can be, as such, an object of mimetic rivalry, of scandal, of lynching, of the reconciliation of all against one, of the divinization of the guilty victim and the exoneration of the violent. It is in this way that I see violence seizing the source of life itself. I acknowledge that this is not obvious, nor easy to make understood. On one side, indeed, it is necessary to give to the Girardian design an application that is already religious in nature and not an unspecified scandal. But it is also necessary to give to the Kantian design in *Religion within the Limits of Reason Alone* an addition that allows it to identify the creative source of the process of the release of goodness. This cannot be done while remaining within the limits of reason alone, but only by crossing the boundaries assigned to pure and practical reason, along the lines opened by the post-Kantians

Fichte and Schelling—Schelling above all. It is this gesture of transgression that will allow me to say something on the properly religious object of mimetic violence and thus religious violence, namely, the pretension to monopolize the source, to appropriate it in rivalry with the other recipients of the source's fundamental generosity. Yes, I found in Schelling's philosophy of religion the powerful theme of the groundless ground, of the *Grund* that is *Abgrund,* the foundation that is abyss. And then, I say to myself: this unsoundable bottom, is this not the very source of life that all receive, but that no one can encompass? And why then is there mimetic rivalry, if not because religion does not exist anywhere in its innocent nudity, in its undivided universality? And if it exists nowhere in its immaculate entirety, is this not because religions are like languages, cultures, political societies, namely, subjected to the inexorable law of plurality, dispersion, and confusion, as is said of languages in the Hebraic myth of Babel? Yes, the Babel of religions. Meaning, invigorating each time for each religious community—the source of life is undoubtedly that. But jealous capture of the source remains the historically attested, disturbing phenomenon. The war of religions and the wars of religion have their origin there. Radical fragmentation—*radical* as was said of evil, that is, radical but not original—is the very given of history. Girard would say: the anthropological fact first. The religious never exists but in religions. And the religions, under the influence of the radical evil of which no one knows the origin, are connected, one to the other, in a relationship of mimetic rivalry, having as object the source of life undivided in its outflow, divided in its receptacles.

If you wish, I will illustrate through a metaphor my idea of the groundless ground that comes to the surface of history only in the competitive plurality of religions, perverted in actual violence. The metaphor is what you might expect, that of the source and the receptacle. The source overflows, but the container would like to collect it all. It would like to lock up the source. Here begins an operation of collecting which requires that the strength of the container's walls be reinforced, as if to compensate for the kind of threat the power of the outflow constitutes. Here violence starts: one will want to enclose the sides, being unable to seal the top. This dialectic of overflow and finitude in the space of reception is lived out mainly at the community level, as Kant pointed out, by coordinating the three moments of the foundational symbol, the adherence of belief, and the mediation of the community. The community, not able to contain everything, will work to exclude people, or worse, it will "compel them to come in," as with the unfortunate principle of St. Augustine that Pierre Bayle worked to refute in the seventeenth century.

Exclusion, forced inclusion, it is the same thing. To reinforce the walls means to contain by force those on the inside, but also to expel those one cannot contain. In connection with the inappropriable object that is the groundless ground, the inexhaustible source, these images of mimetic rivalry are innumerable.

The metaphor that I have just deployed easily allows interpretation in the language I used at the beginning of this presentation, and which expresses well the conceptual thread of all my recent work: the language of capacity. There is with regard to the source of life a finite capacity of reception. It is this finite capacity that shapes the receptacle with the partitions that fear and hatred reinforce. It is this finite capacity that is put to the test in any religious experience, of whatever confession. One could still add to the metaphor of the source and the container, with the idea of Pascalian tonality of disproportion. The foundation, the groundless ground, is too much for our finite capacities of reception. It is through this excess, which I call *foundational excess*, that violence will slip into the Girardian model of mimetic rivalry. Another metaphorical equivalence of disproportion is that of superabundance, as in the proposal of the apostle Paul: "Where sin increased, grace abounded all the more." I find this idea of superabundance in the abovementioned relationship between love and justice—love, which does not count the cost, and justice, which is expressed in the relationships of just proportion, of equivalence, of exact equality, of fair measurement.

Consequences

I would like to finish by examining the consequences of my working hypothesis, of which the majority remain problematic.

The first to be taken into account is that it is necessary to give up the dream of a super-religion. Admittedly, the idea of a source of life that fragments according to the receptive capacity of the containers—to continue with the metaphor—evokes something like a fundamental religion. I even grant quite readily that there are religious sentiments easily transposable and communicable from one religion to another: thus, for example, the feeling of absolute dependence about which Schleiermacher speaks, that I (among others) interpret as precedence of the Word to any word articulated in speech; but also the anteriority of a creative energy with respect to my desire. I speak readily, with Paul Tillich, whom I already evoked once, of an unconditional trust, in spite of all the tragedy, an engagement without restrictions, in spite of any hesitation and doubt;

in the same spirit, I more recently engaged in exploration of the vivid emotional expressions of wishing well, such as admiration for creation, jubilation in the meeting between man and woman, striving for the greater gifts, in the line of the hymn to love in Paul's letter to the Corinthians. Yes, there is a religious sentiment at the root of what I like to call optative happiness. It is the brilliant point of the luminous face of the religious that Kant readily compares to religious madness, *Schmärmerheit*: it is the donation that precedes any collecting, transforming the donation into a threat.

That being granted and even demanded, there remains for reflection and speculation the inappropriable character of the source of life. Schelling's groundless ground does not establish a specific religion, according to the triple articulation of fundamental symbolism, intellectual belief, and the mediation of the community. In this respect, the idea of the groundless ground, the foundation in abyss, remains a limit-idea for understanding. And the feelings themselves relative to the foundation go on to take shape within a framework of high culture, there to be articulated, each time differently, in what I would call a poetics of the good. The verdict must be accepted: the forms of the religious share the same state of dispersion and confusion as languages and cultures, the state recognized in the Babel myth.

This first consequence can be taken as the most honest confession of the trial of veracity in the field of religious belief. Seeking in the sociology of religions the substitute of a core religion—with the Babel myth encouraging its representation as a lost paradise, which never existed on the level of history—is then an attempt to elude and circumvent this confession. The sociology of religions would like to present a picture of the religions where all would be glanced over and placed among the ranks of observed objects, like so many insects on a board. It should then be said that each one is voided as personal engagement and on the three levels considered in the philosophy of religion: the level of imaginary symbolism, intellectual belief, and community practice.

This first set of considerations implies a second: the confession of veracity leads to a confession of perplexity; have we not exchanged the idea of universal truth for that of radical relativism? I answer: yes and no. Yes, if you mean giving up the idea of an absolute point of view, of an overhead perspective that we in fact do not have. No, if you attach to the profession of relativism the profession of a movable perspectivism, by virtue of which I could indifferently adopt one religious point of view or the other. Against this interreligious monadism, I will support the idea that it is always from somewhere, from a particular point, that we perceive, that we observe, that in imagination and sympathy we approach foreign convictions, in a movement of gradual transfer carried as far as this movement of transgressing of my own barriers will allow. I will say for myself, being of the Christian Reformed tradition, that this movement of what I call imagination and sympathy sometimes takes me to the edge of Buddhism. This lateral progression—gradual, as I said—constitutes the exact opposite of an overhead perspective claiming to embrace the totality of the religious field. Moreover, the most solid sociological studies in the sphere of religions confine themselves to a specialized study of this or that religion—at the risk of no longer having criteria for the religious as such. This scientific approach is at once the most modest and the most honest. But it leaves intact the question of the existential truth of the religion, which is the very stake of this study devoted to religious belief in the field of convictions.

Is this to say that we have given up entirely, after this double confession of the absence of an interreligious universal and of a certain relativism that one could ascribe to perspectivism? I would like to add a consideration suggested to me by the Babel analogy, evoked several times even here. If religious groups can be compared with linguistic and cultural groups, can we not call upon the only known remedy for the dispersion and confusion of languages, namely translation? I anticipated this suggestion while speaking just now about a fixed point from which I can gradually consider confessions or religions according to their degree of distance from my own; does that not resemble the relationship between our mother tongue and the languages we call foreign? There also there is no universal language; nevertheless anyone seems capable of learning an additional language, that of a neighboring or distant country. We have always translated: traders, explorers, diplomats, spies, under the supervision of bilinguals, always knew to clear the linguistic barrier by the practice of a foreign language. Indeed, is it not with something similar to this linguistic hospitality that we achieve a gradual understanding of religious beliefs we call foreign, and in general, an understanding of convictions of all kinds, of which the exploration of religious beliefs constitutes only one chapter?

I would like to draw a final conclusion from my interpretation of the phenomenon of religious violence; it is a practical consequence, more certain than the preceding ones and concerning what I call practical wisdom. It relates to the everyday use of tolerance. In light of what I have just said about linguistic hospitality transposed from the level of translation to that of the encounter with other religions and convictions, the path of tolerance can be seen as a progressive initiative. It is not like an easy practice, a one-story house, if I can say that, but like a relatively arduous ascent.

At ground level, tolerance says (and this is the tolerance of the intolerant): "I do not support what you believe, I disapprove of it, but I cannot prevent it. I tolerate it in the sense that I cannot prevent it; I would like to prevent it but I lack the power." It is at this stage that I return to violent rivalry.

At a second, more positive level, tolerance says: "I retain the conviction that it is I who am in possession of the truth, but I recognize, in kindness, your right to profess what I hold to be false; and I do it in the name of the principle of justice. Namely, I recognize that you have a right equal to mine to profess what you believe, although I hold it to be false." This way, it is the right to the error that I recognize; but at this stage I am within myself torn between truth, which I believe I hold unilaterally, and justice, which is a recognition of the other, but on another level than that of truth. I would say that the principle of justice invoked here can be formulated in these terms: every other life is worth as much as mine. But justice then slices into truth.

I take one more step in the direction of a deepening of my relationship with my opposition, my rival in belief. I would say this at this third stage: "Perhaps my adversary also has part of the truth, but I do not know which part." This is the perspectivist version of tolerance: the other sees a side of things that I cannot see, because our positions are not substitutable. It is much like a Zen Buddhist garden I recently visited in Kyoto: fifteen stones are posed on a small sand ocean, but there is no angle from which I can see them all. At this stage the issue is a crisis of the idea of truth, torn within itself; I have passed beyond the simple conflict between truth and justice; I have entered the conflict of truth with itself.

Coming to a still higher level—and it is here that I can hope to overcome violence—at this more advanced stage, I say this: "At the very depth of my own conviction, of my own confession, I recognize that there is a ground which I do not control. I discern in the ground of my adherence a source of inspiration which, by its demand for thought, its strength of practical mobilization, its emotional generosity, exceeds my capacity for reception and comprehension." But then the tolerance that arrives at this peak risks falling down the slope on the other side, that of skepticism: aren't all beliefs worthless? That is to say, do the differences not become indifferent? The difficulty then is to hold myself on the crest where my conviction is at the same time anchored in its soil, like its mother tongue, and open laterally to other beliefs, other convictions, as in the case of foreign languages. It is not easy to hold oneself at this crest. . . .

Translated by Boyd Blundell from "La croyance religieuse: Le difficile chemin du religieux" (Texte de la 334e conférence de l'Université de tous les savoirs, 29 novembre 2000), in Yves Michaud, ed., *Qu'est-ce que la culture?* vol. 6 of *Université de tous les savoirs* (Paris: Odile Jacob, 2001), 461–73.

Remembering Paul Ricoeur

DAVID PELLAUER

Early on he said, "The word is my kingdom and I am not ashamed of it."[1] In a later book, *Memory, History, Forgetting*, he cited this from Vladimir Jankéloevitch as an epigram: "He who has been, from then on cannot not have been: henceforth this mysterious and profoundly obscure fact of having been is his viaticum for all eternity."[2]

It is almost eighteen months now since Ricoeur's death. I believe he would have agreed that as the work of mourning progresses, the balance shifts between what at first is an almost overwhelming sense of grief and an accompanying sense of loss. Grief, for those who feel it, never completely disappears, but it is the sense of loss that most holds its strength. So I do not want to grieve today over Ricoeur's death. Those who knew him could see it coming the last year or so of his life, however much we might have hoped that like Gadamer or Hartshorne he too would live to be a hundred or more—and that we might talk with him one more time, or that he could keep working, as he gave every indication of doing until that last year or so when he really began to slow down. We knew that he didn't fear death, any more than he looked for it, but also that he kept talking of maybe just one more book. Yes, he is gone, but his work remains, and that is what I want to talk about today.

It is easy to say that many members of this society felt respect for Ricoeur. We turned out in great numbers on those occasions when he could participate in our meetings, yet his work did not figure on the program very often over the years as the topic of someone else's paper. There are probably more papers on Ricoeur this year than were given in total over the last five to ten years, which, without meaning to denigrate their authors' efforts, may be as much a result of his death as anything. For Ricoeur never wanted or encouraged a school, and certainly he would have been upset by the idea of a flock of followers or anything like a Ricoeur Society. He chose rather to pursue his own problems and to hope that others would pick up on them. "Talk about my philosophy, about philosophy, not about me," I can hear him saying. Yet his death changes things, and we need to acknowledge this; not in the sense that the time has come for a Ricoeur school or society, but in the sense that the canon, so to speak, has closed. There will be no more new books. Translations? Probably yes, there is still a lot of material already in print out there but not available in English. And maybe these yet-to-come translations can even be put together with a few of the available shorter texts already in English that have been published in obscure, or overlooked, or difficult to obtain journals. Ricoeur would rarely if ever say no when people asked if they could publish the lecture they had just heard, and since he always started over, there were lots of such occasional writings. Sometimes these essays overlapped with other things he was working on; and he wasn't above a bit of cutting and pasting, but often they were brilliant on their own. His essay on human action considered as a text, for example, or the lecture on the fragility of political language immediately come to mind.[3] But now the canon is closed, and we can see that for years we were trying to keep up, if not catch up with him, without really knowing where he was going next. And how often did that next book or essay come as an eye-opening and, to be sure, a thought-provoking surprise. Who among us, for example, could have predicted that at almost the age of ninety he would take up the question of recognition and the politics of identity, which is one of those questions currently in the air? Or that in doing this he would bring to light the all-too-obvious fact that once you look for it, recognition has not been dealt with in the history of philosophy in a way that has produced what philosophers would acknowledge to be a major statement, a class text? This forced him to change his usual search for starting points in the history of philosophy and to turn instead to the dictionary. And who could have anticipated that he would then go on to show that, when dealt with at all—and then usually as an operative rather than a thematic concept—existing philosophical discussions of recognition really only get to the level of reciprocal recognition, not to truly mutual recognition, not to mention that these discussions almost always ignore the side of gratitude that is implicit in reconnaissance. Many of us, I suspect, if we were paying any attention at all, were still back somewhere trying to make sense

be absent from his own philosophical thought? Although Ricoeur claims that "the philosopher as philosopher has to admit that one does not know and cannot say whether this Other, the source of the injunction, is another person . . . my ancestors . . . or God—living God, absent God, or an empty place," thereby bringing philosophical discourse with regard to the Other "to an end,"[24] there is a "point of intersection between the properly philosophical dimension and the properly religious dimension,"[25] where the analogical unity of acting opens onto the analogical unity of being understood as *energeia*, *dunamis*, and *conatus*,[26] and then in turn gives way to the analogical unity of the names of God who acts "for us, to the extent of our acting toward others."[27] Like Russian nesting dolls, these levels of discourse encircle (and/or constitute) the self with forms of language that move from the finite to the infinite by means of attestation of being oneself, of the Essential of being, and the Essential turned toward us. While each of these levels of discourse retains its own irreducibility, none is truly autonomous. Each level opens to the other by way of attestation to a surplus of meaning, to the more-than-possible of superabundance, to "the very source of life that all receive, but which one cannot encompass."[28]

Forgiveness and the Capable Man

The Essential is, according to Ricoeur, manifest in "extreme experiences," such as death, childbirth, joy, happiness, and giving and receiving love, and is particularly evident in his analysis of forgiveness, where we can see how the philosophical opens onto and needs the religious to give a fuller account of the experience of forgiveness.

At the conclusion of his monumental book *Memory, History, Forgetting,* in the epilogue titled "Difficult Forgiveness,"[29] Ricoeur offers us a philosophical reading of forgiveness rooted in a phenomenology of the capable man. In a manner similar to the one he employed in the conclusions of *Oneself as Another, Time and Narrative,* and *Rule of Metaphor,* Ricoeur sketches out a trajectory for a work to come that never arrives; namely, a reflection on the ontological foundation of selfhood. In fact, shortly before his death he had indicated that such was his wish, to write one last book called "*L'homme capable.*"[30] As readers of Ricoeur, we have been pointed in this direction for some time. The theme of the capable man has been mentioned, without significant elaboration, in numerous texts, with the promise of future development. And such is indeed the case in "Difficult Forgiveness," where he gives us a description of the human condition as "the enigma of a fault held to paralyze the power to act of the 'capable being' that we are; and it is, in reply, the enigma of the possible lifting of this existential incapacity, designated by the term 'forgiveness.'"[31]

Ricoeur sets the problem of forgiveness into a disproportion between two infinites that are impossible to bridge on the level of theory. On the one hand, forgiveness is supposed to unbind an action from an agent and no longer hold her accountable for what was done. On the other hand, however, if I am at fault for *what* I have done, then I am faced with an impossible situation; namely, the separation of action from agency, such that when forgiven my fault or action, it is no longer ascribed to *who* I am. If this is the case, then as Ricoeur argues, forgiveness might very well be the destruction of selfhood, which for Ricoeur is always a fundamental relation between *who* I am and *what* I do, between agent and action, and therefore in principle inseparable. Yet it is of the essence of forgiveness to do just that.

If action and agent are inseparable, and an evil action is avowed by an agent who says "I did this!" thereby making the action inseparable from himself and making himself accountable for his evil deed, then we have an impossible condition for unconditional forgiveness. For Ricoeur this is the central paradox of forgiveness: on the one hand, the avowal of all our acts, thereby *binding* them to the agent in the act of responsibility that constitutes a founding act of selfhood; and on the other hand, the *unbinding* of action from agent that is forgiveness. As Ricoeur explains,

> Everything, finally, hangs on the possibility of separating the agent from the action. This unbinding would mark the inscription, in the field of the horizontal disparity between power and act, of the vertical disparity between the great height of forgiveness and the abyss of guilt. The guilty person, rendered capable of beginning again: this would be the figure of unbinding that commands all the others.[32]

To clarify this aporia of the impossible condition of unconditional forgiveness, Ricoeur proceeds in his familiar hermeneutical manner: moving from experience to an analysis of the language that gives rise to reflection on the experience in question. In this case, both the experience of fault and forgiveness give rise to thought through their own unique metaphors. "I shall speak throughout this chapter of a difference in altitude, of a vertical disparity, between the depth of fault and the height of forgiveness. This polarity is constitutive of the equation of forgiveness: below, the avowal of fault; above, the hymn of forgiveness."[33] The language of avowal and the hymn of forgiveness open a space for reflection and philosophical analysis of the "equation" of forgiveness. What is being equated, however, when Ricoeur formulates the "forgiveness equation"?

Ricoeur is careful to point out that this "place" where fault binds action to the self, perhaps making her incapable of acting, is also the place where she is released to act. The debt incurred by means of a fault and the gift of forgiveness have a reciprocal relation—one forgives a fault, and one asks for forgiveness for a fault—but the sheer unconditionality of the demand for forgiveness calls into question the legitimacy of all conditional equations or practical mediations between fault and forgiveness. Ricoeur is well aware of the fragility of the paradox involved in thinking through this problem. "The tension between the avowal and the hymn will be carried almost to a breaking point, the impossibility of forgiveness replying to the unpardonable nature of moral evil."[34]

Hence Ricoeur develops his reflection along two different but intersecting lines: a vertical relation between the depth of fault and the height of forgiveness that *is not subject* to the conditions of calculation; and a horizontal relation of calculated reciprocal exchange and practical necessity where forgiveness *is subject* to the conditions of calculation. The vertical relation is asymmetrical, the horizontal symmetrical; but the real fragility of this disproportion is recognized by Ricoeur as a recovery "at the heart of the horizontal relation of exchange, [of] the vertical asymmetry inherent in the initial equation of forgiveness."[35] So it appears that practical mediations and calculated equations, such as those that are found in the various social and political institutions that seek and/or grant forgiveness (e.g., The Truth and Reconciliation Commission), are inwardly undone by the unconditionality of the height of forgiveness; such mediations, so popular in the realm of political theater and in everyday, practical life, are at best forgiveness *incognito.* Dare I say that Ricoeur's notion of forgiveness might very well be described as auto-deconstructed from within by attestation and hymn that "says: *il y a, es gibt,* there is . . . forgiveness—the form of the universal designating *illéité.* There is forgiveness as there is joy, as there is wisdom, extravagance, love. Love, precisely. Forgiveness belongs to the same family" from on high,[36] and is bound together by love "because it [love] is Height itself."[37]

In describing the place of selfhood distended by the height of forgiveness and the depth of fault, Ricoeur is redeploying a theme from some of his earliest and now often overlooked work, namely the fallible structure of disproportion and the experience of fault as described in *Fallible Man* and *The Symbolism of Evil.* According to Ricoeur, fault is the point of weakness, similar to a geological fault line within the self, where moral fault and evil can irrupt. Fault is always felt at the center of our being. It is a "given of reflection," a "boundary situation," a "nonfortuitous determination . . . implied in every contingent situation and belongs to what we ourselves have designated by the phrase our 'historical condition' on the level of an ontological hermeneutics."[38] As such, like all experience, it gives rise to thought, and the first thought that it offers, according to Ricoeur, is the "fundamental structure . . . of the imputability of our actions . . . that capacity, that aptitude, by virtue of which action can be held to someone's account."[39] In other words, since I am accountable for all my actions and they are imputed to me, I cannot separate my action from who I am. There is a fundamental unity within the self between action and agency; however, *in* the experience of fault as a moral failing, as evil carried out or suffered, there is the wounding of the agent, such that fault opens an "abyss" between the agent and action, between "the 'what' of the actions and the 'who' of the power to act—of agency."[40] Moral failure always seems to include the refusal to own one's actions: "Not me!" "I didn't do it!"; or if I did it, it is of little or no consequence: "Get over it, you're exaggerating." Moral failure and evil open an abyss of disassociation between *who* I am and *what* I have done, between agent and action, that can only be bridged in the avowal of fault, that is, in owning up to acting badly and owning my motivation for doing so. That is why, according to Ricoeur, evil begins a process of the destruction not only of others, but equally so of the self, of the capable man. "Even if guilt is not originary, it is forever radical. It is this adherence of guilt to the human condition that, it seems, renders it not only unforgivable in fact, but unforgivable by right. Stripping guilt from our existence would, it seems, destroy that existence totally."[41]

Since Ricoeur claims that the experience of fault is ultimately a "feeling of the loss of . . . [the self's] own wholeness,"[42] it is the shadow of a more primordial desire,[43] or of an original affirmation for wholeness of the capable man. By making such a claim, Ricoeur gives us some interesting possibilities for reflection. He writes:

> This desire can hardly be expressed except in terms of the desire for wholeness; the latter is better known through failings in the effort to exist than through the approximations of its own most being. We could speak in this regard, if not of an immemorial past, at least of "a past that goes beyond the limits of its memories and of all its empirical history." It is the virtue, as it were, of fault to provide access to this pre-empirical past, but not absent its history, so closely does the experience of fault adhere to this history of desire. So it is with prudence that we speak here of metaphysical experience in order to express the anteriority of defective constitution in relation to the chronology of action. The significance of this anteriority has to remain practical and resist any speculative appropriation.[44]

While the affirmation of this pre-empirical anteriority of action is supposed to remain practical, he nonetheless argues that reflection about the "being proper to desire itself" is a necessary, albeit cautionary, endeavor. What he has in mind here is a kind of ontological reflection of the capable man that is linked to what he formerly called, in the *Rule of Metaphor*, "the ontological vehemence" of discourse about the self,[45] and is tied to the "attestation" of selfhood,[46] which he developed in the tenth chapter of *Oneself as Another*.[47]

Developing his understanding of fault in this way allows Ricoeur to connect the experience of fault with an ontological reflection on the being and nonbeing, or positive and negative excess, of the capable man, as well as to connect fault with the mythical narratives previously elaborated in *The Symbolism of Evil*. The important result of this description of the experience of fault is its connection with "the idea of [a negative] excess, of an unbearable overabundance . . . the unjustifiable . . . excess of the nonvalid, what goes beyond infraction measured by the yardstick of the rules recognized by conscience: a type of cruelty, of baseness, of extreme inequality in social condition."[48] Here the question of accountability is exponentially intensified; if responsibility for evil action could be denied, if evil action could be separated from agency, that would be a moral evil in and of itself. The "avowal" of fault doesn't sever the deed from the doer; rather it inscribes the evil deed in the center of selfhood, whereby I hold myself accountable for what I have done. But that is precisely the problem. If forgiveness no longer holds someone accountable for what he or she has done, doesn't this make forgiveness itself immoral? What hope can Ricoeur hold out for making forgiveness a real possibility and finding some way to bridge the gulf that separates these two infinities? Or should we conclude that evil actions are simply unforgivable? Citing Nicolai Hartmann, Ricoeur sharpens the problem by stating, "Fault in its essence is unforgivable not only in fact but by right. . . . The tie between fault and self, guilt and selfhood seems indissoluble." Hence "the proclamation summed up in the simple phrase: 'There is forgiveness' resonates like an opposing challenge."[49] And yet Ricoeur insists that there is forgiveness; this is what he means by the hymn of forgiveness that attests to its unconditional height as the source from which forgiveness is received.

Even though Ricoeur states that forgiveness is unconditional, he nevertheless tries to give an account of how the unconditional might function in ordinary, practical, conditioned existence. What we see in everyday life and what is most often called forgiveness involves a calculation and an equation between parties who ask and receive forgiveness. The unconditional height of forgiveness demands, however, that we move beyond this market exchange of symmetrical reciprocity that grants forgiveness only for those who ask, or asks for forgiveness from those who can grant it. In other words, if there is forgiveness, Ricoeur insists that we need to find a way to bridge the gap between the conditional and the unconditional, and make forgiveness real. This is why forgiveness is so difficult. Even though the height of forgiveness is asymmetrical and "accompanies us like an enigma that can never be fully plumbed,"[50] we must, nevertheless, "courageously assume" the difficulty of making the unconditional a reality of contingent practice.

So how does Ricoeur suggest we sing this hymn of forgiveness in practical life? "What force makes one capable of asking, of giving, of receiving the word of forgiveness?"[51] What power allows one to believe that when "the wrong is actually admitted; it is actually forgiven,"[52] that "there *is* forgiveness" as a living possibility, even though its unconditionality seems to put it out of reach from each and every historical condition?

For Ricoeur, forgiveness is possible only "on the most secret level of selfhood,"[53] where the capable man attests, confesses, and believes that unbinding an agent from action is possible. Concurring with Derrida that "separating the guilty person from his act, in other words, forgiving the guilty person while condemning his action, would be to forgive a subject other than the one who committed the act,"[54] Ricoeur argues that the unbinding of action from an agent must be a more

> radical uncoupling than that supposed by the argument between a first subject, the one who committed the wrong, and a second subject, the one who is punished, an uncoupling at the heart of our very power to act—of agency—namely, *between the effectuation and the capacity that it actualizes.* This intimate dissociation signifies that the capacity of commitment belonging to the moral subject is not exhausted by its various inscriptions in the affairs of the world. This dissociation expresses an act of faith, a credit addressed to the *resources* of self-regeneration.[55]

Here we see that the experience of fault is also connected with a positive excess through an "ultimate act of trust" in the power to uncouple "effectuation and the capacity that it actualizes." What Ricoeur is arguing for is a radical disconnection more fundamental than the inscription of moral evil within the agent. Regardless of how radical evil may be, Ricoeur claims that good conscience is never rendered completely incapable of genuinely responding to the demand of forgiveness. While action and agent are always coupled together, evil action can be unbound from the heart of selfhood because the heart is never completely incapable of beginning again. Citing Kant, Ricoeur explains that "as radical as evil may be . . . it is not original. Radical is the 'propensity' to evil, original is the 'predisposition' to good."[56] The power of the possible is never rendered completely inoperative. It is always possible, Ricoeur explains, to repent and turn away from a particular course of action, because forgiveness is unconditionally available: "it remains." One can always love again. Forgiveness is the restoration of the power to begin anew, and therefore the "pair forgiveness and repentance" is more suitably linked to the philosophy of the capable man than the stark disproportion that separates fault from unconditional forgiveness.[57] One can always repent and turn away from evil acts.

According to Ricoeur, making such a claim is "not a philosophical aberration"; it is perfectly in line with a philosophy of action based on a philosophical anthropology of the capable man, which is in turn rooted in a fundamental ontology of "the actual and potential ground . . . *conatus* . . . [that] does not mean potentiality but productivity . . . against which selfhood stands out."[58] Therefore, when he explains that "it is in the 'original predisposition to the good' that the possibility of 'the restoration to its power' resides," one would think that such analysis has simply sprung from the resources of philosophy alone. Yet Ricoeur also claims that "this conviction finds a basis in the philosophical rereading of the old myths dealing with the meta- or trans-historical origin of evil," particularly the "Adamic myth in which the fall is recounted as a primordial event inaugurating a time after innocence." Here the philosophical opens onto the religious in a remarkable way, so much so that Ricoeur can further claim:

> The narrative form thus preserves the radical contingency of a historical status now irremediable but in no way inevitable as to its occurrence. This gap with respect to the state of creation holds in reserve the possibility of another history inaugurated in each case by the act of repentance and punctuated by all the irruptions of goodness and of innocence over the course of time. This existential-existentiell possibility, placed under the protection of the narrative origin, is echoed by the predisposition to good upon which the Kantian philosophy of *Religion within the Boundaries of Mere Reason* is constructed. What then can be added in the service of this immense project of restoration would be, on the one hand, the symbols—such as that of the suffering servant and of his Christological expression—that nourish the Jewish and Christian imagination; and, on

> the other hand, the metapolitical institutions—such as, in Christianity, the visible forms of the church placed in the dual position of disciple and guardian with respect to this gift of imagination.[59]

We must be careful to read this correctly. Is Ricoeur simply explaining Kant's position on this issue, or formulating his own position by carefully restating that of Kant's? This is an important question, particularly when Ricoeur closes his analysis of forgiveness with a reference to Kant's assumption concerning the "supernatural cooperation" between the power of the good will and the power of God. Correctly dismissing the significance of the endless "theological debates" on this topic, Ricoeur concludes that

> it does not seem that the vocabulary of the unconditional and the conditional, inherited from the antinomies of the dialectic of pure reason, is appropriate for the problematic of forgiveness and repentance. To disjunction, to dilemma, one must, it seems, oppose paradox. And regarding this paradox, one must give up any attempt to speak in the speculative or transcendental mode. Possessing an irreducibly practical nature it can be uttered only in the grammar of the optative mood.[60]

In other words, Ricoeur is asking us to consider the possibility that the original goodness of the will can allow for the separation of evil moral action from agency by way of forgiveness, if we accept "this dissociation . . . [by] an act of faith, *a credit addressed to the resources of self-regeneration.*"[61] To what resources, however, does he refer? Would they not have to include the power of the good will and the power of height itself? The fact that he brings up the question of "supernatural cooperation" at this juncture, places it within the realm of religious practice, and claims that only optative grammar, or the language of eschatological hope, is suitable to give credit to the power of the possible—doesn't this indicate that his philosophical analysis of forgiveness requires the religious?

There Is Forgiveness

Given Ricoeur's claim of philosophical agnosticism, it would appear that philosophy should ultimately remain silent with regard to religious affirmation. At bottom philosophy can only claim that

> under the sign of forgiveness, the guilty is to be considered capable of something other than his offences and faults. He is held to be restored to his capacity for acting, and action restored to its capacity

> for continuing. . . . The formula for this liberating word, reduced to the bareness of its utterance would be: you are better than your actions.[62]

While Ricoeur's philosophy of the capable man describes the anthropological and ontological conditions for forgiveness to take place, must philosophical discourse remain silent about unconditional forgiveness that sings, "There is forgiveness, it remains"? Such attestation points to resources that are not exclusively the domain of critical philosophy, that open the philosophical onto the religious, allowing both philosophical and religious discourse to sing from the same hymnbook of forgiveness.

In an interview with Richard Kearney, Ricoeur suggests that there may very well be a convergence between philosophy and religion. Explaining that all his hermeneutical-phenomenological studies are tied to a philosophical anthropology of *l'homme capable*, Ricoeur states:

> The ultimate purpose of hermeneutic reflection and attestation, as I see it, is to try to retrace the line of intentional capacity and action behind mere objects (which we tend to focus on exclusively in our natural attitude) so that we may recover the hidden truth of our operative acts—*of being capable*, of being *un homme capable*. So if hermeneutics is right, in the wake of Kant and Gadamer, to stress the finitude and limits of consciousness, it is also wise to remind ourselves of the tacit potencies and acts of our lived existence. My bottom line is a *phenomenology of being able*.[63]

Contrary to substantialist and mechanistic metaphysical derivations of Aristotle's *ousia*, Ricoeur appropriates Aristotle's idea of *dunamis,* Spinoza's *conatus*, and Schelling's and Leibniz's "notions of potentiality (*puissance*)" as a way of developing an ontology "of a dynamic in being that grows towards consciousness, reflection, community."[64] This allows Ricoeur to account for the "capable man," or the "basic capacity of a human being to act and suffer," as a dynamic power linked to an ontology of *Being-as-the-power-of-the-possible*. Ricoeur goes on to state, however, that although "I no longer subscribe to the typically antimetaphysical Protestant lineage of Karl Barth (though it is true that in early works like *The Symbolism of Evil*, I was still somewhat under this influence) . . . I am [now] not sure about the absolute irreconcilability between the God of the Bible and the God of Being."[65] This is an astonishing admission. Is this the "secret eschatology"[66] behind Ricoeur's dual allegiance to philosophy and religious faith?

While I don't think it is possible to uncover the secret religious motivation hiding in anyone's work, I do think Ricoeur offers a suggestion here that opens new meaning in front of his texts, that transforms the entire relation between philosophical and religious thought. Let us suppose for a moment that that which gives *Being-as-the-power-of-the-possible* and the God of Bible are the same. Further, let us assume that it is the power of God that courses through capable subjects, making possible the capacity for love and forgiveness. Now let us read "Difficult Forgiveness" a second time, from a religious point of view. While acts of forgiveness are always contextual and thus conditioned, Ricoeur can attest to the unconditionality of forgiveness because it is another name for the God of the Bible, who forgives unconditionally. He can sing a hymn of the height of forgiveness because it is the expression of height itself, a hymn of extravagance caught up in the love of God who "remains." The disproportion that separates the unconditionality and conditionality of forgiveness is, for Ricoeur, ultimately unsuited to giving a philosophical account of forgiveness because of his conviction concerning the original affirmation of the goodness of the capable man who can and does experience unconditional forgiveness within the fallible heart.

I find it difficult to accept that Ricoeur can account for his understanding of forgiveness without his religious faith. Why should anyone care about unconditional forgiveness, when a calculated exchange makes business as usual flourish once again? Why should I want to sing a hymn to the very height of unconditional forgiveness, when it is far easier to forget the past and carry on life as usual? And why should I want to repent and ask for forgiveness within "the most secret level of selfhood,"[67] unless I believe that it is possible for the God of unconditional love and forgiveness to hear in secret my confessions of repentance spoken deep within my hidden heart?

In other words, when Ricoeur offers his philosophical argument to help us think through "difficult forgiveness," I can imagine a man of deep faith singing a hymn in hope, regardless of fault, that there is forgiveness, and that it remains because God remains. Ricoeur's philosophy of the capable man makes more sense to me as the capacity to move beyond failure and fault, when it is coupled with the belief that we can begin again because love is the very power of beginning and indeed stronger than death and failure. Forgiveness remains because God remains as the power of forgiveness and grace that unbinds us from the past and lets us move forward in freedom. This is a religious affirmation through and through. If Ricoeur's philosophical claims rest in a kind of trust and attestation, then could we not say that Ricoeur's philosophy of attestation is only part of a larger dynamic of affirmation open to the source, the *Grund/Abgrund*, named as God in prayers said in faith? Isn't the heart of faith, expressed in prayer, always an affirmation, and why prayer ends with "Amen"? Therefore Ricoeur's philosophical agnosticism informs us about the anthropological structures required for forgiveness, but is open to the content of his Christian faith. The logic of the conditional and the unconditional folds into religious affirmation and back again, requiring and interpreting each by the other. But if this is the case, why does Ricoeur need to keep them so far apart? Rather than seeing Ricoeur's "double allegiance" as the need to separate philosophy and religion, what we see in Ricoeur's analysis of forgiveness is what has been operative all along, from the very beginning of his work, namely that "the logic of superabundance bursts the logic of equivalence," over and over again.[68] If the God of the Bible and the God who gives *Being-as-the-power-of-the-possible* converge, then it seems to me that Ricoeur's understanding of this logic of excess, surplus, donation, possibility, capability, is another way of naming the "logic" of generosity that Ricoeur finds in "the parables, proverbs, and eschatological sayings" of Jesus, and is therefore very difficult to separate from the source of surplus and donation. While we may concede that the hymn of unconditional forgiveness is closer to Ricoeur's deepest religious commitments, can we not also say that the logic of the surplus of meaning, and the act of creative productivity in discourse, uncovers the phenomenological and linguistic structures in which and through which the believing heart names the source that overflows the fragility of our finite being? If the question of difficult forgiveness is understood as the constant mediation between unconditional excess and conditional equivalence, doesn't this reveal a convergence that not only runs through the center of his understanding of language, but also through all the dialectical mediations that make up the body of his work? That is a question for further investigation; however, at this point it appears to me that Ricoeur's philosophy is one that has long since taken the risk of naming an excess and superabundance that undoes every system and sedimentation of exchange. Even if that name can only be said in so many different ways, imagine if such is made possible by the God who makes the impossible possible. Is that the God of the Bible, or the God who gives *Being-as-the-power-of-the-possible*? I will imagine that they are one and the same, and hope that such unconditional surplus always remains. Nevertheless, this is an eschatological hope attesting to the Essential, to the fundamental groundless ground, the God of the Bible, in whom all religious and philosophical thought find their source, wellspring, and superabundance of meaning.

Ultimately the call that comes from higher and further, when confessed as "a primordial adhesion to the life, the words, the death of Jesus,"[69] places the question of the Essential, or the truth of life, in an act of trust that walking the path of Christ is indeed a trustworthy response to the Essential that opens the present to a future through the "how much more" than possible.[70] So when Ricoeur claims that his adhesion to Christian faith "leads to discerning, to the concern to make sense of, to give the best arguments in situations of confrontation and . . . controversy,"[71] this religious confession of forgiveness, of the Essential, and of God that remains, is an affirmation beyond critical negation that employs a certain type of philosophical competence to understand how such is possible. This is not a secret fideism, but a way to understand how all discourse is open to the infinite, and that the infinite is the source of life itself, whose story is inscribed in the structure of the real made available to philosophical reflection. Ricoeur reminds us, in *Living Up to Death*, that there is a "temporal dimension of the fundamental,"[72] a story that unfolds in time, with a narrative rhythm that "I do not draw . . . out of myself, I find it already inscribed prior to me."[73] To say this about the narratives of Scriptures in which I find myself constituted and through which I am opened to the Essential, to God through "the life, the words, the death, [and resurrection] of Jesus," is not antiphilosophical, but simply a confession that God is the name of the infinite, the Essential, the groundless ground, of which both philosophical and religious discourse speak.

The Golden Rule and Forgiveness

GAËLLE FIASSE

Ethics and the Golden Rule

Mutual and Unilateral Relationships

As is well known, Ricoeur seeks to counter the egological tendencies of philosophies of the subject. With the emphasis he puts on the role of the other, in ethics he belongs to the group of thinkers concerned with otherness within the sphere of ethical thought. But at the same time, he also takes into consideration the excessive weight that this other places on the self. Raising doubts about Emmanuel Levinas's philosophy, while maintaining his admiration of the latter's hyperboles, Ricoeur wishes to underline the definitive aspect of receptivity when encountering the other.[1] There is no "you" without an "I" who is able to hear the call of this other. I am responsible "for and by" another, and I cannot hate myself if I want to stand before this other.[2]

One way to meet this challenge derives from Ricoeur's revival of the ethics of friendship. Through this, he is able to insist on the theme of mutuality. Furthermore, with reference to Aristotle, he also emphasizes that the friend loves the other for being who he is, and not because of mere advantage such as pleasure and utility. Understanding friendship in this manner, Ricoeur introduces the notion of reciprocity, which thus refers to mutual feelings, active benevolence, and the consideration of the other as another self. A friend, another self who trusts me, reveals to me who I am. By loving the best of myself, I can also give the other the best of my humanity. The self who is "acting and suffering"[3] can never ignore the importance of reciprocity. This crucial point needs to be highlighted. Through such a relationship of qualitative value, I experience myself and the other as both being irreplaceable.

In Ricoeur's ethics, the other is not limited to those persons with whom I share immediate and close relationships. In the same way that we are called to take care of our children and to fight against juvenile delinquency, we need to anchor our relationships and at the same time open ourselves up to otherness. As Ricoeur states, the good life is a life that is lived with and for another in just institutions. An ethics of reciprocity thus cannot impede the call of extension toward the third person and the requirement of equality that justice imposes. Ricoeur acknowledges this difficult demand and insists on not reducing the consideration of the other to face-to-face relationships.

This ethical approach, however, which takes into consideration the friend and the third person, is not sufficient for Ricoeur. Ethics needs to turn into "morality."[4] In other words, because our hearts can be biased by wrong desires, imperatives are a necessary route on the way to countering violence and evil. Hannah Arendt, in *The Human Condition*, relates the notion of respect to the theme of political friendship, which is an extended form of benevolence. But respect in Ricoeur appears as the *deontological* side of his notion of self-esteem.

In the development of the *ethical* aim, Ricoeur emphasizes the notion of self-esteem, which unfolds in three different dimensions (I, you, the community)—I am an agent who is able to esteem the goal and the choices of my life; I esteem myself thanks to a friend who believes in me; and I am indebted to a community that gives me standards of excellence by which to evaluate my actions.

This notion of self-esteem is then put to the test through formal rules, with a nod to the Kantian heritage, and is conceived of in terms of respect. The second formulation of the categorical imperative concerns the respect for the other as an end and not as a means. "Act in such a way that you treat humanity in yourself and in the other, never simply as a means, but as an end."[5] For Ricoeur, this echoes the theme of solicitude, in which mutual friendship helps to develop reflective self-esteem as described above. The originality of Ricoeur's presentation of the issue consists in the link between the Aristotelian aim of a good life, also called the teleological perspective, and the Kantian deontological approach, which emphasizes the formal rule of the categorical imperative. Ricoeur does not want to consider them antithetical, but rather complementary, even though he admits the difficulties involved in drawing upon two separate heritages.

One way to build this delicate bridge lies in his interpretation of the Golden Rule.

The Golden Rule serves as a transition from the solicitude of friendship to the formal rule of the Kantian imperative. Its transformational role is inescapable since we are prevented from neglecting genuine otherness as discovered in solicitude. The Golden Rule is therefore immediately tied to an ethics of reciprocity that confers the same value upon the other as upon the self. Furthermore, with respect to the Kantian imperative, it can be seen as the formalization of the Golden Rule.

This Golden Rule thus constitutes a major piece in Ricoeur's ethical puzzle, and one of my goals in this paper is to clarify how Ricoeur interprets it. As is well known, the Golden Rule has two different formulations: a negative one, which forbids us to do to the other what we would hate him to do to us, and a positive expression, which stresses the initiatives taken toward the other—which directs us, that is, to act as we would like the other to act toward us. The Gospel of Luke phrases it as follows: "Treat others as you would like them to treat you."[6] John Stuart Mill writes, in his famous *Utilitarianism*, "In the golden rule of Jesus of Nazareth, we read the complete spirit of the ethics of utility."[7] Many possible interpretations have been offered for the Golden Rule in the history of philosophy and in religious studies. I would like to emphasize, by examining the difficult notion of reciprocity in its light, how Ricoeur understands the Golden Rule. Such an analysis will be helpful in understanding the framework of his developments on forgiveness.

Ricoeur does not ignore the interpretation of the Golden Rule that insists on merely reacting to another action, or expecting something in return. But for him such a view would owe too much to the law of retaliation. It is thus necessary to understand correctly what he means when he refers to the *norm of reciprocity* in the Golden Rule.

Some formulations of the Golden Rule put us into a situation in which we *imagine* how the other is acting toward us, and how we *wish* he would act toward us. The Gospel of Matthew, for instance, expresses this idea as follows: "Whatever you wish that men would do to you, do so to them; for this is the law and the prophets" (Matt. 7:12). The ambiguity concerning a reciprocal "relationship" comes from the difficulty in interpreting this wish.

Strictly speaking, the "wish" does not mean that we act first toward the other as if we were expecting the same behavior on his part. We can act positively toward the other, even when we are unaware of how the other person will behave toward us, or even when this other does not presently act toward us in a benevolent manner. For instance, I may choose not to divulge someone else's secrets even if he or she has not respected my own. This example seems to break the first initiative based on a wish for reciprocity, but this in fact is not the case. The Golden Rule does not involve a logic of reciprocity, as if we were reacting to the other's behavior. Rather, it only suggests that an agent's wish to be respected should be construed as an inspiration to be benevolent toward this other.

It is thus becomes clear that the "norm of reciprocity" in the Golden Rule refers to a level other than reciprocal benevolence.[8] Indeed, I can act according to the Golden Rule before being in a reciprocal relationship, but I nonetheless act toward the other by imagining that he or she is the same as me. Inasmuch as I can imagine, I never consider myself as ruler over subordinated people, since I imagine that the other must be considered as oneself.[9] I thus treat the other with respect, and I overcome my selfish tendency, which could lead me to consider only my own interests and nothing else. We thus see that the Golden Rule is not intrinsically grounded on reciprocity as such, but includes the respect for the other as oneself and the altruistic dimension that comes along with this, in that the subject does not focus on his egoistic advantages, but on the other's benefit.[10]

These two elements, the other as oneself, and the non-egoistic perspective, can paradoxically be better understood by drawing an analogy with friendship. I have insisted that Ricoeur links the Golden Rule to the notion of solicitude. Let us focus on the similarity and dissimilarity between agency in the Golden Rule and action in friendship. Friendship is a conscious awareness between friends of mutual benevolence for each other's sake. With the Golden Rule, by contrast, the agent transposes himself into a situation where there is no knowledge of mutual feelings and intentions. A point of similarity nonetheless exists between the two, which helps us to understand the norm of reciprocity to which Ricoeur refers. In both cases, the other is considered as oneself; we do not see him in terms of our advantages, and we wish the best for the other.

In his discussion of friendship, Ricoeur asserts, "it averts any subsequent egological leanings: it is constitutive of mutuality."[11] The emphasis on reciprocity thus has a broader meaning than a strictly mutual relationship. Reciprocity is not only applicable to the relationship between friends (which is not present in the Golden Rule), but also to the other as a person to be treated with respect. In the Golden Rule, this latter meaning of reciprocity appears. I put myself in a situation where I see the effects of my action. My scope is not limited to the possibility of *my* power over the other. As in a mirror, I look at the *reciprocated image* of my behavior. In this sense, I am not concerned only with my primary advantages; rather,

I am able to take into consideration the person who will be affected by my actions. The norm of reciprocity, as expressed by Ricoeur, refers to this other side of action (i.e., the passive side, or the impact upon the other), and not to direct mutual feelings.

Interestingly, Ricoeur at times uses the term *asymmetry*, and at other times uses the term *dissymmetry*, to express this nonreciprocity and the absolute respect of the individuality of each person. *Asymmetry* means the absence of symmetry. In the same vein, *dissymmetry* shows the two-sided relationship of such an asymmetry; each has the possibility to act on the other. By acknowledging the dissymmetry initiated by my behavior, and by imagining how I could myself be a victim, given the passive form of such an action, I am led to see the manifold possibilities of violence. While the point of departure of the Golden Rule has been the notion of solicitude, especially expressed in the Gospel formula "*love* your neighbor as yourself," the point of arrival is now the prohibition to murder. The Golden Rule underlines at the same time both the norm of reciprocity and dissymmetry.[12] As Ricoeur more precisely puts it, "The Golden Rule and the imperative of the respect owed to persons also have the same aim: to establish reciprocity wherever there is a lack of reciprocity."[13] Emphasis on this last element demonstrates even more clearly in which sense the norm of reciprocity used to qualify the Golden Rule does not mean the concrete situation of a shared interpersonal relationship, but the respect owed to the other as "oneself" and yet first as "another." As asserted in Ricoeur's last book, *The Course of Recognition*, one is not the other, and the asymmetry protects the relationship against the trap of fusion (*union fusionnelle*).[14]

The term *reciprocity* may be understood in the French sense of "la *réciproque* d'une action," which means the *reverse* of the action—that is, its passive element. Reciprocity also concerns the perspective I have on the other as a self, and the rejection of an egoistic perspective. At issue here is "the rule of reciprocity which balances patient and agent," both as agents deserving respect.[15]

To better undersand this particular meaning of reciprocity, we can refer to the famous Ricoeurian "logic of equivalence." Ricoeur does not consider the purpose of the action to be a *do ut des* ("I give in order that you will give"), as if we were first focusing on what to get from the other. This would be a failed perspective, since we could never be sure of any response from the other at all (were this kind of argument needed). Such a calculation of returns would furthermore be biased in its intention. We must take the other into consideration for his or her own sake, and this demand is precisely what leads Ricoeur to criticize the abstraction of the second formulation of the categorical imperative. A Kantian formal rule can lead to an underestimation of genuine otherness, since it examines "humanity" in general and not "persons" who are different. Secondly, this second formulation of the categorical imperative is primarily subordinated to the first one, the formal principle of autonomy: "Act only according to that maxim by which you can at the same time will that it should become a universal law." Ricoeur thus puts forward this argument of "otherness" to express his skepticism and unease about Kant's formalisation. He does not aim at denying the Kantian heritage, but at grounding it in a teleological approach where the value of genuine otherness is fully endorsed.

It is thus important to acknowledge what Ricoeur means by a logic of equivalence, which considers the self under the binomial relationship "agent-patient." Such a logic permeates two major elements of Ricoeur's "little ethics": love and justice. As we have seen, Ricoeur puts strong emphasis on friendship, a reciprocal relationship in which each agent esteems the other as another self. The meaning of this equivalence seems to be more complex in the case of justice, because Ricoeur holds a double goal. He wants justice to be understood as a mutual disinterest for the interest of others, in which impartiality dominates, but he also links justice to the meaning of total interdependence, close to the notion of total responsibility. The first task of justice clearly appears when Ricoeur comments on John Rawls's theory of justice. The second is tied to Ricoeur's insistence on our mutual indebtedness toward others.

This double meaning is indicated by the play on the words and phrases *part, just parts,* and *taking part.* Ricoeur insists on our participation in institutions. The moral agent does not only benefit from equal shares or *parts* of distribution; rather, he also *takes part* in the life of the state. We are all, accordingly, indebted. To paraphrase the Stoics, nothing human is alien to us. Or to refer to one of Ricoeur's early writings, the just person appears not only under the figure of the "socius," the relationship mediated by institutions, but also under the figure of the "neighbor."

The author of "love and justice," however, does not wish to ignore the anonymity of our institutions and the rules of the social contract, which help us to treat everybody equally. Rather, this anonymity—which takes the form of a relationship of impartial indifference in the mouths of economists—becomes in Ricoeur a relationship of indebtedness, similar to that expressed in Levinas's vocabulary. This ambivalence is highlighted by Ricoeur himself, and it can help us to understand how his notion of justice problematizes the expression "economy of the gift," whose ambiguity has recently attracted the attention of W. David Hall.[16] As Ricoeur says, we encounter the tension between bilateral justice and unilateral love.

On the one hand, such as in fair distribution, the focus lies in a demand for reciprocity where all agents are supposed to act in the same manner, in the sense that all receive duties and responsibilities. Ricoeur is well aware that "to lend without expecting anything in return" could never become the standard of ethics.[17] On the other hand, Ricoeur points out the perverse interpretation of the logic of equivalence that could lead to a self-interested position. His consideration of justice leans toward indebtedness and not toward the utilitarian interpretation, as his full endorsement of Rawls's criticism of John Stuart Mill attests. Ricoeur never neglects the side of the weak, "the fragile" and unfortunate in society. This analysis of justice helps us understand why Ricoeur cannot conceive the Golden Rule as a law that must first favor our self-interest or rest upon a calculation of returns.

Now to better emphasize that the Golden Rule cannot be reduced to a resultant reaction preceding a given action, or to an anticipation of the other's behavior, I will turn to Ricoeur's logic of superabundance. We will see how this other logic informs his notion of the gift in his correlative expression, "economy of the gift."

The Supreme Gift and the Answer to a Call

According to Ricoeur, the Golden Rule cannot be understood only within a logic of equivalence. A logic of superabundance allows us to have a better grasp of it. Ricoeur even refers to the command to love one's enemies to illustrate this new interpretation of the ancient precept. Such a reading gives us, first, the possibility to emphasize even more than previously the altruistic side of the Golden Rule: it is not to be conceived in the sense of giving in order to be given to.[18] Second, the love of enemies will lead us to another difficulty, as Ricoeur also highly values the quality of reciprocal relationships. The radicalism of this command concerns our action toward an enemy, who by definition is not benevolent toward us. Is such an ethics incompatible with the benefits of a shared relationship where both agents are responsible for one another? I will show how Ricoeur tries to answer this challenge.

The starting point of his analysis lies in the Gospel of Luke, in the so-called Sermon on the Plain. For Ricoeur, the Golden Rule appears with all its splendor as a logic of equivalence—"As you wish that men would do to you, do so to them"—even though, as we mentioned, this equivalence rests on a wish and not on a concrete reciprocal relationship. In the next verse, the Sermon immediately draws upon a logic of superabundance, mentioning that there is no merit in only loving those who love us; on the contrary, "love your enemies, and do good, and lend, expecting nothing in return" (Luke 6:35). Ricoeur acknowledges the break this new command to love our enemies represents with respect to the opposition neighbor/enemy, in contrast to a reciprocal relationship based on equivalence. He therefore immediately situates this verse from Luke within a context of love. The end of the verse mentions that God is also kind to the ungrateful and selfish. Accordingly, Ricoeur highlights the particular context of such a harsh command: that of love as a gift.

In his article "Love and Justice," Ricoeur's point of reference becomes Franz Rosenzweig's interpretation in *The Star of Redemption*. The imperative of love is not interpreted as the figure of a God-judge who imposes a law from above, but is to be read as a loving answer, finding its expression in the Song of Songs by "love me." Drawing from the Latin or French phraseology "le commandement *de l'amour*," which can be translated as "the command *to* love" or "the command *of* love," Ricoeur plays on the double significance of this verbal noun complement. With the command to love (objective genitive), love is the object, whereas with the command of love (subjective genitive), love is the subject. Instead of being a mere "command to love," a duty or an imperative, it can thus also be read as a subjective genitive; "love" commands in a more positive sense. Love itself has the initiative, God, who has first loved us.[19] Or as Franz Rosenzweig states, "As he loves you, so shall you love."[20] The command to love our enemies is thus not a unilateral commandment, since it proceeds from love itself. Ricoeur emphasizes this starting point by turning to Christ himself, who does not only obey his father, but gives his own life.[21]

Before being a command to love (objective genitive), this imperative is a loving answer. I thus do not act toward the other "in order" to get a favorable return, which in the case of an enemy does not even appear plausible. But I act toward the other from love "because" love was given to me by God. The gift calls for another gift, but gratuitousness prevails over any kind of obligation or calculation of returns. It is here that the delicate point of reciprocity arises, and here that our analysis sheds light on the perplexities of commentators who do not see that a gift can call for another gift, without being a calculation of returns.[22]

Now, even taking into consideration the inseparability of love for God and love for the neighbor, we might object that this loving answer is directed toward God who has loved us first. Thus, following this objection, reciprocity with the enemy would seem definitely impossible. In answer to that, we may focus on Ricoeur's attention to how perverted would be an ethics that could not take reciprocity into consideration. He stresses that neglect of a reciprocal relationship could lead the receiver into a terrible debt. A "tension" thus needs to be maintained. First, we do not act in order to be given to, since our first intention is directed toward the other, and is not motivated by our selfish interests. Secondly, a hope remains, which itself belongs to the economy of the gift. This hope concerns the unknown possibilities of the agent—that is, his capabilities in spite of his fallibilities.

I offer two examples in order to clarify this perspective: a gift to a friend and the pacifist movement. When we offer a gift to a dear friend, we do not do it because we seek a gift in return. We do it for him or her. Now, love is such that we can wish this gift to be appreciated and to give rise to a reciprocated movement. The hope is thus there, but it is not the source of the motivation. Nonviolent action is similar. When Martin Luther King Jr. invites his brothers to love their enemies, he emphasizes the necessity of breaking the chain of violence and retaliation in the inner self. He knows that nonviolent agents must deal with people who do not endorse their principles. His first motivation cannot be to act in the same way others do. Nonetheless, for him the nonviolent attitude remains a power of action. Love can transform the enemy. Hope for such a move is thus maintained, even though it is not the original intention.

Forgiveness

The norm of reciprocity, the dissymmetry, the economy of the gift, and the hope in the other are keys to understanding Ricoeur's consideration of forgiveness. The title of his epilogue to *Memory, History, Forgetting,* "Difficult Forgiveness," is not a coincidence. Ricoeur does not want to start with an impossible forgiveness, as does Derrida, but neither does he adopt a naïve position. He knows that forgiving is difficult, even sometimes impossible, or "(almost) impossible." Furthermore, he also considers the dangers of minimizing the reality of the fault. Forgiveness must not be confused with forgetting. The dilemma of forgiveness resides on one hand in the recognition of the negative action, and on the other hand in the possibility of unbinding the agent from his action. Ricoeur combines the horizontal equation of forgiveness between the two protagonists, and the height of forgiveness. This process is similar to his interpretation of the Golden Rule, which is not a calculation, but which never neglects the wish for reciprocity. As with the Golden Rule, I will show how the notions of binomial reciprocity, dissymmetry, and hope apply to Ricoeur's understanding of forgiveness by focusing on the difference between depth and height, and the distinction between agent and action.

The Gift of Forgiveness

Our use of the word *forgiveness* refers to two poles of a complex reality: on one side the person who is in a position to forgive the wrong that was committed against him or her, and on the other side the person who may request forgiveness and who may be forgiven. Ricoeur maintains both the unconditionality of forgiveness—translated in his language by the *height* of forgiveness—and the necessity to take into consideration the avowal and the repentance of the offender. This ambivalence can only be understood, however, in the light of Ricoeur's economy of the gift.

Ricoeur's insistence on the height of forgiveness may be seen as a positive echo to the Derridian concern that forgiveness could be misused and biased by ulterior motives. Forgiveness is not a horizontal transaction, or a mere exchange mediated by a request and a return. In this sense, "forgiveness is unconditional: it comes before any expectation, any petition."[23] Similarly, the one who asks for forgiveness must be ready to also receive a negative answer, such as "no, I cannot forgive." This assessment is parallel to the criticism of a utilitarian interpretation of the Golden Rule. Forgiveness cannot be an interested exchange. Ricoeur insists on the distance that exists between the depth of the fault and the height of forgiveness.

Ricoeur also refers to the analysis of Hannah Arendt, who draws a parallel between forgiveness and a promise. Arendt wishes to show that action can be paralyzed by unpredictability and by irreversibility.[24] A promise counters the first risk by giving stability. Through making a commitment with a promise, my action can endure. Forgiveness answers the second risk. It delivers the agent from the consequences of his action. While Arendt is interested in the temporal dimension of action, Ricoeur focuses his attention on the particular link between the agent and the action. He adopts Arendt's expression of the bond, but he does not adhere to the strict parallel she draws between promising and forgiving in terms of human faculties. Arendt argues in favor of this human power by referring to the importance of forgiving in order to be forgiven in the Christian prayer to God the father. Ricoeur, on the contrary, while acknowledging the positive aspects of Arendt's remarks, insists more on the height of forgiveness than on the human faculty.

Such a distance also allows him to spotlight the depth of the fault, which cannot be neglected. The fault is *de jure* unforgivable; "There is something irreparable in human affairs."[25] Such a recognition explains why forgiving cannot be confused with forgetting. Forgiveness confronts fault and is linked to memory. We cannot get rid of the traces, but we may hope to be "delivered from their mischievousness." We may here refer to the whole work of Ricoeur, *Memory, History, Forgetting*. Forgiveness appears as the eschatological horizon of memory, history, and forgetting. We may recover the "lightness of existence," not by forgetting the debt, but by lifting it. By recognizing the depth of the fault, we may see that forgiveness is always a height. The author uses the expression *there is forgiveness* to assert that forgiveness, like love, remains. As Ricoeur states, the vocabulary of forgiveness belongs to philosophy, theology, and poetry. We cannot say whether it comes from above or from humans. "There is forgiveness," as there is love, even when we seem unable to forgive.[26]

Although Ricoeur maintains this height of forgiveness, he does not ignore the risk that an ethics unable to take reciprocity into consideration might make itself present. Here, we find the other aporia that came to light in the context of the economy of the gift. In the same way that solicitude was recognized as a major ethical step, we cannot deny the correlation between forgiveness requested and forgiveness granted.[27] It even belongs to our recognition of the other's dignity that we maintain our expectation that he will recognize his fault. Of course, Ricoeur is not unaware of the tendency toward victimization and all the difficulties involved in declaring oneself guilty. Still, his insistence on keeping forgiveness within a binomial relationship leads to his taking into consideration the admission of guilt and the avowal on one side and the receptivity of forgiveness on the other side.

We all know from experience that it is easier to forgive somebody who recognizes he is at fault. In this way, the expectation of such an admission makes sense, as does the request for forgiveness. The logic of superabundance is not intended to create inequality. We have seen that reciprocity was maintained in the love command as a hope for the enemy. In the same vein, as humanitarian aid can place too heavy a burden on the receiver, forgiveness can be corrupted by denying the critical role of dialogue.

The height of forgiveness does not mean a condescending superiority; that is why it cannot neglect the importance of avowal, repentance, and even reparation. The hope that forgiveness may be requested and received remains. Forgiveness must be thought of in terms of a gift that answers to love, an act that may inspire a "giving back," but that is not motivated by it, contrary to mere calculation of competing interests. As we have seen, the example of love for an enemy can clearly illustrate this position as well. While forgiveness acts first and foremost from the sole motivation of breaking the reaction of revenge, and not because we initially want to be loved by the enemy, such an attitude highlights the power of action and does not discard the hope that a transformation will occur in the enemy as well. We are not motivated by what we will get from the other, but it would at the same time be wrong to have no wish or hope for a conversion.[28] Avowal, repentance, and even reparation can thus be welcomed.

The Action and the Agent

Now the recognition of guilt must face yet another of Derrida's objections. For him, forgiving after avowal would imply forgiving somebody different from the one who committed the original crime, since the person who repents, just through the act of repentance, is already a better person. Ricoeur answers this problem by insisting on the different possibilities of the capable man. As he has continually shown in his previous writings, the human being is "acting and suffering." Here, Ricoeur turns to the practical dimension of freedom, not to its theoretical presupposition. We can only attest to our freedom through actions that bear witness to it. This attestation is also an act of faith, a belief in the different powers of the self, which counters the "proud foundation of the subject."[29] Ricoeur rejects the category of substance because he fears that a metaphysical core might predetermine the subject. But he maintains the category of being as "power and act" in order to give an ontological dimension to his philosophy of action. He insists more on the power to act than on accomplishments. This approach appears in his answer to Derrida. Ricoeur suggests that both the "capacity" and "effectuation" at the heart of our very power to act be decoupled.[30] He does not wish to deny the unforgivable character of the guilty self. In response, the Kantian distinction between radical evil and an original disposition to good are put forward. The imputability of our actions cannot be separated from the experience of the fault. An intimate bond "unites the agent to the action, the guilty to the crime."[31] But if evil is radical, the original disposition to good is primary. Turning to Kant's *Religion within the Boundaries of Mere Reason*, he accentuates this predisposition to good and the project of liberation of such goodness in human beings. Such a process may also be perceived as "an act of faith, a credit addressed to the resources of self-regeneration."[32] It should also be noted that Ricoeur insists on the Kantian philosophical arguments, while maintaining that the theme of forgiveness cannot escape "theological contamination."

In his developments within the judicial sphere, Ricoeur emphasizes that there is no forgiveness for the courts. Forgiveness can be granted only by persons toward persons. To consider forgiveness at the level of institutions would create impunity, which is a great injustice. Nonetheless, he dares to speak of a spirit of forgiveness, or, borrowing the expression of Klaus Kodalle, an "incognito" of forgiveness.[33] While judging the fault, we need to keep the consideration of the guilty person's human dignity. In an article in which he analyses the question of criminal delinquency, Ricoeur even speaks about an *imago dei* that can never be destroyed, even in the most ruined being.[34] We can thus see that theology is never far from his conviction. On the ultimate horizon, the notion of hope remains a crucial point. "Because God is the God of hope, the goodness of creation becomes the sense of a direction."[35] Forgiveness granted is thus really addressed to the agent whose humanity can never totally be abolished. Ricoeur observes, however, that if we are not able to express our consideration to the authors of abominable crimes, it is a sign of our limited ability to love absolutely. The difficulty of forgiving thus acutely makes itself felt. If forgiveness can be seen as the horizon of memory, it does not mean that the scars are to be erased. The loss is thus real, and the work of mourning necessary. In this sense, if life is carried on under the reign of memory and forgetting, we are nonetheless always confronted with incompletion, which is also the last word of Ricoeur's *Memory, History, Forgetting.*

Toward Which Recognition?

JEAN GREISCH

The last book that Paul Ricoeur published in his life bears the beautiful title *The Course of Recognition.*[1] I do not know whether it has already been translated into German, or if it has been, under what title. In my view, the translation that would best do justice to the work of thought to which Ricoeur invites his readers would be *Unterwegs zum Anerkennen.*

Since the philosopher's death, this title takes on new connotations that transform the task of reading and appropriating his work into a "course of recognition," with its own risks and dangers, which each reader will carry out while wondering who this philosopher was who occupies a singular place in twentieth-century philosophy, which kind of recognition of oneself "as another" he made possible, and how the major themes of his thought can contribute to promoting a culture of mutual recognition that is not reduced to a mortal combat admitting but a single victor.

Read in this way, the title is itself transformed into an invitation to reread Ricoeur's philosophical path as the slow and patient beginning of an unfinished, and by definition unfinishable, work of recognition. If we accept this invitation, the three conceptual foci around which this final work revolves—recognition-identification, self-recognition, mutual recognition opening onto the problematic of gratitude and gift—are enriched by a fourth dimension that would deserve its own study: recognition-exploration.

During one of our last conversations, Ricoeur himself recalled this dimension in telling me an anecdote. During the "phony war," his commander ordered: "Ricoeur, go scout the forest over there, to make sure there are no Germans hiding!" "I carried out the order," said Ricoeur, "and I returned five years later!" This anecdote seems to me to mesh well with a style of thought I characterize as a "philosophy of detour." Despite everything that separates Ricoeur and Hegel, the two thinkers share the conviction that "the way of the spirit is primarily mediation, it is detour." If they part ways, it is because Ricoeur excludes the possibility of a total mediation, where absolute Spirit would be the final master and guarantor of the project.

There are obviously many ways "to recognize," that is, to explore and navigate, the immense philosophical territory that Ricoeur left behind. The three studies gathered together in his last work lead to a negative report: the absence of a philosophical theory of recognition analogous to other theories of knowledge. The formulation "the course of my survey" indicates that Ricoeur does not have as an ambition the bridging of such a considerable gap.[2] It is a matter of showing, more modestly, under which conditions one can "confer on the sequence of known philosophical occurrences of the word *recognition* the coherence of a rule-governed polysemy capable of serving as a rejoinder to that found on the lexical plane."[3] The preface and introduction to *The Course of Recognition*, in which Ricoeur to some extent "reads aloud" the notes that the *Littré* and the *Grand Robert* devote to this concept, would deserve to be included in the remarkable *Vocabulaire européen de philosophie* recently published by Barbara Cassin, which rightly does not include a corresponding entry. Indeed, as the French language gathers under the single verb *reconnaître* no less than twenty different definitions, one can easily imagine the problems of translation that result from it, which the translator of *The Course of Recognition* must resolve.

From Fallible Man to a Self Capable of Recognition

The three studies that mark out this course are underlain by the conviction that "philosophy does not advance by a lexical improvement dedicated to the description of ordinary language as it is commonly used," that its task is dictated to it by "the emergence of properly philosophical problems that slice through the simple regulating of the ordinary language in terms of its use,"[4] to the point that they constitute true "thought events" inaugurating "a new way of asking questions."[5] Before examining in greater detail the way in which Ricoeur establishes his "course of recognition," it seems useful to me, in the spirit of recognition-exploration mentioned above, to ask from the outset what connection this work maintains with the rest of the author's philosophical work.

In the absence of any explicit indication provided by Ricoeur himself, I will formulate three hypotheses.

1. The first is related to the initial hermeneutic breakthrough of 1960, which occurs in the two-part work *Fallible Man* and *The Symbolism of Evil.* If the "symbol gives rise to thought," it is because it is, by definition, a symbol of recognition, as Plato emphasizes in the *Symposium*: "Each one of us is thus a symbol of man, cut as it were like a fish, the splitting of a unity; and each always seeks its other half, the symbol of himself."[6] A hermeneutics of the symbol cannot be satisfied with analyzing the various planes of symbolic manifestation—oneiric, cosmic, poetic—or with making the symbol a second-order sign. It must also be interested in the fundamental function of the symbol, which, as Edmond Ortigues emphasized in *Le discours et le symbole*, is mainly a function of recognition, independent of the diversity of the symbolized contents. In this sense, one can wonder whether the hermeneutics of the symbol that Ricoeur sought to develop through the 1960s does not already contain the seed of the problem of recognition.

2. This bond is made more explicit in the 1990s, in the works that come in the wake of *Oneself as Another*. What Ricoeur modestly calls the "little ethics" developed in studies 7 to 9 of that book—which is, needless to say, actually an ethics of a great sort—culminates with the idea of a "critical" *phronèsis* that seeks to understand how situational moral judgment, whose notable trait is comparable to sense intuition,[7] takes shape through public debate, friendly discussion, and shared convictions. This daring attempt "at reconciling Aristotle's *phronēsis*, by way of Kant's *Moralität*, with Hegel's *Sittlichkeit*"[8] seems to me to deserve being labeled as Ricoeur's first "work of recognition."

Oneself as Another takes as its task the deployment of the quadruple range of the questions: "Who is speaking? Who is acting? Who is telling his or her story? Who is the moral subject of imputation?"[9] It does so by examining the various figures of the self that emerge over the course of an investigation initially ordered by the dialectic of selfhood and sameness, then by the dialectic of selfhood and otherness. The investigation leads to the thesis according to which otherness does not come to be added from outside to a selfhood already armed from head to toe, "as though to prevent its solipsistic drift," but rather belongs "to the tenor of meaning and to the ontological constitution of selfhood."[10]

The work has no apparent conclusion if it is not the declaration, made "in the tone of socratic irony," that the three methods of otherness that constitute the three great experiences of passivity-otherness—namely, that of the body itself, the other, and the moral conscience—must be recognized each one in its specificity, instead of being reduced to a common denominator. But one should not forget that the ninth study of the book, where Ricoeur completes what he calls his "phenomenologico-hermeneutic cycle," contains, from its side, a kind of conclusion in the form of a rereading of the course completed up to that point, very much in the style of the conclusions of the author's great works. Ricoeur shows there that the three problems stated in the introduction to the book—"the detour of the reflection on 'who?' by the analysis of 'what? why? how?'; concordance and discordance between *idem*-identity and *ipse*-identity; the dialectic of the self and the other than self"[11]—are each able to be connected to an emblematic term borrowed from ancient and modern moral philosophy, which the hermeneutics of the self then enables to be enriched and specified.

At the crossroads of esteeming the goals of action characterized by the predicates *good* and *obligatory* and self-esteem, one encounters the concept of *imputability*, defined as "the ascription of action to its agent, *under the condition of the ethical and moral predicates* which characterize the action as good, just, conforming to duty, done out of duty, and, finally, as being the wisest in the case of conflictual situations."[12]

The second crossroads, at the intersection of the concepts of selfhood and sameness, is shaped by the concept of responsibility. As Ricoeur had shown in the fifth and sixth studies of *Oneself as Another*, the true nature of narrative identity appears only in the light of the dialectic of selfhood and sameness. Narrative identity interlaces the perseveration of character with the permanence of creative fidelity, while prohibiting the confusion of constancy and continuity. With respect to the problems of the ethical act, the same dialectic finds expression in the concept of *responsibility*, which Ricoeur inflects in the triple register of relationship to the future, to the past, and to the present. Can a self be said to be "responsible" that assumes the future consequences of its acts, including the most remote consequences, on which Hans Jonas lays the stress in *The Imperative of Responsibility*? But Ricoeur does not hesitate to speak as much about a responsibility for the past "that affects us without its being entirely our own work."[13] The responsibility in this case takes the form of a recognized debt. The third enrichment the hermeneutics of the self brings to the concept of responsibility concerns the relationship of the self to the present, which ceases to appear as a purely specific instant.

The final suggestion of this brief rereading of the phenomenologico-hermeneutic cycle that frames the first nine studies of *Oneself as Another* needs only one paragraph. Ricoeur affirms there that in the dialectic between oneself and the other, that the self finds its adequate expression in the category of *recognition*, so dear to Hegel in the Jena period. One can thus consider that the thesis on which this rereading concludes is also the germinal cell of *The Course of Recognition*: "Recognition is a structure of the self reflecting on the movement that carries self-esteem toward solicitude and solicitude toward justice. Recognition introduces the dyad and plurality in the very constitution of the self. Reciprocity in friendship and proportional equality in justice, when they are reflected in self-consciousness, make self-esteem a figure of recognition."[14]

The fact that this allusion to the philosophical importance of the category of recognition is paired with a reference to Hegel invites us to give to *The Course of Recognition* the sense of a combat course. It is a matter, for Ricoeur's part, of an ultimate "fight for recognition," taking this expression in the sense given it by Pierre-Jean Labarrière and Gwendoline Jarczyk in their translation and commentary on the chapter of *Phenomenology of Spirit* traditionally entitled "The Master-Slave Dialectic," a chapter that, as a careful look at the overall economy of *Phenomenology of Spirit* indeed suggests, can be read as a first fight for recognition.

3. *Oneself as Another* opens the ultimate major philosophical building site of Ricoeur, designated by the heading "phenomenology of the capable human." The fact that the second study of *The Course of Recognition* consists of a whole chapter that retrieves the same formula only proves that the capacity of recognition, with the triple sense of recognition-identification, recognition of oneself, and mutual recognition whose highest expression is gratitude, forms a decisive link for such a phenomenology.

A formula from the preface to *The Course of Recognition* recapitulates the whole trajectory of the book: it is a question of adopting "the dynamic which presides first over the promotion of recognition-identification, then over the transition from this identification of something in general to the recognition of those entities specified by ipseity, then from self-recognition to mutual recognition, and finally to the ultimate equating of recognition and gratitude, which French is one of the few languages to honor."[15] Neither the choice of *terminus a quo*: identity-identification, nor that of *terminus ad quem*: the request for recognition, comes from oneself. They are philosophical choices in the strong sense of the term, so it is important to determine the stakes by bringing them back to "a philosophical history of philosophical questioning."[16]

Noting "the absence of a grand unified philosophy of recognition," Ricoeur chooses to concern himself with three major philosophical spaces that constitute major intellectual events on the path to problematizing the concept: the Kantian space of *Rekognition*, in the first edition of the *Critique of Pure Reason*; the Bergsonian space of the "recognition of memories," in *Matter and Memory*, a space already visited by Ricoeur in the first part of *Memory, History, Forgetting*; and, *last but not least*, the Hegelian space of *Anerkennung*, in the *Realphilosophie* of Hegel at Jena. The disparity of terms is less important than the disparity of the respective philosophical styles, which take us in succession from a transcendental philosophy to a reflexive psychology to a speculative philosophy of spirit.

One measures the audacity of Ricoeur's wager, which consists of wanting to balance this manifest disparity of problematics, at ease with conceptual transitions between philosophemes as distinct as mountain peaks. This audacity may be recognized again by another symptom: the decision to climb each of the three peaks not by following a chronological order, but rather by following an order of problematization that gives priority to Kantian recognition over Bergsonian recognition and Hegelian *Anerkennung*. Beginning with the problematic of recognition-identification is justified by the conviction that "it is indeed our most authentic identity, the one that makes us who we are, that demands to be recognized."[17] So long as this identity is not "identified," that is to say recognized for what it is, neither does one know what is at stake in the mutual recognition referred to by Hegel's celebrated expression in the *Phenomenology Spirit*: "self-consciousness attains its satisfaction only in another self-consciousness."[18]

Instead of being simply a pure I, the living self-consciousness is "*a self-consciousness for a self-consciousness*,"[19] which, says Hegel, corresponds to "the experience of that which is spirit," that of "*I* who [is] we, and *we* who is *I*." Thus opens the specific order of the desire for recognition, which, for Hegel, enters us into the "spiritual daylight of what is completely present."[20] This "spiritual daylight" is reserved for those who have taken full measure of the implications of the term *Anerkennung*, namely a relationship in which the self-consciousness is so closely "interlaced" (*Verschränkung*) with the consciousness of the other that it must be said that it "only exists . . . insofar as it is acknowledged."[21] Hegel takes care to specify that it is about an "interlacing in multiple aspects and multiple senses" (*eine vielseitige und vieldeutige Verschränkung*); therefore it should be taken into account if one wants to clarify the tenor of sense of "for" in the guiding formula "self-consciousness for a self-consciousness." Emmanuel Levinas will interpret this *Verschränkung* as an ethical "intrigue" of otherness that clarifies the structure of "the one for the other." Just as one can ask what Levinasian "intrigue" adds to Hegelian *Verschränkung*, one can ask how Ricoeur's *The Course of Recognition* modifies what Hegel calls "the movement of *recognition* " that is also a "*doing*" (*Tun*). In entering into the order of recognition, the consciousness is torn from itself, in such a way that there is for it from then on another consciousness external to it. Perhaps it has not been sufficiently noticed that, in *Phenomenology of Spirit*, the movement of recognition brings forth a "oneself" that is defined as "*oneself* in *the other*" (*sich selbst im Anderen*).

Is this the "oneself as another" that Ricoeur seeks to close in on in his hermeneutics of the self? Here is not the place to tackle such a thorny question. It is enough for us to note that the formula "to renounce Hegel," which Ricoeur made use of in *Time and Narrative, III* to express the way in which that book took its distance from the Hegelian philosophy of history without giving up the project of thinking history, retains all its topicality in the third study of *The Course of Recognition*. In fact, the problem is knowing what sense a hermeneutics that gave up the presuppositions of a philosophy of spirit—that is, a philosophy of total mediation—can give to the Hegelian formula that recapitulates a movement of redoubling (*Verdoppelung*) in multiple directions: the double direction of being-other; the double direction of the sublation (*Aufheben*); the double direction of the return into oneself: "*They are recognized as mutually recognizing*" (Sie *anerkennen* sich als *gegenseitig sich anerkennend*), the formula that summarizes, according to Hegel, "the pure concept of recognition."

The Test of the Unrecognizable and the Small Miracle of Recognition-Identification

Each of the three studies in Ricoeur's work is preceded by an epigraph that tells us much about the spirit of his investigation.

The first study, which treats recognition as identification, is deployed under the aegis of a declaration of Pascal, excerpted from "Conversation with M. de Saci": "The essence of any mistake consists in not knowing it." From the outset, this formula draws our attention to the difference between a mistake and simple ignorance. A mistake is more than a simple error of judgment. We could say that it is an error of judgment that has its source in an erroneous identification—a universal experience if ever there was one, which can be set alongside what Schleiermacher said about the universality of misrecognition.

This explains why Ricoeur chooses to take as his point of departure not Kant but Descartes. This Cartesian detour confronts us with a problem of identification in which identifying comes down to distinguishing, whereas for Kant, to identify means to connect. One can certainly see there an obligatory tip of the hat to the ancestor of reflexive philosophies, a line to which Ricoeur attaches his own hermeneutic project. But there is a deeper reason: Descartes is not only one of the great philosophers of judgment, who deserves a place of honor in a "phenomenology of judgment";[22] the shadow cast by "the threat of error that runs through Cartesian discourse"[23] also accompanies the attempt to work out a philosophical theory of recognition that must, in some way or other, grant its entire place to the experience of the mistake.

As Ricoeur emphasizes, such a theory cannot be truly rooted in Cartesian ground, because the subject beset by doubt (or, what is more Cartesian, the subject who decides to doubt for good, radically and hyperbolically) does not discover the need for distinguishing the operations of knowledge and recognition unless the mistake finds its source not in a simple subjective hesitation, but takes on an objective aspect. This is what occurs when, in the presence of a man devastated by Alzheimer's disease (or disfigured by anguish), we exclaim: "He became unrecognizable."

This type of statement helps us to understand the Kantian facet of judgment, that is, the capacity for the connection of understanding that enables us "to grasp a unified meaning through thought," in other words, to recognize by identifying.[24] What in certain cases renders this work of recognition very difficult or even impossible is nothing other than the distorting power of time: "It is no longer how it was!" It is indeed time and "the idea of identification understood as a connection in time"[25] that is in question in the Kantian analysis of the "synthesis of recognition in the concept" which comes to prolong the "synthesis of apprehension in intuition" and the "synthesis of reproduction in imagination."[26]

Without going into detail on the interpretation of such important Kantian topics as transcendental imagination and the doctrines of schematism that Ricoeur outlines throughout the pages he devotes to Kant, I will retain above all the confession that opens the third section of *The Course of Recognition*: "The question of moving beyond Kant is a difficult one."[27] It is tempting to connect this statement with the similar point made in the chapter "Should We Renounce Hegel?" in *Time and Narrative, III.* On both sides, the difficulty is due to the fact that wanting "to correct" these intellectual giants is as vain and futile as returning a paper to a student with the comment, "Could do better!" Whether with respect to Kant or Hegel, it is essential to say "just what it is that one is breaking with, and how radical that break may be."[28]

In fact it is a matter, for Ricoeur, "by the same gesture to refuse the Copernican reversal and to move out of this magic circle of representation."[29] His allies in leading this combat for "the ruin of the representation"[30] (using Levinas's formula) are many and, in a sense, perhaps even a little too numerous: in addition to Levinas, Ricoeur evokes Husserl and Heidegger, to which one could add Michel Henry. On this point, the reader of *The Course of Recognition* is left a little unsatisfied, wishing to know with more precision which strategy Ricoeur himself implements to avoid the imperialism of representation.

It is in the name of a philosophy of being-in-the-world, capable of differentiating several modes of being (*Seinsweisen*, as Heidegger would say) to which correspond as many distinct modes of temporalization, that the primacy of the representation is broken. One day I happened to recognize somebody whom I had lost track of—not his facial features, but the way in which I recalled his name. Whereas the simple mistake arose from the confusion of two representations (my scanner confused the letter *L* and number *1* or the letter *I*), the misrecognition rises to another level, which transforms the reappearance of the same, if not into a "small miracle,"[31] at least into a small victory over the universal inconsistency, and gives a touching gift to the disillusioned wisdom of Qohelet in the Bible.

One thus understands better why Ricoeur completes his first study in the pages of Proust's *Time Regained*. It is the episode of the illustrious dinner party in which the narrator finds, for the length of one dinner, familiar characters from his past made unrecognizable by the outrages inflicted by age. Does the modern novelist here pay his tribute to the long tradition of *memento mori* and the *dance macabre*? What is more unrecognizable than a skeleton? Ricoeur wonders: "Has recognition reached its apex, at least as identification, when it has to be won from the unrecognizable?"[32] The question seems to be rhetorical, because it is enough for anyone to recall the moments when confronted with "the test of the unrecognizable" to understand that, in certain cases, recognition can be transformed into a truly Sisyphian task.

The solution of the dilemma raised by Proust recalls the formula Ricoeur himself makes use of to define what one might call his "second hermeneutics," which move the accent from the symbol toward the text. Its guiding formula: "To understand is to understand oneself in front of the text . . . exposing ourselves to the text and receiving from it an enlarged self."[33] This resonates strongly with the words of Proust: "The writer's work is merely a kind of optical instrument which he offers to the reader to enable him to discern what, without this book, he would perhaps never have perceived in himself." It will be noticed, however, that

Proust's thesis, "The recognition by the reader in his own self of what the book says is the proof of its veracity, the contrary also being true," is moderated by "at least to a certain extent," a nuance whose weight must be measured.

Before analyzing the way in which Ricoeur himself envisions this "different sort of recognition,"[34] I will conclude this analysis of the first study with a remark that puts me at odds with the funeral image of the dinner party.

Even if the expression *it is unrecognizable* usually refers to a disfiguration that makes identification difficult, can the opposite not be considered, where the misrecognition has as its source a "transfiguration"? "I wouldn't have recognized her" can also be the expression of astonishment when faced with the "small miracle" of a successful transformation. A reader of the New Testament will not fail to see this possibility in the way in which the evangelists speak about the appearances of the resurrected Christ in front of his disciples. If their eyes "are prevented from recognizing Him," it is not because they deal with a ghost, but with a "sur-vivor." Perhaps the fact that the Lukan account of the disciples on the road to Emmaus several times uses the verb *to recognize* invites us to concern ourselves with this very singular "course of recognition" that was necessary for them to complete.

To Recognize Oneself as Another

The second study of *The Course of Recognition* has as its epigraph a sentence from Arthur Rimbaud, taken from a letter to George Izambard: "I recognized myself as poet." It is enough to replace the word *poet* with that of *philosopher* to guess the sense it might have for Ricoeur himself. The short draft of an intellectual autobiography published under the title *Réflexion faite* could have as a subtitle, *How I Recognized Myself as Philosopher.*

The way in which Ricoeur develops the concept of the recognition of oneself is even more disconcerting than the strategy he adopted in the first study. The first surprise for the reader concerns his decision to mobilize "the Greek sources," notwithstanding the fact, strongly emphasized by Rémi Brague in *Aristote et la question du monde*, that the Greeks seem to have been unaware of "oneself" as a philosophical problem.[35] This rehabilitation of the Greek inheritance, which Ricoeur shares with Bernard Williams, begins with Homer and finishes with the Aristotelian conception of deliberation. All this happens as though the phenomenology of the capable human, which Ricoeur summarizes briefly in the second chapter of this study, must first declare its Greek sources before being able to turn to the modern theorists of self-consciousness, transcendental or empirical.

The readers of Ricoeur who accompanied him through his reflections on the connections between the philosophical and extraphilosophical—connections that never lead to genre confusion—or who contemplated the interlude entitled "Tragic Action" in *Oneself as Another,* will not be particularly surprised by the place occupied by the Homeric account of Ulysses's return to Ithaca and Sophocles's *Oedipus at Colonus* in this reconstitution of the Greek contribution to the problems of self-recognition. What holds Ricoeur's attention in the famous passage of the *Odyssey* are "the verbal formulas of recognition, the role of the marks of recognition, and that of disguises."[36] *Larvatus prodeo*: it is as Ulysses presents himself at his home, provoking on the part of his friends and relatives a work of recognition resting on different signs, of which some are other-than-simple traces, such as the scar by which the old servant recognizes her master. Over the course of this "tale of recognition," there unfolds a whole semiotics of recognition that would deserve a study of its own by someone well versed in the work on a "hermeneutics of the trace," which, unlike the hermeneutics of signs and symbols and the hermeneutics of texts, exists for now only in a state of outline.

Why does Ricoeur stop precisely with *Oedipus at Colonus*, rather than with *Oedipus Rex*, in his meditation on the Greek conception of recognition of responsibility as an elementary form of self-recognition? It is a question of showing that the tragic character, crushed as he is by the disastrous destiny that has fallen upon him, remains a capable subject in the precise sense that he "remains the author of that innermost action consisting of evaluating his acts, particularly retrospectively."[37] *Oedipus at Colonus* draws a singular course of recognition that transforms misfortune undergone into misfortune assumed, by showing that misfortune can become "a dimension of the action itself, in the sense of being endured in a responsible manner."[38] The "lesson" is deep, and invites us to read differently *Agamemnon*'s famous "to learn while suffering"—perhaps endured suffering is itself less a "school of wisdom" than a "school of the recognition of oneself."

It is as the extension of this tragic "school of the recognition of oneself" that Ricoeur places the Aristotelian design of practical wisdom dominated by the key terms *phronèsis* and *phronimos*, terms that above all must not be disconnected. Their reciprocal implication gives a specific coloring to the idea of a practical wisdom that "is *this discernment, this quick glance, in a situation of uncertainty, in the direction of suitable action*,"[39] practical wisdom in which Ricoeur thinks of being able "to discern retrospectively a hint of such reflexive philosophy."[40]

Aristotle's ethics is thus used as a prelude and entryway to the picture of a capable human, of whom this second section presents the general features, by recalling that the phenomenology of the capable human only extends the role recognized as attestation in *Oneself as Another*. If, as is emphasized in the introduction to the book, attestation is the secret password of all the hermeneutics of self,[41] one can say that only those who understand this password will be able to adopt the perspective of the phenomenology of the capable human who is the self recognized in its capacities. It is a question, as Ricoeur emphasizes, of providing the foundations of a "philosophical anthropology"[42] that has as its background the concept *human action*—in other words, a practical philosophy elevated to the level of a second-order philosophy. One would be wrong to oppose the first "philosophical anthropology" of Ricoeur, as contained in *Fallible Man*, against this second "philosophical anthropology," as though it were necessary to choose between the fallible human and the capable human. The true difference is elsewhere, and is due to two features: the transformation of the question "*What is* the human?" into the question "*Who* is the capable self?"; and the more "practical" orientation of the latter anthropology.

Whereas the second section can be read as a resumption of the fundamental questions that underlay *Oneself as Another*, the third shows that the "three-masted ship" that forms *Memory, History, Forgetting* is well equipped for new navigations, like that of *The Course of Recognition*. In the third section Ricoeur places memory and promises, where "the problematic of self-recognition reaches two high points simultaneously."[43] If these capacities deserve shared treatment, it is because it is not given to just anyone to be able to scale these two precipitous peaks of recognition of oneself. Indeed, the various capacities enumerated in the preceding chapter—to speak, to act, to narrate one's story, to take responsibility for one's actions—could still give the impression that the self-recognition they imply is evident, which is not the case with these new capacities.

One could obviously wonder whether the "threat of something negative"[44]—which, in the case of memory and promising, assumes the face of the lapse of memory, and the face of treason—does not already weigh on the first four capacities, where it takes the form of silence, of the passivity of this or that which drags behind existence like dead weight, of the incapacity to translate lived inconsistency into a thoughtful narrative, and finally of irresponsibility, incapable of recognizing the authorship of its acts (including, in certain cases, authorship full stop!). Is it not obvious that all these "not-capacities" are themselves also constitutive of the meaning of these capacities, just as in the case of memory and promising, in which "[t]heir opposite is part of their meaning"?[45]

To this perplexity I will add a second: how to explain the fact that in this reconstruction of the most remarkable figures of "I can," which enable Ricoeur to honor the "Bergsonian moment," he overlooks the capacity to forgive, which completes the epilogue of *Memory, History, Forgetting*? If, as Hannah Arendt suggests, one pairs the capacity to promise with the capacity to forgive, are there not good reasons to wonder whether this faculty does not in its own way clarify both the recognition of oneself and mutual recognition? Perhaps it will be objected that the question is premature, because one can only forgive others, but not oneself. One who says "I do not forgive myself for having done that," however, is himself also engaged in a work of self-recognition, whose highest expression—and for this reason also the most difficult, ultimate "struggle for recognition," to express it in Hegelian terms—is the request for forgiveness.

Ricoeur shows himself especially anxious to protect his phenomenology from the "capacities that each person has the certitude and confidence of being able to exercise"[46] against the reproach of being a disguised egology, interested exclusively in the individual expressions of "I can." This is why he takes care to stress that the "I" of "I can" could equally be "we," equipped with a certain number of "capabilities," in the sense given this term by economist Amartya Sen. This broadening, which enables the move from the individual to the social forms of the power to act, pays the price of a certain epistemological and notional heterogeneity related to the difference "between those identities which imply personal capacities and those identities relating to the instituting of the social bond."[47] Ricoeur puts his finger on the essential difference when he stresses that "recognition-attestation" does not have a strict equivalent on the plane of collective action.

Mutual Recognition beyond the Master-Slave Dialectic

The third study develops under the aegis of a sentence of Rousseau's from *On the Origin of Language*: "As soon as one man was recognized by another as a sentient, thinking Being similar to himself, the desire or the need to communicate feelings and thoughts to him made the first man look for ways to do so."[48] Here also, one might be astonished that an attempt to explain the Hegelian moment of *Anerkennung* is introduced with an epigraph from the philosopher of immediacy. In fact, the "Rousseauian moment" is not a link in the chain of "events of thought" that Ricoeur climbs to reach the Hegelian summit. From the start, the epigraph puts its readers on guard against inappropriate praise for reciprocity as mutuality, which would be the "originary" and "insurmountable" difference between the idea of the one and the idea of the other indicated by the expression that is at the same time a "categorical structure": "one another."[49]

Far from constituting an originary phenomenon, as Rousseau seems to suppose, reciprocity is a derived category that has as background the dissymmetry original to the ego and alter ego. Ricoeur illustrates the difficulty with the example of the fifth of Husserl's *Cartesian Meditations* and Levinas's *Totality and Infinity* and *Otherwise than Being, or Beyond Essence*. First, he retains the idea that reciprocity concerns a second-degree constitution: "The other must be my analogue, so that beyond my experience of myself I come to terms with that of others on a basis of reciprocity, even though this chain of constitutions draws its basic meaning from me as ego."[50] The same dissymmetry presents a very different face (of course!) if one chooses, as Levinas does, to start directly from the pole of otherness that reveals itself in the face of the other. It is not only the otherness of the other that remains forever "resistant to concept," because all that I can understand of it does not succeed in neutralizing its irreducible externality. Also, others, "under the sign of the stranger," as Levinas likes to put it, are a "spoilsport" coming to disturb, not to say to torment, the "ethical slumber" of ego anxious to preserve itself in Being. Even if the difference between the Husserlian treatment and the Levinasian treatment of the problem of the relation of me to the other seems to be abyssal, Ricoeur refuses to be trapped by a choice between the alternatives of "Husserl or Levinas, which of the two to choose?" What enables him to challenge this choice between alternatives is the fact that, on both sides, "it is a question each time of comparing incomparables and hence of *equalizing* them."[51] From this point of view at least, Husserl and Levinas are equally anti-Rousseauians.

Hanging over this third course of recognition is the persistent shadow of the "refusal to recognize," taking over from the ignorance of the first course of recognition and from the self-deception that inevitably generates mistakes about others,[52] and whose second course breaks down the various facets—secrecy, inhibition, resistance, disguise, lying, hypocrisy, and so forth—to which we must now add self-hatred, understood in the sense of the passage of Bernanos that provided the title of Ricoeur's *Oneself as Another* and that he declares he wishes to assume for himself: "It is easier than one thinks to hate oneself. Grace means forgetting oneself. But if all pride were dead in us, the grace of the graces would be to love oneself humbly, as one would any of the suffering members of Jesus-Christ."[53] Even if the word *recognition* does not appear in this quotation, it invites us to ask ourselves whether *self-recognition*, as defined by Ricoeur, does not give a new currency to the classical virtue of humility.

In Ricoeur's view, the Hegelian *Anerkennung* has for finality first to bring a moral counterpart to the challenge of the naturalist interpretation of politics that Hobbes proposes in his *Leviathan*. What in the end grounds living-together? For Hobbes, it is a certain idea of the state of nature that dissociates humans "in making them capable of attacking and killing one another." There is no trouble measuring the challenge that such an idea presents to a phenomenology of the capable human, who has perhaps a certain difficulty in accepting that humans are capable of the worst as well as the best. What would become the list of the "capacities that each person has the certitude and confidence of being able to exercise," if one added the "capacity to attack and kill one another"? If humans are capable of all that, then, facing the possibility of "the war of all against all," one understands well the need to limit the damage by delegating a share of our capacities to the State, "this *mortal god,* to which we owe under the *immortal god,* our peace and our defense." At the end of a packed analysis, in the form of *explication de texte,* Ricoeur suggests that the only way to take up Hobbes's challenge is to restore others, as does Leibniz, to the heart of the rights relationship, by showing how the very idea of rights requires the link and cooperation between selfhood and otherness.

As a result, one must take an interest in the role played in living-together by the desire to be recognized, which was precisely Hegel's great concern during the Jena period. In the way in which this desire develops the concept of *Anerkennung,* what holds Ricoeur's attention is, initially, the very narrow way it associates self-consciousness and orientation towards the other; then, its processual point of view, in which contempt is transformed into consideration and injustice into respect; and finally, the care to distinguish a multiplicity of institutions that have as their responsibility guaranteeing or promoting this recognition. This institutional pluralization has as counterpart an awareness of the historicity of the entire process. The struggles for recognition are never won in advance, but always carry us to ever new battlefields. Despite Ricoeur's fascination with the great texts of *Realphilosophie,* which have the merit of definitively inscribing the topic of recognition into the hollow of political philosophy, he signals his reservations about the Hegelian concept of Spirit: "the way in which the Spirit finds itself in its other remains fundamentally a relation of a self to itself."[54] The objection is important, because it has as its background the "renunciation of Hegel" already mentioned above. Can the desire for recognition be restructured, if one no longer adheres to the presuppositions of a metaphysics of absolute Spirit?

The question is as much addressed to Ricoeur as to Axel Honneth, who is his principal interlocutor in the fourth chapter of *The Course of Recognition*, where the immanent *explication de textes* gives way to a dialogue with this interpreter of Hegel with whom Ricoeur shares concern for a systematic reactualization of the Hegelian theme. What holds his attention in Honneth's *The Struggle for Recognition* are the three models of intersubjective recognition—love, rights, and social respect—to which correspond three distinct figures from the refusal to recognize.

Before examining those, I will note Ricoeur's remark concerning the way Honneth associates Hegel and George Herbert Mead in his project to constitute a social theory with normative content. This association is the "model for an interweaving of a speculative conceptualization and the testing of experience."[55] In the absence of a strong speculative structure, the topic of recognition is likely to find itself "slipping into banality, as today is more and more the case." But the opposite is also true: in the absence of empirical ballast, the concept of recognition is likely to spin its wheels.

Is what is said here about the need for a meshing of the speculative and the empirical not also equally applicable to the very project of a hermeneutics of the self? One indeed notices the insistence with which, in *Oneself as Another,* Ricoeur emphasizes the conceptual orientation of his investigation, while avoiding or circumventing the "psychological" problems of identification. The reference to the positive effects of the linkage between Hegel and Mead (who, let us recall, was a disciple of Dilthey) encourages us to ask whether, sooner or later, these brackets will not have to be removed.

It is initially on the plane of erotic, friend, and family relationships that Ricoeur and Honneth seek to detect the first springs of the desire for recognition, to which correspond the no less profound figures of the refusal to recognize that assume the form of humiliation, coming to betray "more complex kinds of threats than those relating to mere physical integrity."[56] Ricoeur extends the reflections of Honneth by stressing the family unit and the phenomenon of filiation (phenomena that had also captured the attention of Gaston Fessard in his reading of the *Phenomenology of Spirit*). Quoting the works of Pierre Legendre, Ricoeur restores to them a particular form of the desire for recognition: the capacity of "recognizing oneself in one's lineage."[57] This has as its background a preliminary recognition, often mediated by a familial, civil, or religious ritual: "Because I was recognized as the son or daughter of . . . , I recognize myself as such, and I *am*, as such, *this* inestimable object of transmission."[58]

Onto this formula of Pierre Legendre, Ricoeur grafts two more personal considerations.

The first relates to the difficulty in reflecting on birth, which confronts us with the enigma of an origin that is not confused with a simple beginning. It is the miracle of "natality" (*Gebürtigkeit*) in Hannah Arendt's sense that constitutes, as Claude Romano demonstrated in *L'événement et le monde*, an original "*événemential*," transforming *Dasein* in its happening. One could apply to it the couplet of Angelus Silesius that Ricoeur quotes: from its birth, *Dasein* is without why, it exists because it exists!

The second consideration relates to the prohibition of incest. The function, which could be described as transcendental, of this ban is to make possible the genealogical principle of "*self-recognition through filiation*,"[59] while learning with each bird "to sing on a particular branch of its family tree," to quote the beautiful image of Cocteau. However it may be as the absolute foundation of this genealogical principle, Ricoeur argues that "the experience of recognizing oneself through filiation . . . is sufficient for confronting the fantasy of being all-powerful, as well as for revealing the mystery of birth and testifying to the objection that the genealogical principle makes against the incest drive as the bearer of nondistinction."[60] Ulrich, the "hero" of Robert Musil's *The Man Without Qualities*, is certainly not a man "without character"—quite the opposite! What he is missing, as the first confrontation with his father shows, is precisely the capacity to recognize himself in his lineage. The fact that, later in the book, the same Ulrich engages in an incestuous relation with his sister Agatha shows that his "lack of qualities" means especially the inability to recognize himself in his lineage.

This "lineage" is not only that of the filiation that attaches one to one's parent; it is more broadly that of the Viennese culture in Austria at the beginning of the century. In this sense, one can prolong these reflections on "the inestimable object of transmission" while reflecting on the work of recognition implied by any attempt to recognize oneself in an intellectual or spiritual lineage. Is it an accident that, in Germany more than in France, one announces one's academic identity by saying of which master one is a disciple? More than once, during my stays in Germany, I have *had to resist* the temptation to present myself to my colleagues by saying, "*Ich bin ein Ricoeurschüler*"!

Anyone who has considered the theses that Ricoeur defends in the two volumes he devotes to the notion of the Just will not be surprised by the interest he takes in the legal aspects of the struggle for recognition. They draw their specificity from the fact that the predicate *free* comes to replace the capacity to be alone on the emotional plane, just as respect takes the place of trust. Even if Ricoeur resists the "Habermasian" manner of opposing "conventional" and "post-conventional" morals, which goes hand in hand with the dichotomy of conviction and argumentation, he agrees with Honneth in distinguishing between civil, political, and social rights, with correspondingly distinct figures stemming from the refusal of recognition: "humiliation that relates to a denial of civil rights," "the frustration that relates to not being able to participate in the shaping of the public will," and the "feeling of exclusion that results from the refusal of any to the most basic goods."[61] The common denominator that connects all these negative experiences to one another is nothing other than the feeling of indignation, which Ricoeur had already stressed the importance of in *Oneself as Another* and *The Just*. What the third study of *The Course of Recognition* adds is the argument that indignation ceases being demobilizing if it is united with responsibility, understood as "self-assertion" and "recognition of the equal right of others to contribute to advances in the rule of law and of rights."[62]

What characterizes the juridical order of recognition is the fact that the rise to a universal is a historical process with two complementary facets, according to whether one takes into account the specificity of each sphere of rights, or takes an interest in the way in which these rights are applied to new categories of people or groups. Beyond this juridical sphere extends the vast field of social respect, which defines a third model of mutual recognition.

It is on this point that Ricoeur advances most beyond the analyses of Honneth, by raising three equally important questions: that of the normative requirement able to satisfy social respect, that of the specific forms of conflict proper to this sphere, and that of the personal capacities required by this social regard and the contiguous concepts, such as prestige and consideration. To solve these problems, Ricoeur depends on some theoretical works that approach the same concept from a particular angle.

It is first of all about the way Jean-Marc Ferry characterizes the various organizational or institutional "orders of recognition" that make the social recognition of others possible and to which correspond specific modes of communication: socioenonomic, sociopolitical, and sociocultural complexes. Arnold Gehlen's *Anthropology*, which is, with those of Max Scheler and Helmuth Plessner, one of the three classics of philosophical anthropology of the first half of the twentieth century, thus finds a new relevance.

But it is especially close to the way Luc Boltanski and Laurent Thévenot distinguish the six "economies of size" proper to the "city of inspiration," the "city of opinion," the "domestic city," the "civic city," the "commercial city," and the "industrial city" that occupies Ricoeur. We can understand why: it is not only that each one of these "cities" (or, what, in a more phenomenological language, one could call each social *Lebenswelt*) incorporates its own tests of justification and its own forms of refusing recognition. More importantly, as each one of us belongs, in one way or another, to each of these "cities," and there is no pre-established harmony between them, their relation is fundamentally "critical" in both senses of the word: I can always criticize a city in the name of the values and criteria of justification of another; but perhaps is it more productive to negotiate an acceptable and livable compromise in a given situation. It is precisely this solution that is lauded by Ricoeur when he defines compromise not as a cowardly concession, but as the expression of "mutual recognition in the situations of conflict and dispute resulting from the plurality of economies of standing."[63] In this very way, one sees taking shape a new figure of the one capable of recognition: on the level of social regard, one must be shown as able to understand another world than that in which one has chosen to reside, and, at the same time, one must prove one's "capacity to recognize oneself as one figure in the passage from one city to another," by avoiding the double temptation of disillusioned relativism and simplistic accusation.

The way Ricoeur, following Charles Taylor's lead, tackles the problem of multiculturalism and the political problem of recognition of the distinct identity of disadvantaged cultural minorities recalls the way he defines the idea of tolerance in other writings.[64] The link between the two problems leaps to the eye: the struggle for recognition merges on this level with the fight for more tolerance. But the reverse is also true: on both sides, it is necessary to resist the temptation of a banalization that makes the differences so different that they become indifferent. With respect to these currents, which elude the shadow of the intolerable that accompanies speeches on tolerance, in whichever order, it is important to find the right balance which, in certain cases, is also a negotiated compromise between the homogenizing effects of the universally identical and a particularism disguised as universal principle. In the end, no society that calls itself democratic can evade the following question: "Tell me how you treat your minorities, even those who do not share your values, and tell me what rights you grant to all your members, so that I might recognize you as a truly democratic society!"

What could have been the conclusion of this third study takes a new and unforeseen turn with the question: when "does a subject deem him- or herself to be truly recognized?"[65] Whatever may be the legitimacy of the various "struggles for recognition," past and future, the philosopher can hardly elude the question of knowing whether the various petitions that demarcate these struggles—self-confidence, respect, self-esteem—can be achieved through hard-won fights. Ricoeur finds suspect the temptation to flee in the face of the indefinite that Hegel denotes as "bad infinite," and which finds its expression in the figure of the "unhappy consciousness" whose economy is summarized in the formula: *Ziehen der Linien der Sehnsucht ins Leere hinaus.* That this temptation is by no means hypothetical is shown in our contemporary experience, where we meet from time to time on our path protesters who judge that they have never received the recognition to which they have a right.

With regard to this kind of situation, individual or collective, it is good and salutary to put forward "peaceful experiences of mutual recognition" that prove that the "small miracle" of recognition actually took place.[66] But the philosopher could not be satisfied with invoking these states of ever-provisional peace, similar to truces or armistices. If they give us courage to continue the fight, they do not answer the properly conceptual difficulty related to the very idea of reciprocity: is recognition always and in all cases synonymous with reciprocity ("I recognize you because you recognize me, and I recognize you only under this condition")?

To move this question forward, Ricoeur proposes to compare three distinct concepts, each implying a different model of successful mutual recognition: the Aristotelian *philia* that finds its expression in friendship, the Platonic *Eros* that is animated by a desire for spiritual ascension, and the biblical *agape* that is able to give without being paid in return. It is by comparing love with justice that Ricoeur tries to answer the provocative questions raised by Luc Boltanski in the second part of his *L'Amour et la justice comme compétences*: does the sociology of action have the means of proving that people are capable of love? In other words, is the concept of *agape* an operational concept enabling it to qualify certain actions, or is it simply a case of an ideal to which one aspires without being able to fully achieve it, the case, even, of a Utopia or a fraud, as Marx and Engels would maintain?

For Ricoeur, the only way to answer these questions is to consider the way in which *agape* speaks, or rather—because true *agape* is mostly mute—the way in which it is spoken about, as does the apostle Paul in his paean to charity of the First Epistle to the Corinthians: it is a hymnic discourse of praise. It is only as a second step that one can raise the question of the possibility of a bridge "between the poetics of *agape* and the prose of justice, between the hymn and the formal rule."[67]

In vigorously defending the possibility of building such a bridge, Ricoeur finds himself once again in the role of the "*pontifex maximus*" of contemporary philosophy. This bridge can be crossed only if the person of the "first gesture," which is the person of *agape*, and the person of the "second gesture," that of justice, are ready to make concessions and to negotiate an acceptable compromise between the pure generosity that is excluded from the world and the safety based on the single rule of equivalence. But if on the path of these two incommensurable kinds of mutual recognition the misunderstandings are legion, one might fear that this bridge is reduced to a thin wire passable only by tightrope walkers.

What restores a certain solidity to the bridge is the way Ricoeur, following Marcel Hénaff, rehabilitates the Maussian categories of gift and counter-gift. Even if, in our societies that are ever more subjected to a commercial logic requiring that all have a price, the exchange of ceremonial gifts seems to elevate these marginal behaviors, "the struggle for recognition would lose itself in the unhappy consciousness if it were not given to humans to accede to an actual, albeit symbolic, experience of mutual recognition, following the model of the reciprocal ceremonial gift."[68]

The "ceremonial" qualifier is by no means superfluous in this context. On the contrary, it suggests that certain methods of recognition need rituals and ceremonies in order to be achieved. Even if, in certain circumstances, for example during the exchange of gifts during the visit of a foreign head of state, the comedy of power is not far off, one cannot forget that these rituals mean first to signify the quality of the relationship established by the exchange of gifts. It is what the family meal illustrates well, which deserve to hold the attention not only of the sociologists, as is the case today, but also of the phenomenologist who discovers a rich and complex method of mutual recognition within a familial clan. The legendary conflicts that tarnish these festivals show that in this field also, mutual recognition—inseparable from the way in which one recognizes, or does not recognize, oneself in a lineage—is never guaranteed in advance.

Most important of all is the symbolic effect of the gift, incommensurable with its commercial value. The symbolic value of the gift depends finally on what it expresses of the personality of the giver. Conversely, the trilogy give-receive-return enables us to discover one of the most original aspects of a phenomenology of the capable person: the *capacity*, which is sometimes a true art, to *receive*.

It is with this suggestion that I will conclude this analysis, to which I wanted to give the bearing of a simple "flight of recognition," of the last book of Paul Ricoeur. This reading also corresponds to an attempt to offer an answer to the question of the sense the formula "I recognized myself as philosopher" had in the life and the work of the philosopher who has just left us. By casting a retrospective glance over *The Course of Recognition*, I wonder whether the way Ricoeur asks that each citizen of the six cities mentioned possess the "capacity to recognize oneself as one figure in the passage from one city to another" does not likewise correspond to a certain "Socratic" idea of the philosophical vocation.

The way that Ricoeur, in *Time and Narrative, III*, has defined the ethicopolitical task as consisting in making our spaces of experience more malleable and our horizons of expectation more determinate reinforces his warning against the double temptation of disillusioned relativism and simplistic accusation. The real question is how the philosopher, who is recognized as being of Socratic lineage, can play the part of border escort between these different worlds. Most of the time, the philosopher recognizes him- or herself as a citizen of the "city of inspiration" or the "city of opinion," rather than as a captain of industry or a banker. Precisely because of this, it is important to resist the temptation of a superficial criticism of the other orders of greatness. To amuse the crowd by treating the politician, the economist, or the businessman as "scum" is easier than one might think. Such snap judgments do not help us to refine our understanding of the complexity of reality. Ricoeur's formulation, which speaks of "the capacity to awaken the actors of one world to the values of another world through criticism, even if it means changing the world,"[69] seems to me not only applicable to the critical function of philosophy, but also illustrates the way he recognized himself as philosopher. It is what gives his thought a particular *authority*—provided that one takes this term in the Arendtian and Gadamerian sense of recognition of a superiority that, far from requiring an act of submission and abdication of reason, finds an exemplary illustration in the master-disciple relationship.

Translated by Boyd Blundell from "Vers quelle reconnaissance?" *Revue de Metaphysique et de Morale*, no. 50 (2006, issue 2): 149–71.

Paul Ricoeur and Development Ethics

DAVID M. KAPLAN

What do Paul Ricoeur and Amartya Sen have to do with one another? On the surface, not much. Ricoeur is a French hermeneutic philosopher and theologian; Sen is a Nobel Prize–winning Indian economist. Ricoeur researches such topics as subjectivity, imagination, and memory; Sen, poverty, development, and famine. But beneath their surface differences lies a fundamental similarity in their respective projects. Both take the notion of human capability as the central descriptive and normative feature of human existence. For Ricoeur, the capable human being (*l'homme capable*) is the ultimate subject of philosophical analysis. For Sen, the right to capabilities forms the basis for a theory of social justice in economic development.[1] The connection between the two, however, hinges on more than a shared use of the term *capabilities*. In Ricoeur's last major work, *The Course of Recognition*, he enthusiastically cites Sen's *capabilities approach* in development ethics as crucial for connecting individual capacities for action to social capacities for collective action.[2] Sen's work forms a bridge in Ricoeur's analysis between social agency and social responsibility. But the reference to Sen and the capabilities approach is even more rich and provocative than I think even Ricoeur acknowledges. It marks the opening of a dialogue between two worlds of theory and practice: a hermeneutics of the self and international development ethics. I want to briefly explore this relationship to demonstrate what each has to offer to the other. At the end of this exploration, we should have a richer and more nuanced understanding of what development ethics is, and what it means to be a capable human being.

L'homme capable and Human Capability

The notion of human capability is the guiding thread that runs through Ricoeur's philosophical career, unifying his seemingly disconnected works: from his early phenomenology of the will in the 1950s, to his investigation of psychoanalysis in the 1960s, to his studies on metaphor and narrative in the 1970s and 1980s, to his studies on the nature of selfhood in the 1990s, to his recent examination of memory and forgiveness, recognition and reconciliation in the early 2000s. Echoing Kant, Ricoeur believes that to be a human being is to be capable of thinking, choosing, and acting for oneself. Yet he goes beyond Kant and affirms a wider range of human capabilities. He does so by analyzing the various ways that the verb *I can* is modified and realized in the ways that *I can speak*, *I can act*, *I can tell a story*, and *I can be responsible*. Ricoeur argues that the notion of capability forms a link between our actions, our language, and the worlds we live in. It relates actors to patients, agency to suffering, and capability to vulnerability. Capabilities are always bound to various figures of otherness (such as other people and our own bodies) that both enable and constrain us, delimiting who and what we are, as well as what we may hope to become. Ricoeur explains that *l'homme capable* is a "thin but continuous" thread running through his work: "It is only very recently that I felt allowed to give a name to this overarching problematic. I meant the problem of human capability, capability as the cornerstone of philosophical anthropology."[3] *L'homme capable* is both descriptive and normative: it is what we are and what we should try to become.

It took Ricoeur a lifetime to unravel this rich concept of capability and its web of related phenomena. He endeavored to show how *l'homme capable* implies:

a notion of the will as embodied, free, and receptive;
a relation to the unconscious, desire, dreams, and myths;
a relation to language through which we relate to the world, initially described in terms of symbols, then texts, then narratives, then translation, as successive models of linguistic mediation;
a relation to literature, poetry, and other imaginary realms;
a relation to group and national identities;
a relation to other selves, to social practices, and to history;

moral relationships with others to whom we are accountable, individually and collectively;

a relation to memory, forgetting, and forgiving, the interrelated concepts that attest equally to our capacities and achievements and to our vulnerabilities and finitude.

L'homme capable in each of its various manifestations is, for Ricoeur, both the starting point and destination of philosophical analysis. It is the starting point because being capable defines who and what we are as individuals and members of groups; it is the destination because we only know ourselves as capable agents after we have taken "the long route" to self-knowledge—a *detour* through the symbols, myths, narratives, bodies, and other people to which we are always related and in terms of which we always understand ourselves. Capability, for Ricoeur, is human nature, a term that is pregnant with meaning and open to interpretation.

Capability, for Sen, is a somewhat less complicated term. It simply means the freedom to live a worthwhile life. Sen's contribution to our understanding of capabilities lies in his claim that we have rights to capabilities. This notion of capability forms the cornerstone for his version of development ethics, a field concerned with evaluating the moral dimensions of socioeconomic change, primarily in poor countries. Development ethics seeks to formulate ethical principles relevant to social change, to analyze and assess the moral dimensions of development theories, and to resolve moral dilemmas in development policymaking and practice. It aims to help render development actions humane—to ensure that the changes enacted under the banner of improvement do not destroy cultures or cause undue suffering to individuals or groups.

The term *development*, like capabilities, has both descriptive and normative senses. In the descriptive sense, development is usually identified as the processes of economic growth, industrialization, and modernization that aim to produce a higher gross domestic product. In the normative sense, development refers to the process of realizing worthwhile social goals, such as the overcoming of economic and social deprivation or the achievement of social well-being. Development ethicists typically attempt not merely to understand development, but also to argue for and promote specific conceptions of desirable social change.

Sen argues that economic development should not be understood as narrowly construed economic growth, but as the rightful expansion of people's "valuable capabilities and functionings."Functionings are "the various things a person may value doing or being"; capabilities are "the alternative combinations of functionings that are feasible for her to achieve."[4] A capability is the freedom to achieve goods and valued states of being. Development should be concerned with, as Sen says, "what people can or cannot do, e.g., whether they can live long, escape avoidable morbidity, be well nourished, be able to read and write and communicate, take part in literary and scientific pursuits, and so forth."[5] Development, on this model, is not seen as a means to an end, but an end in itself.

Sen argues that this freedom-based approach is the key to understanding social and economic progress: underdevelopment should be seen as unfreedom, and development as a process of removing unfreedoms and extending substantive freedoms to people who value them. Poverty, on this model, is understood as capability deprivation; prosperity is the realization of substantive freedoms. The capabilities approach in development ethics focuses on what people are actually able to do and able to be, and what they should be able to do and to be.

American philosopher Martha Nussbaum builds on Sen by more explicitly connecting the language of capabilities with the language of rights. Her version of the capabilities approach has more unabashedly universalist aspirations, arguing for a list of "central human capabilities."[6] Nussbaum's list of capabilities forms the basis for the political principles that any government should guarantee to its citizens through its constitution. The central capabilities are:

Life: Being able to live for the span normal for the species.

Bodily health: Being able to have good health (and adequate nourishment and shelter).

Bodily integrity: Being able to be physically secure, and with rights over one's own body.

Senses, imagination, and thought: Being able to use the senses, imagine, think and reason, and to do this in a truly human way: educated, informed, and free from repression.

Emotions: Being able to have attachments and feelings for other people and things.

Practical reason: Being able to form a conception of the good and to engage in critical reflection about the planning of one's life.

Affiliation: a) Being able to interact well with other people and empathize with their situations; b) Having the social bases for self-respect and non-humiliation (not being discriminated against on the basis of race, sex, etc.).

Other species: Being able to live with concern for the natural world.

Play: Being able to play and laugh.

Control over one's environment: a) Being able to participate effectively in political processes; b) Being able to have possessions, and to seek employment.

This list, for Nussbaum, represents the bare minimum of what respect for human dignity requires.

The idea of a right to capabilities is a powerful criterion for social justice that links individual capacities to act with governments that have a responsibility to protect our rights. The policies, institutions, and welfare of a society should be measured by how well they enable opportunities for people to develop their full human capacities. Since 1990 this approach has been institutionalized within the UN Development Programme to measure global progress even in advanced industrialized nations.

Ricoeur is attracted to three aspects of Sen's version of human capabilities. 1) We have rights to capabilities; governments have an obligation to secure them. The very idea of a right to a capability is unusual: it bridges the deontological and the teleological. Sen explains that we have the right to capabilities in relation to and because of our "evaluations of situations." That is to say, we have rights and liberties within an evaluative, interpretive framework that shapes and constrains what those rights and liberties are and how we ought to exercise them. The right and the good, abstract universal and concrete particular, come together in the notion of rights to capabilities—a contextualized notion of human rights.

2) Rights to capabilities are bound up with social practices. The claim that we have rights to capabilities implies an internal relationship to other people and to social institutions and traditions in which our rights gain recognition. Capabilities are always social capabilities: we always act and are acted on within a socially effected context. Furthermore, groups and collectives are also capable of speech and action, and, therefore, capable of recognition and misrecognition. Rights and identity/recognition concerns apply not only to individuals but also to groups and collectives. The right to capabilities extends beyond individuals to include "social capabilities."

3) Capabilities imply responsibilities. Just as rights imply duties, so do collective rights imply collective responsibilities. The latter are required to ensure that individual liberty flourishes. In turn, liberty (i.e., the right to capabilities) is the key moral-political criterion of social justice used by the UN to evaluate and compare political regimes and development policies. For Ricoeur, Sen's contribution to the notion of human capability is "his having associated the idea of freedom on the one hand with a life choice and on the other with collective responsibility."[7] Groups have rights, within social contexts; they deserve recognition, *and* can be held responsible.

In *The Course of Recognition*, Ricoeur uses the idea of social capabilities as a transitional concept to link the epistemological sense of recognition to its moral-political sense. The term *recognition* can mean either 1) to grasp (an object) with the mind, to distinguish or identify a judgment or action, to know it by memory; 2) to accept, acknowledge, take to be true; or 3) to bear witness, through gratitude, that one is indebted to someone for something.[8] In its active voice, *to recognize* is to have knowledge; in its passive voice, *to be recognized* is to enter into a reciprocal relation with another. One can recognize things, persons, oneself, others, and one another; one can also be recognized and ask for recognition. Both depend upon one's agency and capacity to act. Ricoeur examines each sense of recognition, first as in the epistemological sense of identification, next in the anthropological sense of human capacity to know and to act, and finally (thanks to Sen) in the full moral-political sense of mutual recognition and respect.

Following the trail begun by Hegel, Ricoeur develops a model for mutual recognition that is less a struggle in a state of law than a receptive experience of the other in a state of peace. This model is based less on a conflict between master and slave than on a reciprocal relationship among friends exchanging gifts. One's very identity as an individual and citizen is bound up with others. Ricoeur asks, "Is it not my genuine identity that demands to be recognized? And if, happily, this happens, does not my gratitude go to those who in one way or another have, in recognizing me, recognized my identity?"[9] Ricoeur's course of recognition takes us from knowledge, to agency, to capability and social practices, to reciprocity, respect, and gratitude. At each stage, the active sense of recognition is always limited by its passive sense, because human beings are always both active and receptive, agents and patients, capable and vulnerable.

Ricoeur and Sen share the idea that our human capabilities are social capabilities that are always related to social practices, institutions, and political authority. Both affirm that we have rights to capabilities and that freedom is inseparable from the good life. And both argue that human capabilities define our humanity as it is and as it should become. But because they each develop a version of capabilities in relation to different philosophical and practical concerns, each version expands the scope and vision of the other's project. Ricoeur gives to development ethics a rich notion of *l'homme capable*, which expands the notion of human being and extends the implications of our rights to capabilities. Development ethics gives to readers of Ricoeur an entire research project of applying various aspects of his works to issues related to economic development, social justice, poverty, and suffering—a research project very much in the spirit of the one Ricoeur himself undertook.

How Ricoeur Contributes to Development Ethics

Ricoeur's work complements and enhances the capabilities approach in development ethics. Three themes stand out: imagination, vulnerability, and the paradoxical nature of political authority.

1) The imagination directs and affects capabilities. The imagination, for Ricoeur, relates to both discourse and action. Like a Kantian matrix of understanding, the imagination schematizes, constitutes, and creates new meanings. The key feature of the imagination is "semantic innovation." Myths, poems, metaphors, and other creative discourses express new meanings and capture experience in ways that ordinary language cannot. A metaphor, for example, is a "heuristic fiction" that "redescribes" reality by referring to the world in terms of something imaginative, which allows us to learn about reality from fiction. A metaphor involves an unusual predication—a metaphorical twist—that is understood when we grasp figurative and literal meanings together. The imagination lets us both see-as and see-as-not. Semantic innovation bridges the worlds of fiction and fact, creation and interpretation.[10]

In *Time and Narrative,* Ricoeur further develops the notion of semantic innovation.[11] Like a metaphor, a narrative synthesizes, integrates, and relates experience into a coherent whole. This unity is achieved by means of a plot, which orders actions, intentions, events, and settings into a story that says more than the sum of its parts. The structuring activity of the plot is what gives the story a meaning and what allows it to make its point. As a story unfolds, the experience of the reader or listener is influenced by the way events are configured by the plot. Telling and interpreting stories form a circle: the imagination constructs meanings as they are told and as they are understood.

Semantic innovation in metaphor and narrative also figures our actions. The imagination has what Ricoeur calls a "projective function" that is a part of the very "dynamism of acting." "Without imagination," he says, "there is no action."[12] It operates in one's projects, in one's motivation, and in one's capacity to act. At the level of projects, an actor orients himself toward the future and imagines a thing to be done, projecting and trying out different possible courses of action. At the level of motivation, the imagination is involved in figuring out whatever might contribute to the motives and desires for an action. Imagination creates a realm for comparison and evaluation of the elements that act as motivating forces. At the level of initiative (or the power to act), the imagination mediates one's self-estimation of what one is capable of. I can, for example, only determine what I could do by imaginative variations of what I can do. I impute my own power to act by depicting to myself imaginative variations of what I can do, what I could do, and what I could have done had I wished otherwise. Ricoeur explains that "I take possession of the immediate certainty of my power only through the imaginative variations that mediate this certainty."[13] The imagination thus figures into the determination of my projects, my motives, and my capabilities, helping me understand what I am to do, why I am doing it, and what I can do.

The imagination may be projected either into individual or social action. Every society has its imaginative ideas, stories, and images that form interpretive schemas, what Cornelius Castoriadis calls the "cultural imagination."[14] This form of the imagination is like an interpretive grid that organizes the meaning of social action, shaping who we are as members of society and affecting what we are capable of knowing and doing. The cultural imagination is the socially constructed background and context from which we think and act. But there's more to it than that: for Ricoeur, the two opposite extremes of the cultural imagination are ideology and utopia. They represent imaginary, false, "noncongruent" perspectives that are nonetheless vital for members of a community. Ideology and utopia are omnipresent, ineliminable features of social life. Ideology acts to consolidate, integrate, and order a society; utopia calls a society into question. Both are ultimately about power: ideology attempts to legitimate power, while utopia attempts to replace power with something else.[15]

Ricoeur's notion of the imagination has tremendous relevance for development ethics. Imagination, so conceived, is fundamental to human experience. It is essential for cognition and volition. As a result, any notion of human rights, typically understood as derivative of the basic right to think, choose, and act for oneself, implies the right to imagination. In the exercise of any right, individuals and groups also exercise their imaginative capacities to create new expressions and new interpretations, and to engage in new actions. The right to imagination is another way of saying "right to freedom" or "right to life." It is part of being human.

This notion of the right to imagination is found in Nussbaum's version of the capabilities approach. Individuals have the right to imagination, senses, and thought: to be free to think, choose, and act using the full resources of one's creative capacities. According to Nussbaum, this right to a capability consists of the following:

> Being able to use the senses, to imagine, think, and reason—and to do these things in a "truly human" way, a way informed and cultivated by an adequate education, including, but by no means limited to, literacy and basic mathematical and scientific training. Being

> able to use imagination and thought in connection with experiencing and producing works and events of one's own choice, religious, literary, musical, and so forth. Being able to use one's mind in ways protected by guarantees of freedom of expression with respect to both political and artistic speech, and freedom of religious exercise. Being able to have pleasurable experiences and to avoid non-beneficial pain.[16]

Governments therefore have the obligation to protect the right to imagine, sense, and think, and to ensure that no one's capacities to do so fall below the minimally acceptable level needed to realize one's full human potential. The precise way in which the right to imagination (leaving out for the moment sensation, thought, and reason) should be guaranteed is, of course, difficult to specify in advance of any knowledge of the exact nature of the social-cultural context in which that capability would be realized. That is, the right to imagination would be secured differently depending on the needs and aspirations of the members of a society, the cultural practices into which members are socialized, the nature of the dominant institutions, and the availability of resources. It is one thing to affirm the right to creativity in thought and action; it is quite another thing to create policies that would protect such a vast, wide-ranging capability. At very least, the right to imagination implies the obligation of governments to protect free speech, freedom of the press, freedom of assembly, and other typical liberal rights. But it also implies the positive responsibility of a government to create the conditions that would enable the development and free exercise of the imagination.

One problem with affirming the right to imagination is that the imagination is a broader category than the kinds of political discourse and action typically ensured and protected. The imagination constitutes, among other things, our full creative capacities to read and write fiction and poetry, to play and listen to music, to create and enjoy the arts, to exercise and to participate in sports, and to live creatively in relation to customs and traditions. Where conditions for the exercise of these rights are lacking, they should be developed, creating the conditions conducive to our full imaginative flourishing. The aim of development policy might be to ensure that governments foster, nourish, and protect the rights of individuals and groups to realize their imaginative potentials. A policy that fails to foster the right to imagination fails to respect human dignity.

Nussbaum is particularly eloquent on the importance of the imagination to the cultivation of humanity. According to her, reading fiction helps to develop a "narrative imagination," a propadeutic for moral interaction. The narrative imagination helps one to understand the perspectives of others, appreciate how circumstances shape actions, consider what could happen, and see oneself as another. We learn about the experiences and suffering of others through stories, poems, and songs. Creative discourses of all kinds, she argues, help us to identify with others and otherness, perceive invisible members of the world, recognize virtue, comprehend other people's motives and choices, and challenge conventional wisdom and values. A developed narrative imagination fosters a critical examination of oneself and one's traditions, and lets us see ourselves as humans bonded to all other human beings by ties of recognition and concern.[17]

Ricoeur's notion of the "political imagination" is very similar to Nussbaum's narrative imagination. Developing a political imagination is the key for creating new political institutions that would bring together nations, peoples, and groups without failing to respect the differences among us. Ricoeur offers three related models to help reconcile nations, peoples, and groups while preserving our differences.[18] The first model is a "translation ethos" or an "ethics of linguistic hospitality" that would help us to reach out to people who speak other languages and prevent all of us from withdrawing and retreating into our own linguistic traditions. Ricoeur proposes both bilingual education and "cultural bilingualists" capable of translating traditions, beliefs, and convictions from one culture to another. The second model is the "exchange of memories" or "crossed narration." To translate is to take account of and recognize perspectives of others, including the stories they tell about themselves and tell about us. Understanding the stories of others opens the way for an exchange of memories that, in turn, helps us interpret and recount ourselves differently. The third model is the "model of forgiveness." Through an exchange of memories may come forgiveness, which is a specific act of reinterpreting the past concerned with understanding the suffering of others. Forgiveness "consists in shattering the law of the irreversibility of time by changing the past, not as a record of all that has happened but in terms of its meaning for us today."[19] Ricoeur maintains that individuals and groups must learn to remember events differently if they wish to achieve recognition and potentially reconcile.

Nussbaum also speaks of the role of the imagination in contributing to the "undoing of retributive anger."[20] She explains the role of remembering events differently for the sake of making peace with the past and (potentially) with others for the sake of justice and reconciliation. She too emphasizes the role of literacy in the development of our critical capacities, and she very neatly connects the imagination to policymaking. Nussbaum relates the imagination, capabilities, and development policy far more adequately than Ricoeur does, of course.

Yet Ricoeur shows how the imagination not only affects meaning but also figures into action, and thus adds a vital component missing from Nussbaum. Creativity suffuses what we say and what we do. It is not just a cognitive category, but a practical category that belongs to moral and political philosophy as well as to aesthetics. Ricoeur further reminds us that the imagination is social. It belongs to groups and to nations as well as to individuals. Consequently, the specters of ideology and utopia always haunt social action, rendering the social bonds that hold us together unreliable, untrustworthy, and too often in the service of illegitimate power and authority. The thesis of ideology and utopia is (like Ricoeur himself) quietly radical: ideology and utopia are operative, but never totally thematic; they are not derivative of social reality, but constitute it; we think and act from them, rather than about them; no vantage point exists that is entirely free from either ideology or utopia. From Ricoeur's perspective, Nussbaum's conception of the imagination appears naïve—even Pollyannaish. She ignores its strategic dimensions, overlooks its perverse effects, and whitewashes its dark side. The imagination not only enhances capabilities and promotes understanding and affiliation, but also erodes capabilities and fosters ignorance.

The importance of this chastened notion of the imagination for development ethics is to remind theorists, practitioners, and policymakers of the highly interpretive nature of social understanding. No discourse and action—no matter how reasoned, just, or well-intentioned—is ever entirely free from the specters of ideology or utopia. That means that any proposed transformations are mediated by the possibly harmful effects of the imagination just as much as they are animated by its creative potential. Development ethicists should, therefore, affirm the right to imagination, but with the understanding that, while individual and groups are free and deserve protection, they are also distorted and deserve criticism.

2) Capabilities are always tied to vulnerabilities. Our capabilities are always framed by our incapabilities—not only from external constraints, poor government, or economic deprivation, but from the inevitable limitations of being human. *L'homme capable* is vulnerable and fragile, capable of suffering as well as acting. We are patients just as much as we are agents. Ricoeur explains that "suffering is not defined solely by physical pain, nor even by mental pain, but by the reduction, even the destruction, of the

capacity for acting, of being-able-to-act, experienced as a violation of self-integrity."[21] That is, we suffer when our capabilities become vulnerabilities. Or to put it in terms of capabilities, we are capable of being acted upon, of being wounded, and of being taken advantage of. We can be injured, we forget, we age and grow enfeebled, and ultimately we die. Our rights to capabilities are important precisely because of what we are incapable of doing and being: we need help, we need protection, we need recognition, and we need love. Ricoeur calls it the "paradox of autonomy and vulnerability." "It is the same human being who is both of these things from different points of view. What is more, not simply opposed to each other, our two terms go together: the autonomy in question is that of a fragile, vulnerable being."[22]

The idea that humans are both capable yet vulnerable is a hallmark of Ricoeur's philosophical anthropology. Each of his major works addresses the limits of being human and the way that philosophy might respond to our limitations. For example, in *Freedom and Nature* he argues that voluntary acts are both the realization of freedom and the reception of necessity. When a person decides and acts, she must consent or acquiesce to the act of willing and confront the absolutely involuntary: one's character type, the unconscious, and one's life as a biological organism that form the very situation of the will. Activity is therefore tied to passivity. In *Fallible Man*, Ricoeur examines the gap between our limited *bios* (our bodies, passions, and desires) and unlimited *logos* (reason capable of grasping universals), and how we are rendered fragile, fallible, and therefore susceptible to temptation, evil, and sin.[23] In *Freud and Philosophy*, he argues that immediate, transparent consciousness is limited by deception and delusion, rendering self-knowledge uncertain and incapable of clear articulation. The full sense of the *wounded Cogito* can only be expressed in dreams, symbols, and myths.[24] In both the *Rule of Metaphor* and *Time and Narrative*, Ricoeur continues the search for a poetic language that is capable of interpreting and expressing the "dream of innocence" that would reconcile the limited, breached nature of selfhood. In *Oneself as Another* and *The Just*, Ricoeur examines human suffering in relation to the notions of agency and capability in moral, political, and legal contexts. And the recent studies on memory, forgetting, and recognition show how human capability is always tied to limitation, fragility, and incapability.

Our vulnerabilities are even more numerous than our capabilities. There are innumerable ways in which individuals and groups can be rendered powerless and helpless. Most of these vulnerabilities are context-bound, passing, and trivial. Yet some vulnerabilities are persistent, essential, and nontrivial. Ricoeur affirms that autonomy is more fundamental than vulnerability. It endures while vulnerability passes.

> Autonomy offers features of universality more relevant than does vulnerability, which moreover modulates its originary passivity through the cultural circumstances that history unfolds. As both presupposition and task, autonomy raises a claim to universality that is part of its constitution in principle, whereas the signs of vulnerability are inscribed in a history of passivity that confers upon vulnerability an irreducible history.[25]

And yet, while most vulnerabilities are obviously contextual, some are not. Some are tied to our human condition, as Ricoeur himself details again and again throughout his career. Among the basic vulnerabilities that we all potentially share are sickness, injury, disability, aging, hunger, poverty, incarceration, and violence. Children, indigenous people, minorities, refugees, and women are typically vulnerable. Other states of vulnerability include sleep, exploitation, mental illness, illiteracy, homosexuality, and homelessness. Some of these vulnerabilities are permanent features of our finitude; others are tied to particular historical contexts that make them appear as vulnerabilities. The former represent enduring conditions we must all cope with; the latter represent contingent social conditions that can be changed. Since the capabilities approach to social justice requires that all forms of capability deprivation be remediated, the task is to identify the vulnerabilities that threaten well-being and to develop policies to limit suffering.

One of the implications of *l'homme capable* for development ethics is that the capabilities approach should be completed by a *vulnerabilities approach*. Our vulnerabilities are just as basic as our capabilities; suffering is as basic as acting. Vulnerabilities are part of being human, they have moral-political significance, and they can be affected by development policy. Ricoeur himself has hinted in this direction while framing the issue in terms of redressing "asymmetrical relations" between actors and patients. "The whole problem of justice," he writes, "finds its starting point there because justice is concerned with the kinds of institutions or structured actions which attempt to redress this asymmetry by saying that there is a basic equality between men."[26] The task for development ethics is not only to eliminate unjust asymmetries and to enhance capabilities, but also to protect the vulnerable and eliminate as many contingent, nonessential vulnerabilities as possible. If our rights to capabilities deserve respect, then so do our vulnerabilities. At very least, vulnerabilities should not be exploited or taken advantage of. At best, the conditions that create vulnerabilities should be mitigated or eliminated. Ricoeur reminds development ethicists that their focus on autonomy is one sided and that our incapabilities are just as important for policy as our capabilities. People need both opportunities and protection.

3) Political power is paradoxical. The paradox is that, on one hand, political authority is legitimate if it comes from the rational consent of the governed; on the other hand, political practice is often so violent and coercive that it is something to which individuals, in principle, cannot consent. The paradox of authority is permanent. Any attempt to eliminate it is mistaken. Political power, according to Ricoeur, can never be entirely legitimate because it is potentially too violent to be entirely just. The political sphere is a mixture of authority and domination, reason and tradition held together in a fragile balance. The fragility of politics stems from the fragility of political language, situated in what Ricoeur calls a "vulnerable zone" between rational argumentation and rhetoric. It is vulnerable because ideology and utopia are permanent features of our social life, always present in politics, frustrating any attempt to purify our language into a vehicle for transparent political representation. Consequently, Ricoeur advocates for an impure democracy, one that is always tied to particular situations, specific institutions and practices, and, above all, ineliminable conflicts. The conversation about legitimate political power is interminable because so are its conflicts.

Ricoeur identifies three kinds of conflicts (hence three kinds of vulnerabilities) in democratic political institutions.[27] 1) There is a conflict between reason and rhetoric in political deliberation. Neither the rules of discourse, nor subject matter, nor participants, nor conclusions can ever be chosen in a completely free and impartial manner. 2) There are conflicts over the proper ends of government. Terms like *equality*, *freedom*, and *justice* are essential to the liberal tradition, yet problematic because they are ambiguous, open to interpretation, and subject to ideological appropriation. 3) There are conflicts over competing ideas of the good life. We are free to pursue happiness, yet the ends of our lives often seem opaque and unknowable, a condition Ricoeur attributes to the secular nature of modernity. He explains that "from such conflict, such a plurality of ends, and such a fundamental ambivalence come the fragility of political language."[28] This fragility makes it impossible to eliminate the use of political language as rhetorical sophistry. Politics is fragile because we are fragile.[29] At best we are flawed, fallible, and often mistaken; at worst we are self-centered, manipulative, and malicious.

Any institution or regime on which the authority to use force has been conferred is inherently dangerous. Ricoeur wisely links the fragility of everything political with the political responsibility held by every member of society to exercise prudence and judgment, given the enormous powers of governments. Political societies render us responsible because they are ultimately based on a "fiduciary bond." Citizens should "feel particularly responsible for the constitutive horizontal bond of the will to live together. In short, he or she must ascribe public safety to the vitality of the associate life which regenerates the will to live together."[30] Because we live together and have to trust to one another in order to survive and flourish, we are also responsible for one another. We need to be especially vigilant about the powers we confer upon political institutions, precisely because of the vital role they play in holding us together. Owning up to the fragility of politics means that we should do our best to find balance between argument and rhetoric, individual rights and membership in communities. Ricoeur implores us to be at once more ambitious and more humble in our political aspirations. We should work equally to develop global political institutions and to limit their powers.

One lesson or implication of the political paradox for development ethicists is to exercise humility in the face of proposed policy changes. However noble the call to expand the notion of capabilities might be, we should be wary of the authority that would enforce such an expanded notion of rights. We should be cautious in support of policymakers extending their scope of concern so deeply into the realm of human capabilities—not to mention vulnerabilities. As more aspects of our lives are politicized, we become susceptible to more political abuses. In light of the political paradox, the appeal to extend of the capabilities approach is a mixed blessing. The notion of capability enhancement is a powerful and promising moral-political principle that is gaining traction within both development ethics communities and policymaking agencies. Yet as more and more aspects of our humanity become the subject of development policy, the more we become exposed to institutional interventions. Once vulnerabilities are including as the proper subject matter of theory and practice, then we have invited policymakers to penetrate far deeper into our lives than policy typically reaches. Ricoeur, of course, is no libertarian or Foucauldian skeptic of bureaucratic administrations. He does not question political power entirely. But he does urge us to exercise a healthy skepticism—toward any absolute claim—while, at the same time, calling on us all to act responsibly in our political activities.

No one has examined the meaning of being human more thoroughly than Paul Ricoeur. His notion of *l'homme capable* is an exceptionally textured notion of human nature that gives development ethics new research projects that also have policy implications. Development ethics theorists and practitioners would be well served were they to include Ricoeur in the conversation and consider his works as valuable a resource as Sen's and Nussbaum's.

How Development Ethics Contributes to Ricoeur

Had Ricoeur followed Sen faithfully and taken a detour through the world of development ethics, his discussion of capabilities would have looked considerably different. Ricoeur already took a global view of social justice and the international institutions that could promote our rights to capabilities. But he never explicitly took on problems of development, nor did he explicitly address human deprivation and misery in poor countries. He never related our right to capabilities to a critique of political economy, to a critique of social and cultural life, to problems of resource and environmental management, or to questions of the meaning and nature of civilization itself. Those were not his explicit philosophical or political concerns.

Of course, it is hardly fair to criticize a man for what he did not address when he published and lectured on so much over his sixty-year career, producing thirty-five books and more than five hundred articles. The burden now falls on his readers if they wish to continue research that thinks with and against him. One fruitful path for his readers to take is a detour through development ethics in order to open up new opportunities to apply Ricoeur's insights to pressing theoretical and practical matters such as poverty reduction, peace and security, unfair distributions of goods, unequal burden of the costs of change, preserving natural environments, national and global governance, agriculture and energy policy, and technology transfer and colonialism. Ricoeur believed that philosophy needs to address the "hard cases" of politics and law and to confront the difficult choices citizens, political leaders, and judges face in liberal democracies. Few issues are as hard and intractable as how best to deal with massive, remediable, undeserved suffering and to improve the lives of as many as possible using means that are just, fair, and culturally appropriate. It is a matter that Ricoeur took seriously but never addressed as explicitly or as concretely as some of his readers might have liked. The work of Sen and Nussbaum points the way for readers of Ricoeur back to the rough ground of applied ethics, toward some of the hardest cases we confront today.

For those of us who respect and admire not only Ricoeur's works but the man himself, I can think of no better way to show our respect and admiration than to take up the themes of capability, vulnerability, and politics that mattered so much to him, but extend his analysis outside of a European and liberal context to the developing and exploited parts of the world, where the injustices and daily suffering are unimaginable. This is where philosophers might want to take a detour if they wish to be relevant and to honor the life and works of Paul Ricoeur.

Narrative Matters among the Mlabri

Interpretive Anthropology in International Development

ELLEN A. HERDA

The most persuasive moment of Paul Ricoeur's work for the development anthropologist is his idea of narrative imagination. This concept, applied to the development act of working together with the other who faces marginalization, fear, famine, and isolation, provides a medium for both the anthropologist and the local to emplot history and fiction into a social reality that brings each to a new place. Far from static, this new place is an emerging plot that enables movement from shame and hunger to self-sustainability on the part of the local, and movement from the confinement of Western individualism to an ontological state that allows the westerner to see herself as the other. Moreover, the relationships created in this place bring narrative to bear on an ethical plane that includes remembrance, re-telling, and choosing one's actions. These, in turn, open even further imagined places and lay the groundwork for attestation and appropriation. There is no development orientation for the economist, the anthropologist, the policymaker, or the developer that entails the possible, the plot, or the potential for solicitude as does narrative imagination housed in narrative identity. It is this aspect of Paul Ricoeur's work that I have used for the past several years in the field of international development.

In this essay I delineate in highly abbreviated form those concepts drawn from Ricoeur's work that most pertain to working in the applied world of international development. I do so, quite aware that I do not fully bring into discussion the theoretical implications of the ideas drawn from critical hermeneutics and their application to the social realities inherent in the field of international development. This long-time intellectual and practical endeavor will proceed as people with whom I work continue to teach me and work with me on how to move a mimetic reality into projects and assessment protocols, and into new trucks, expanding rice fields, and burgeoning organic fish ponds. These projects are initiated secretly under the blurred eyes of one government that is militaristic, and another government that wants to keep the "tribals" in comic regalia for voyeuristic tourists who pay to see them.

Several years ago, I was encouraged in a conversation with Professor Ricoeur to apply his theories to the field of development. His enthusiasm for such an application provided a momentum that I value both in memory and in action. He was kind enough to come the following year to the University of San Francisco, where I teach, to lecture to and have conversations with my graduate students, and a few years later his student Richard Kearney followed suit. Since then I have worked through Ricoeur's theories as well as those of allied writers in lectures, dissertations, publications, and in application, in concert with several indigenous people groups, most particularly the Mlabri and Akha in Southeast Asia. Many of my graduate students have worked, and walked, alongside me in my efforts to bring aspects of Paul Ricoeur's work to bear on critical hermeneutic inquiry design and collective research, and, in the field, on the capacity of each of us to recognize the other.[1]

In this essay I select our relationship and our work with the Mlabri people group to portray an ongoing story of critical hermeneutic field research and development amid an almost disappearing group of about 350–400 people scattered among three countries, Laos, Thailand, and Burma. The greater part of this overall project has taken place in Thailand. I will use the word *development* in this essay because it is the only one the literature offers at this point. Development implies a linear, successive movement. This is not how people's lives change for the better. Another word is needed; perhaps *appropriation*. For now I will use the word *development*, and I imply by its use a change in the lives of the poor that leads to an ameliorated state of being.

Below, I briefly set forth the development concerns that comprise the general context in which today's field developer works. This backdrop indicates that many development theorists now know that the way things were done, and in many cases still are done, in the name of development falls short of ameliorating world poverty. While the current discussions rarely, if ever, rely on notions of imagination and narrative identity, emerging critique encourages new directions. Before my discussion, drawn from Ricoeur's work, on the application of time, imagination, identity and plot, I provide an overview of today's development issues. Preceding each of these discussions is a brief ethnographic account of the Mlabri people, which may help concretize both current development views and the application of Ricoeur's ideas to working in the field.

The Mlabri

Since 1999, I have worked with the Mlabri people and neighboring Hmong people in supporting development practice. I travel to the Mlabri village in Nan Province, Thailand, several times a year. In the spring of 2006, I spent several weeks living with them in a nearby Hmong village. There is no conclusive evidence on the origin and/or migration patterns of the Mlabri, nor have any connections to other, earlier people been made with certainty.[2] One speculation is that the Mlabri migrated to Thailand from Sayabury Province in what is now the Lao People's Democratic Republic (the Lao PDR, or Laos) during the late 1800s;[3] they were documented in Thailand in 1919 and 1924.[4] More recently, genetic research carried out among selected Mlabri has provided additional speculation about their origin and past living styles.[5] It has been suggested that several hundred years ago there were thousands of Mlabri.[6] Today, in Thailand, these people are slowly emerging as agriculturists, whereas in Laos they remain hunters and gatherers; those who may be in Burma would most likely be hunters and gatherers.

Due to deforestation, the forests in Thailand can no longer support the Mlabri's previous migratory lifestyle. Deforestation is also taking place in the Lao PDR, which makes it extremely difficult for the remaining fifteen Mlabri there to survive. Both large and small animals have disappeared, and the edible roots and medicinal herbs once supported by the forest floor are now virtually impossible to find. The Mlabri in Thailand have been required to live closer to other people groups, particularly the Hmong, who are agriculturists. The Mlabri work as laborers for the Hmong in exchange for food, and in very recent years, for actual wages. The Mlabri have small frames, and the work they do is extremely difficult for them. Both men and women perform this manual labor in order to have enough to eat. One young Mlabri woman told me, "We used to hunt for food, now we hunt for money." Earlier, it was easier for the neighboring farmers to get by with giving the Mlabri rags or a small amount of rice for their labors, since the Mlabri did not use a numbering system—"one," "two," and "many" sufficed. (The Mlabri have words for numbers in their language, but rarely use them.) Cheating them out of pay was a simple matter. Now the Mlabri use the Thai language for counting and have asked to be paid in currency for their work. Increasingly, the Hmong farmers pay the Mlabri laborers in Thai baht.

A few of the Mlabri still dress traditionally and sit for tourists, who come view them for five minutes, take pictures, and then leave. A Hmong tourist agency sets up this circus-like environment and pays the Mlabri with a pig or a minimal amount of Thai baht. I first met the Mlabri in Nan Province in 1999 in these humiliating circumstances, and at that time decided to work toward helping them adopt a different lifestyle.

In a conversation with TaTaw, the leader of the Mlabri living in Nan Province in northern Thailand, we discussed why there is no communication between the Mlabri in Thailand and those in Laos. He told me what I had heard earlier: there was an argument long ago between two men who wanted the same woman; the result was a split between these groups. In this account, however, a new ending appeared. TaTaw said, "We are Mlabri and we should no longer have this rift. I would like to talk with them. I would like to go see them. I know they are poor. We could help them." Such a meeting could be difficult to arrange, since the governments of both Thailand and Laos control the comings and goings of the Mlabri, with no small amount of covetousness imbedded in their actions.

The adult Mlabri are nonliterate, both in their own language and in the Thai language. (Many of the men speak Thai well. Some of the adult Mlabri are multilingual, and a few speak five or more languages.) This is an unfortunate condition that could have been redressed by foreign missionaries who came to live with the Mlabri three decades ago. During this long period, one of the missionaries transcribed the Mlabri language, using the Thai alphabet. This missionary and his family speak Thai and Mlabri—an ideal situation for teaching the adult Mlabri to read and write Thai, a language they already speak. It is essential for the Mlabri to know Thai in order to obtain driver's licenses and buy land. Their lack of Thai literacy seems to be an inexcusable state of affairs, in light of the Mlabri's natural gift for learning languages. Moreover, having been acknowledged recently as humans living in the country of Thailand—not evil spirits, as many Thai formerly believed them to be—they have the right to have identification (ID) cards, which are a mark of citizenship. They have been forced by the government, however, to take on Thai names. Consequently the Mlabri have ID cards with names that are not theirs, written in a language they cannot read. Upon being asked by the police for their ID cards, for example, they show cards that identify them as Thai persons. Identifying them as Thai, however, carries with it tension, since the Mlabri do not look Thai; they look Mlabri—or like "Spirits of the Yellow Leaf," as the Thai refer to them.

There is limited literature on current Mlabri culture and changing lifestyles.[7] Ethnographic data in the case of this present work has been key to development efforts among the Mlabri. I anticipate that ethnography will make inroads into international development designs, since cultural understanding currently is considered more important in international development than it was even a few years ago. International development for the past several decades was marked primarily by economic considerations. Today, policymakers and development planners are becoming more attuned to the idea that structure, programs, and implanted markets may not be the sole, or even the best, progenitors of successful development. The phrase *people-centered development* is one example of a slowly emerging paradigm shift in development theory. Below is a view of some of yesterday's and today's considerations in international development. The following discussion is a broad overview of the ways in which people think about development. The reason we might be interested in this portrayal is reflected in the nature of the problems being addressed. Their nature cannot be reflected in simple, or complex, data retrieval and display. The nature of the problem is a philosophical one that can be addressed only in practices other than those we have been using. Paul Ricoeur's anthropology both accounts for the nature of human suffering and provides a direction toward another means of thinking about assuming responsibility for addressing the issues at hand.

Portraying Development

Worldwide, more than 20,000 people each day perish of extreme poverty. The West has tried for decades to care for the poor, the sick, and the disheartened. These attempts have been carried out under the auspices of security, democracy, and aid. Governments, private foundations, religious organizations, and nongovernmental agencies have all taken a stand in the development arena. Two primary motifs may be noted in the practices through which those who work in development have tried, over the last seven decades, to answer the call for aid among marginalized people of the world: the top-down approach and the bottom-up approach, through participation. The poor are still with us, however, and are increasing in number.

Top-Down Development

Since the 1940s, development has become professionalized and institutionalized. The professional stance casts the problems of the poor in terms of the neutral realms of science and the Westernized version of modernity. This approach removed the problems of the poor from the political, cultural, and personal realms and placed them in the hands of the foreign expert.

The term *Third World*, as a way to refer to the poor, gave a name to a new social and political problem that was made evident with the increase of a market economy. Arturo Escobar writes that with "the consolidation of capitalism, systematic pauperization became inevitable."[8] The poor were thought of as a social problem that needed to be managed; control mechanisms were to be played out through interventions in health care, education, cultural improvement, and new ideas about work for the poor in the Third World (such as "work hard and save money"). Moreover, the poor emerged as the domain of development at the same time that politics assumed a binary arrangement between the East and the West, between the Soviet Union and the United States. After the Second World War, anti-Communist sentiments contributed to the emerging doctrines of national security, which, in turn, served as motivation for the conceptual and actual practices of intervention development.

Capital investment from rich countries purportedly moved into poor countries through intervention programs and international organizations, most notably the World Bank, the International Monetary Fund, and development arms of the United Nations such as the United Nations Development Programme (UNDP). Armed with scientific knowledge and labels, the experts depicted Third World peoples as deficient subjects in need of intervention and treatment.

There was little fit, however, between the research and the application, because the design, strategy, and leadership were imported from developed nations. Furthermore, the designs and strategies were developed within research methodologies that perpetuated the gap between theory and practice and retained power relations not advantageous to local recipients of development policy. The research designs were for the most part created by sociologists whose work was housed in a quantitative paradigm. The recipients of the projects were counted as data and analyzed in ways that made sense to the Western developer. For all the time and the intellectual, monetary, and human resources spent on modernizing the poor, the move out of poverty seemed to elude the very people for whom these resources were expended. As Amartya Sen recently pointed out in remarking on the above period, the "process of economic growth is a rather poor basis for judging the progress of a country; it is not, of course, irrelevant, but it is only one factor among many."[9] International funding organizations, government agencies, and policy planners and implementers, among others, thought it was time to change direction. The answer to the problems inherent in the top-down approach was, naturally, to move to a bottom-up approach.

Bottom-Up Development

The lack of expected change, or modernization, led to an almost wholesale buying-in to various grass-roots approaches by activists for human rights, developers, anthropologists, and others wanting to improve the plight of people in the so-called Third World countries. The top-down approach toward eliminating poverty through modernizing the poor was becoming a faint dream, the efforts toward which had cost governments and international-development-oriented organizations both money and loss of face. One organization in particular spent an exorbitant amount of money: since the 1960s the World Bank had spent over one trillion dollars, only to meet with scathing criticism that its efforts to mitigate poverty had failed to have any significant impact.[10]

Throughout the 1990s and early 2000s, participatory research in myriad and tangential forms became a mantra among many of those interested in field-based development.[11] As it turns out, participatory research can be carried out using any number of theoretical orientations, ranging from positivism to quasi structuralism. These approaches rely, however, on a concept of identity that houses only one facet of a human being—that of self as a singular entity. When personal and community change is required, as it is in development settings, with this sense of self one ends up counting numbers of people saying yes or no in surveys, or simply responding to choices provided by Westerners. It is believed that if enough people agree on what to do, then development will take place. Agreement is something that makes our work in development easier, but agreements only have staying power if a group of people change who they believe they are and hold on to what they believe they can do, both on a personal and communal level. The self, for Ricoeur, is "I am" and includes "I can." Each person needs to hold to the belief that he or she can inhabit a proposed world. When we embrace the idea of self that is appropriate for work with others, namely, a self that is constituted by one's material and cultural aspects, yet is capable of initiating something different, we can then understand that this duality—the physical and intentional—is the very requisite needed for people to work together in development.

Some core concepts discussed by Ricoeur and others—freedom, ethics, and well-being, and morality, ethics, and capabilities—have found their way into development parlance.[12] To date, however, to my knowledge there has been no application of narrative imagination and narrative identity as posited by Ricoeur to the remembered world, the present world, or the anticipated worlds of local people groups. The development act among the Mlabri discussed below embraced several ideas from Ricoeur's work in order to help the Mlabri move from a highly communal life to one where individuals see themselves as selves in relationship to various others capable of changing their lives.

An Interpretive Development Act among the Mlabri

For an anthropological base through which to explore his ideas, Ricoeur used ancient world thinkers, philosophy, and literature. As a development anthropologist, I find his study of the human both provocative and provisional. He offers a philosophical context in which to locate the core of our humanness, along with parameters that provide guideposts to action in the field. The idea of validity of attestation rather than empirical verification is central to Ricoeur's work, and to the work of the interpretive development anthropologist. The distinction between humans and things is basic to both. Humans have belief far more often than they have certitude. All the empirical verification gathered in whatever modality available will not form the basis for changing one's life. To intervene in the order of an impoverished life, or any life, a person must believe that she is capable of so doing. How to inaugurate one's capability invokes the notions of time, imagination, narrative identity, and plot. Ricoeur's anthropology of the capable person provides a living text[13] from which to draw when working with the destitute and stricken, an aim toward "the 'good life' with and for others in just institutions"[14] and communities.

In my first meeting with TaTaw, the leader of the Mlabri, he stood before me drunk and angry. My students and I had brought clothing and food, including canned fish and fruit. I wanted to meet the leader. One of the older men went to find him. This was our first visit to their village and our second visit to see them. In our first encounter with the Mlabri, they were in the forest and dressed for tourist viewing: TaTaw was not, however, one of the Mlabri posing for tourists. When TaTaw finally arrived, he stood in front of me, spit on the ground, and told me that if I ever came back I needed to bring him a television. I told him "*Taa, kuhn mai mee fai*" (But you don't have electricity). He turned away angrily and stumbled back to his hut. Now, nearly ten years later, he is a farmer who quietly encourages others to start up farming so as not to be compelled to work as laborers for the Hmong farmers; he has bought a motorcycle, he cares for people in his community, and he is my good friend. He is faithful to a Mlabri woman, Nit, who has her own voice and works alongside him as his partner.

My first challenge was to have a conversation with TaTaw. By *conversation* I mean an exchange in which the topic at hand takes over the movement of talk between myself and the other—where there is the sense of "play" that Gadamer talks about.[15] This did not take place easily. It took several trips to his village before he was willing to talk with me. When he did, I asked him to tell his story of his family and his forefathers, of living in the forest, of moving to the countryside, and what he wanted for the future. In these questions I was looking for his history, his predecessors, how he thought about the present, and what he imagined for the future. It turned out to be only an interview, not a conversation. He told me of hunting exploits that called for communal bravery on the part of several men to kill a large animal. He told me of the pain of working long hours for little money in the Hmong fields. He did not say anything about the future. I asked again what he would like to see happen in the future. He did not answer. He merely repeated what he had already said about something that he had done in the past. It seemed as if he did not know what to say about a future. Moreover, I had the sense that there was very little reason for him to hope for anything, much less imagine something that might take place.

After several interviews (not conversations), he finally indicated that he wanted his children to go to school to learn to read and write—something related to the future. There was no indication that he had any vision for himself or for other adults in his community. The primary consideration was food to eat today. The forest they once lived in gave them food one day at a time. There was no need to store food. Tomorrow never came up as an issue. In their nomadic movements, an event of planning to leave their camp would not come up, since the Mlabri could depart in five minutes without leaving a trace.

A question arises as to the conditions that allow people to move into conversation, as opposed to simply undergoing an interview. TaTaw and I now have conversations. We have come to know each other and to trust each other. And we are both oriented toward reaching an understanding. Habermas's idea of validity claims, which serve as a guide in communicative action, can be redeemed only if the hearer and speaker are in a relationship oriented toward reaching understanding.[16] This idea of relationship, in addition to Gadamer's idea of play, contributed to my understanding of how to carry out a conversation as opposed to simply conducting an interview. To help create a relationship oriented toward reaching understanding required my comprehending TaTaw's idea of time, and creating a different framework of time that could become part of TaTaw's worldview. Without a different framework of time, it would have been difficult for him to imagine another kind of life. Conversation about change, in his and others' lives, requires the ability to imagine a future in which our past grounds us and gives us perspective. Kearney tells us of the need to reflect and understand the past in order to "recreate ourselves in a new future."[17] TaTaw needed to recognize his past, not just remember it as a linear series of events and hunting exploits. One's idea of time plays a role in such recognition. It may be that recognition is achieved in narrative, which holds the capacity to represent our human experience of time as well as the capacity to enhance, or re-plot, our experience of time.

In *Time and Narrative* Ricoeur points out that there are two modes of time, in which we experience time in two different ways: cosmological time and phenomenological time. In cosmological time we experience time in a linear fashion—a succession of events in the passing days and seasons and in the progression of our lives. In contrast, phenomenological time is experienced in terms of the yesterday, today, and tomorrow, as a succession of time in terms of what has been, what is, and what will be. Ricoeur argues that the past, the present, and the future presuppose cosmological time, but that in order for us to understand human existence we must use a composite framework of time, which is only possible in a narrative whose expression relies on imagination. People invent ways to interweave these two concepts of time, such as through the use of calendars. The calendar notes time in an ongoing, anonymous fashion, but a date becomes noteworthy when it is marked on the calendar. Actions take on meaning when we interweave these two times, which are reflected in our lives as historical time. When action is set into historical time, the action is placed in a meaningful context. It is a response to something in the past and it anticipates that in the future there will be another response.

The idea of historical time is a critical aspect of those actions that are embodied in appropriate development. Unless we help locals create a space for experience and also for expectation, they are more likely to let someone else tell them what to do tomorrow. If the reward is inviting enough, they will certainly do it, whether or not they believe it is right. When the "essential tensions" between cosmological time and phenomenological time and between self and other are played out in a meaningful space, development occurs. In other words, when the past is made present through the recognition of meaningful events, it provides a place for a new plan or action that opens expectations and lays the groundwork for exploration of how to go about doing something. The past experience of someone and their sense of the possible mutually enhance each other. Of course, there are myriad ways in which the possible can come alive. There is no determinative relationship between past experiences and future possibilities. Development action in the present comes out of both the past and the future.

What happens, to whom it happens, when it takes place, and how it is assessed call for narrative discourse. For the preliterate person, the telling and re-telling of a story to another holds the potential for connecting and unifying many actions over time. When more than one person tells and re-tells the stories, different viewpoints and assessments of the ethical action in question come into view. These actions pass through the moral aim of the Mlabri, expressed in the following obligation: keep people fed and alive.

When there are new things to talk about, and men and women dare to imagine, lives can change for the better. In a setting in the middle of a village, in this case, the more coherent and inclusive the plot of the story, the more people there are who will listen. They will then be encouraged to tell their own story. The story will answer the question, "who is the agent in the development act?" The narrative holds the answer to the "who," a starting place in development; the next question is the "what?" In the move from asking "who" to asking "what," the social scientist places the focus of her work on the move from the person, the "who," telling about a possible world, to the person recounting something about the possible world, to the "what." This is the "what" of action, because in recounting it as though it were past, Ricoeur explains, "the 'as though it actually happened' is part of the meaning we attach to every narrative."[18] He refers to the recounting of the plot and characters as a "quasi events" and "quasi characters" that are part of a "quasi past." Through fictional narratives of possible worlds, these stories are "authorized to detect unactualized potentialities of the historical past, in the mode of imaginative variations."[19] This is Ricoeur's response to Arendt's question: "How do we know the 'what' of action?" His answer elevates action to its appropriate sphere: "It is action, as a model of actuality, that bears narrative to its proper sphere."[20] This model for action is the "proper sphere" and a fulcrum for development. In past development ideas, there is most assuredly an emphasis on the "who." But in the character of verisimilitude there resides a powerful "force of discovery, of revelation from the deep structures of temporal experience" which embodies a model for our actions.[21] Here the "what" of development is found in the depths of the stories of the humanity we say we want to help. The realist narrativist is comparable to the developer who brings her own plot to the field and believes that no one else's plot counts. In neither example is there a space for action whose reference resides in the lives of real people—those beings with whom we claim we are striving to develop relationships.

Ricoeur, at the point of acknowledging how various proposals of ethical justice are brought forth, points out that it is at the juncture of telling and acting that the "notion of narrative identity encounters its limits and has to link up with nonnarrative components in the formation of an acting subject."[22] In the case of the development act among the Mlabri, it is the oral narratives and related actions that create a development identity and a "wholesome" circle of telling, acting, and re-telling—"[i]n a word, narrative identity is the poetic resolution of the hermeneutic circle."[23]

Narrative identity is not a seamless identity, and it is possible for many plots to emerge from the same set of incidents (not appropriately called the same *events*). It is always possible to weave different plots about our lives in an "exchange of roles between history and fiction."[24] Narrative identity does not exhaust the question of the self-constancy of a subject, whether a particular individual or a community of individuals. The power of the act of reading, whether in oral or written form, resides in what Ricoeur calls a "thought experience by means of which we try to inhabit worlds foreign to us."[25] Herein, Ricoeur posits, "narrative exercises the imagination more than the will."[26] The person or persons moving in a social imagination that can house the opposition between imagination and will is in a moment of both stasis and impetus. It is due to this inclusion of impetus that the moment becomes a provocation to be and to act differently.[27] Ricoeur describes the development act when he says this "impetus is transformed into action only through a decision whereby a person says: Here I stand!"[28] This declaration reflects a decision and ethical responsibility. TaTaw makes a decision that has grand implications for the amelioration of his village. I describe below the context in which he made the decision to farm.

The Mlabri, not only the leader but others as well, are commonly found to be faithful to and caring toward others. Rare is the person who wants to retain autonomy and individuality. There would be considerable pressure on this person to move in concert with others. I have not seen this done in a forceful way, but rather through patience with one another. The Mlabri avoid violence. The group sees that when life is better for all, it is better for each one. But this is going ahead of the story. Encouraging TaTaw to risk re-remembering his past and to further risk thinking and talking about the future was a necessary move in order to bring his capabilities into reality, rather than simply have them remain in potentiality.

The personal identity of TaTaw appeared to be grounded only in the *idem* or, even more so, in a perdurable insignificant self in a locked space and time dimension. Perhaps, in actuality, this was never the case. Had I been a close-to-native speaker and had I lived in their community for a long time, I believe that I would have seen his selfhood, or ipseity, in light of my being the Other; and, in seeing his selfhood in this way, in turn I would have seen this aspect of his *ipse* identity in our everyday life. But as a Caucasian foreign female arriving as an outsider with moderate Thai language ability (I made use of Thai-English translators), it was unlikely that I would receive a view of any side of TaTaw other than the nonpersonal self that he placed before me. It took time for both of us to change in our own selves and in relationship to each other, and for each to come into a different narrative identity, an identity that sustained both a tension and a harmony in each of our selves and in relation to each other. At such a point, as Ricoeur points out, drawing from Proust, the individual then "appears both as a reader[/listener] and the writer[/teller] of its own life."[29] The stories of each of our lives, and the lives of those in the Mlabri community, continue to be refigured in the development act by our history and our fictive stories about our self and selves. It was through a process of the telling of stories and the re-telling of them that TaTaw saw something different both in his past and in the future. From a new vantage point, new relationships were established and new actions began to take on meaning in a space that housed both stasis and impetus.

This process began on one of my visits when TaTaw, a translator, and I began talking about the land that belonged to Hmong farmers. We saw some of the Mlabri trekking up the hill to the village after having worked many hours for the Hmong farmers. I asked TaTaw to tell me about the lives of Mlabri today and how they were different than their lives while they were still nomadic. He told stories filled with travels from one place to another, visiting other Mlabri families. (They usually lived in bands of four or five families, since this was the number the forest could support in one area for a certain amount of time.) Life was not easy, but it was free. They had access to land. They did not own land but they used it. (It is against their traditional belief system to own land—they believe it is unethical. There is no word for ownership in their language. When the forest came under protection by the Thai government, the Mlabri were forced to remain stationary.) Although it was difficult to live in the forest as it decreased in density and they increasingly suffered hunger and fear, TaTaw acknowledged that it became more difficult when they were forced to remain in bush land in the midst of Hmong farmers and work for the farmers under extremely harsh conditions. Their suffering, their passive action, only increased over time.

I asked TaTaw if he thought there could be another shift—from their living on land as workers, to working their own land.This question would not have been heard a few years ago, since people owning land, working the land, and then buying things they might want or need, was foreign to them. TaTaw acknowledged that his life and the lives of his people were only becoming more difficult. A Hmong farmer named Sornkiri, who had befriended the Mlabri, was with us, and he also spoke of owning land. He told of the land in the area and the possibility of the Mlabri farming some of it. There was no settled plan, however, at that time. We ended our day with pleasantries and a goodbye.

A few weeks later, I returned to the village. Before returning, I had developed some of my own ideas of what would need to be done in order to have even one person begin farming. This person would make the difficult decision to break with the community after a twenty-five-year tradition of working for the Hmong in their fields, going against the ethical grain of the Mlabri community. This person would need some basic farming tools and seed. Besides, one person cannot do all the work alone: there would need to be at least one other person involved who knew how to farm and who was willing to teach. Working for someone else and working your own land require different conceptual frameworks, including the idea of time—waiting for the rice to grow so you can eat. In the forest you had food as soon as you were successful in your hunt. When working for the farmer, you received pay every few days or weeks. There were many problems and unknowns among the people in the village as they discussed the possibility of farming their own land. And whose land would they farm? They had no land of their own, and most still believed that it was wrong to claim land for one's own or the community's own purposes.

More conversations ensued. Some people left the area in which we were talking, staying off to the side, sitting on their haunches, staring at those talking. Nothing seemed to hold, no plot emerged, and only problems surfaced as to why this could not work. There was only confusion. And hovering in the back of some minds, I am sure, was the fear of the majority of Hmong farmers, who certainly did not want the Mlabri to farm for themselves. Who would work in their fields for as low wages as the Mlabri? Some of the Hmong farmers might become angry and threaten the Mlabri as they had done in the past, by calling the police to report either a real or fabricated infraction. Mlabri are extremely afraid of the police because they carry guns.

Over the course of a few weeks, discussions were ongoing. One person said he did not know how to do this work, and he was answered by Sornkiri, who said he would teach him; the Hmong friend's father said he would provide the land for the Mlabri to use at no cost to them; and I had been able to secure a small amount of funding to support three or four families with rice and other supplies while they readied the land, planted, and waited for the harvest. It came time to cut down the bush on the land that was made available to them in order not to miss the planting season for mountain rice. In the end, only TaTaw and Nit were willing to try farming. TaTaw was willing to take a stand based on the past occurrences of hunger and suffering, anticipating the supply of food a field of rice would provide. No one else wanted to try. This was a brave act on the part of TaTaw. He could fail, and he separated himself to some extent from his fellow villagers, but he was prompted to try some part of a life that was previously outside his experience. He suffered a past that was not of his own making, and he imagined a future that would dramatically alter his life. He started to talk about his decision by telling a story of how he would do this farming step by step and why it was a good idea. A plot took hold and people listened. The force of discovery and revelation that drew upon his temporal experience provided the model of action that undergirded his act of farming.

At the end of the rice harvest, TaTaw and Nit received some benefit from their inaugural work. But the harvest was not bountiful. Their harvested rice was stored in their one-room hut and most of the villagers came to ask for food, since they were always short of rice and the Mlabri custom is to share what you have equally among the others. This was a difficult time for TaTaw. He was the leader. His actions toward all others were expected to be of the highest good. He gave his rice away but told and re-told why it would be better for them to plant their own. He would place the people who came to ask for rice into the stories he told, as potential benefactors of their own work, and he illustrated how they might live differently if they pursued a new direction.

The next season placed TaTaw and Nit in the same fields, but this was the year to plant corn. One other husband-and-wife team joined them. Each team had a bumper crop. The stories, now of the two couples, were heeded by three other families the following year. I brought these stories back to the United States, and they prompted the renewal of a nonprofit organization which today is headed by former and current graduate students of mine. Each year for several years, a group of graduate students and friends has joined me in working on site with the Mlabri in Thailand. We have provided basic necessities—food, clothing, health supplies—and raised funds in the United States to buy land and support an ongoing rice program for children. We have also set up a small learning center, built a dormitory for Mlabri students in a nearby Hmong village so that they can attend school, provided tin roofing for some huts, and set up a water-tank system that draws water from nearby mountains. One of the most significant projects is our agriculture mentoring program, which offers the Mlabri the possibility of a new way of making a living. None of this work would have been possible without creating conditions under which this new life could emerge, incited by the decision of TaTaw, who placed his history and tradition into the practical dimension of caring for his people. Developers in the field are learning that care and responsibility are crucial elements in appropriate international development practice.[30]

TaTaw's person is that of one who is responsible uniting someone "counting on" him and "being accountable for." He is the response to the question, "Where are you?" asked by another who needs him. His response in return, judging from my experience in being with him, would be "Here I am!"[31] The permanence in time of character and of self-constancy comprise a leadership narrative, one that TaTaw authors.

The decisions of those who came into farming later rather than earlier certainly did not require as much bravery as was exhibited by TaTaw when he risked imagining a future. The impetus for taking a stand against tradition and for a better life was much stronger in the case of TaTaw than it was among his village fellows. TaTaw saw the possibility of freedom, and his action reflects the sense of possibility expressed in Kearney's words: "The imaginary liberates the prisoners of our lived experience into possible worlds."[32]

The most powerful narrative emerged early on in this development story, as TaTaw first told others of the potential benefits of farming. He saw through many obstacles; he had conversations with Sornkiri and with myself. He created a future whose past will soon form even better bases for socially imagined future lives for individuals and for the entire village. Now, when some of the children are asked what they want to do in the future, they are ready to imagine completely new lives, very different than the ones they have been living. Some want to become teachers, others nurses.

If one asks various Mlabri to tell their stories about farming, each story is somewhat different, since into each narrative are woven the challenges the tellers faced, the unanticipated gifts they received, the unexpected help from an outsider, the family problems with sickness, and the result of having harvested their own crop, which they sold in order to buy a new roof or clothes or a pair of shoes, plus myriad more details that can be brought to light in another telling. Each story holds the teller's personal identity—an idem-identity and an ipse-identity—which is housed in a narrative identity. In their stories, each teller is still Mlabri, a human with a unique history through which he or she has come to be, among other things, a farmer. The concern of narrative, however, is coherence and plot, not a particular experience. In this light, there is the possibility of another re-telling of what happened, in a narrative of becoming a farmer and further imagining a life inspired by hope that can shape a different and potentially better future—this is the context of development.

If the new narrative does not cohere, however, this is a sign that one must pay attention to the personal and overall story of a community. With the loss of coherence comes the inability to regard oneself as worthy of the good life—the aim of development. Ricoeur suggests that our life has an ethical aim. Further, our aim in life is self-esteem, and how we interpret ourselves and our actions are the telling aspects of our ethics. Self-esteem is an important feature of the evaluation process. A major question in development is how best to evaluate our projects. Narrative assessment is more time-consuming than using, for example, a Likert scale, but it provides meaningful data that can set the direction for action.

I have looked at TaTaw as the main person of interest at this time; he is the subject of his actions, and he is responsible for what he did and what he continues to do, both as a member of the village community and as their chosen leader. He is the one to whom his actions can be imputed and whose character is interpreted in view of such actions. In further conversations with TaTaw, I want to explore with him how he would describe his life now. I will ask him to tell me another story about what has recently happened and what he thinks could happen in the future. His past is now significantly different in the telling than it was a few years ago. I want to try to discover his ideas on responsibility and justice and try to understand how he would tell someone else about living an ethical life by "aiming at the 'good life' with and for others in just [communities]."[33]

There is today a historical context for a conversation with TaTaw about how to move people to exercise their capabilities in everyday life. Does he see himself in others? In what ways does he see himself as similar to others? Or different from others? I am interested in learning how to ask questions that may spark such topics for conversation. There may even be a possibility for a conversation about how one becomes who one is through relationships with the Other based in friendship and love.

The power to act on the part of TaTaw came from his belief that he could. He needed to believe that he (in self-recognition) could begin the daunting task of farming. One can say that the context in which he lived was far from just. The Mlabri were recognized as fodder for the tourist industry, and they were considered mere serfs by their neighbors. There was no certainty that TaTaw would succeed, but he believed he could. The part of his identity that led to this attestation is noted when Ricoeur writes that the "proud assertion 'I will do it' expresses in language the risky posture of ipseity, as self-constancy that goes beyond the safety of mere sameness."[34] To move beyond the safety of sameness requires the invocation of the narrative imagination—learning how to narrate oneself, and in so doing, learning how to narrate oneself in other ways—which, when carried out in action with others, is what the development act is.

The Place of Remembrance

Reflections on Paul Ricoeur's Theory of Collective Memory

JEFFREY ANDREW BARASH

The theme of collective memory, conceived as a source of social cohesion, has come to assume a unique importance in the heterogeneous context of our contemporary societies. The public function of collective memory, in the form of commemorations or museums, as in the evocation of traumatic memories shared by entire social groups, has become a topic of lively debate in a large number of theoretical areas, ranging from cognitive science to sociology, political theory, history, and other disciplines of social inquiry. It is the singular achievement of the recent work of Paul Ricoeur, *Memory, History, Forgetting,* to take a wide variety of arguments into consideration stemming from each of these fields. In the essay that follows, however, my concern will focus less on the diversity of perspectives in which he examines the theme of memory than on the profound intention arising from the moral philosophy that inspires his concept of memory and informs the work as a whole. On the first page of the introduction to the work, Ricoeur clearly formulates this intention:

> I remain troubled by the worrisome spectacle arising from an excess of memory at some points, from lapses into forgetfulness at others, and this without even speaking of the influence of commemorations and of the abuse of memory (*abus de mémoire*)—and of forgetting. The idea of a politics of just memory is in this respect one of my explicit themes of civic concern (*un de mes thèmes civiques avoués*).[1]

Ricoeur here expresses a broad ambition: in *Memory, History, Forgetting,* he concerns himself with memory or forgetting not only in relation to individuals or small groups, but also in relation to the political order, in the fundamental sense of the word. In conceiving the theme of a "just memory" as a genuine "civic concern," he extends his analysis to the political field of national communities and of the different groups that constitute them, organized in terms of the vast political orders that are familiar to us in our contemporary world. At this level of analysis, how should we understand the moral injunction to reestablish a "just memory" through the application to vast political communities of the categories "too much" memory or "too much" forgetting? In what sense is this moral intention appropriate when applied to the domain of politics? In the following paper I will attempt to answer these questions in terms of critical reflection on the work of Ricoeur in *Memory, History, Forgetting.*

I

Beginning in the first part of the book, entitled "On Memory and Reminiscence," Ricoeur emphasizes a fundamental problem that reflection on the political scope of memory must confront: he examines the possibility, in terms of the original experience of memory rooted in the intimate sphere of personal life, of accounting for the "collective memory" of national groups. What principle of social cohesion, indeed, allows us to identify a "collective memory" in this sense, permitting us to ascribe to it an excess of memory or of forgetting?

In order to answer this question concerning the features of such large-scale remembrance, Ricoeur draws upon previous traditions of reflection on the role of memory in the constitution of human identity. In a precise manner he examines the principal philosophical investigations of memory and the fundamental role they have played in modern interpretations both of personal and collective identities. He recalls in this context the significance of Locke's reflection, which, in rejecting metaphysical theories of the substantial soul that had predominated since antiquity, posited as the sole foundation of personal identity the experience that each individual has of him- or herself, as "the same thinking thing in different times and different places."[2] According to Locke, personal identity extends as far as self-consciousness of past actions and thoughts. Thus, through consciousness of the self that encompasses the different moments of its experience, each person constitutes the unity of his or her own identity; and, on the basis of memory of oneself in the past, one recognizes the sameness of self in different times and places.[3] The question of the link between different individuals, however—between the different memories constitutive of different personal identities—did not pose any particular problem for Locke, who, to weld together collective existence, emphasized the role of economic interaction and the contract established among atomistic individuals in a framework provided by political institutions. For Ricoeur, nonetheless, this perspective of social atomism and political contractualism can hardly account for the complex lines of cohesion that unite vast modern collectivities. And beyond a series of individual identities constituted by personal recollections, he continues the search for an appropriate principle of social cohesion.

While aware of the limits of Lockean empiricism and of Whig liberalism, Ricoeur does not for this reason advocate the opposite tendency, which would deny that, in the act of remembrance, personal experience is the "authentic subject."[4] Here he directs his critical analysis to the theory of collective memory elaborated by Maurice Halbwachs, above all in his works *Les cadres sociaux de la mémoire* and *La mémoire collective*. Halbwachs sought to demonstrate that collective memory, far from comprising a series of individual memories, is on the contrary the wellspring of personal memory and individual consciousness. This analysis, as Ricoeur emphasizes, attempts to account for personal consciousness in terms of collective factors, namely the social framework from which it supposedly arises: our social milieu expresses itself in us, even when we are not conscious of its influence, to the point that our most intimate thoughts and recollections depend upon a network of significations that originate in collective life.

In attempting to steer between these alternative accounts of memory, Ricoeur intensifies his quest for a principle of cohesion capable of accounting both for personal experience in its autonomy[5] and for the extrapersonal dimension of communal experience with which it is interwoven. He finds the point of orientation for this search in one of the earliest sources of his philosophical work, the phenomenology of Edmund Husserl, above all in the fifth of Husserl's *Cartesian Meditations*, which examines the possibility of comprehending other persons. For Husserl, the condition of possibility of grasping the other lies in an *a priori* appresentation, or in what Husserl terms an *analogical apperception* of the other in terms of the self; and Husserl conceives of this constitution of the other "in me, yet as other" not as a simple perception of a plurality of atomized individuals, but as a possibility of immediate apprehension of others as communal others.[6] This constitutive act serves as the starting point for a theory of intersubjectivity at the different levels of articulation of the social world, from interpersonal interaction to the "higher intersubjective communities" that designate larger collectivities. Ricoeur is well aware that Husserl did not rely for this analysis on any notion of communal memory to support his theory of the constitution of communities.[7] Moreover, since Husserl ultimately grounded his principle of cohesion of collective identity on the presupposition of the transcendental ego, serving as the absolute source of meaningful interaction in the common lifeworld, the role of collective memory could never be fundamental in his theoretical perspective. For this reason, if Ricoeur adopts the vocabulary of the Husserlian theory of intersubjectivity, he remains skeptical concerning the claims of transcendental idealism, which placed the sovereignty of the cogito at the basis of understanding of the other and of the configuration of intersubjective meaning. Beginning with his first works, Ricoeur's hermeneutic philosophy rejected this idea of the sovereignty of the cogito in all of its forms, while seeking to limit its role in the constitution of the sense of its experience. He refers to this more humble status of the self as the "wounded cogito" or the "broken cogito."[8] Nonetheless, he maintains the paradigmatic role that Husserl attributed to the analogy between personal consciousness and community, and he employs it to elaborate his conception of social cohesion and collective memory. Hence he writes: "it is by analogy alone, and in relation to the individual consciousness and its memory that one takes collective memory to be a collection of traces left by events which have affected the course of the history of given groups, and in virtue of which we attribute to it the capacity to represent these shared memories during festivals, rites, and public celebrations."[9] This principle of analogy between individuals and groups comes to expression in the two principle categories of analysis of memory that Ricoeur adopts: on one hand, the moral category of the "debt" and of the "obligation to remember," and on the other hand, that of the "work" of memory, modeled on psychoanalytic therapy.

This consideration leads me to a more precise formulation of my initial question: does this conception of an analogical relation between individual and society permit us to situate the "place" of collective memory? Does recourse to this analogy allow us to identify the principle of social cohesion? We must analyze in this light Ricoeur's constant tendency to draw analogical parallels between collective and personal memory and examine the legitimacy of his ambition to identify, on this basis, the deeper levels of cohesion of collective memory. If Ricoeur refuses to accept the presupposition of transcendental idealism according to which all meaning derives from the constitutive acts of the cogito, does the privilege he continues to accord to the analogical relation between individual and community not lead him to run another risk: that of obscuring those dimensions of collective identity that escape characterization in terms of analogy with personal identity? At this point in my analysis, it is necessary to examine more closely this notion of collective signification that, as a source of communal identity, might resist any definition in terms of analogical parallels with personal consciousness and personal memory. For this purpose, before returning to an analysis of the work of Ricoeur, I will focus on the significance of collective memory as such and on its claim to ground the tie between different members of a community.

II

What is collective memory? The attempt to respond to this question, which has been subject to lively debate over the course of the past decades, faces very different and even contradictory kinds of response according to the ways in which it is analyzed in the various disciplines of the humanities and the social and cognitive sciences. In each case the term "collective memory" signifies the transmission of shared experience that has been retained by a group. But even this rudimentary qualification raises difficulties that immediately come to mind: first, memory necessarily refers to the original sphere of personal experience and to the intimacy of personal life; to speak of "collective memory," then, necessarily presupposes a principle of cohesion of singular personal memories within an overarching whole. The definition of this principle is by no means an easy task. Secondly, when we refer to group experience with which personal life is interwoven, memory assumes a very different role in the perspective of a small group, such as a family or a professional association, than in that of a more extended collectivity, such as the public sphere of national commemoration. Oftentimes comprehension of the word *memory* is obscured when it is applied indifferently to personal or collective experience, on one hand, and to small or to very large groups, on the other. It is in this light that we raise the question concerning the meaning of "collective memory" and the "place" in which it might be found. We are reminded of St. Augustine's famous description of personal memory in quest of its hidden source in book X of the *Confessions*, in which he likened memory to the soul itself and described it as being in a "place which is not a place."[10] And beyond the personal sphere, this same question of "place," of "locus," is all the more complex in relation to collective memory.

An initial attempt to locate collective memory, as I conceive of it, must situate it at different levels according to whether it is shared by smaller or larger groups. At the most elementary level we can speak of the experience of a family, of a school class, or of a professional group. Here the description of shared memories may be quite simple: an important event, for example, may characterize the personal reminiscences of each of the members of the group over the course of their lives. Beyond memories retained by small groups, we may refer to memories shared by larger collectivities that recall events that draw on collective practices much older than any of the members of the group and, as such, constitute a fundamental source of their identities. We may take as examples political or religious ceremonies, which follow symbolic patterns of behavior. As a sign of patriotism, the members of a group who share the same nationality, upon hearing the national anthem of their country, rise to their feet. The Pesach Seder enjoins each of the participants to reenact in memory the flight from Egypt by which a mighty hand led the Jewish people to freedom. Similarly, the members of the Catholic Church celebrate the ritual of the Eucharist in remembering the words of Christ: "This is my body, which is for you; do this in memory of me." In such examples, the identities of smaller groups, family or other gatherings, incorporate the memories of larger preexisting groups and draw on symbolic practices that are at the root of all collective experience as such.

In terms of such phenomenological description, the characterization of collective memory, in spite of the variety of levels at which it may be situated, indicates in a preliminary way that the possibility of referring memory beyond the sphere of personal experience arises in the communicative power of *symbols*.[11] It is in deploying potent symbols that flags in political experience, wine in religious ritual, evoke collectively meaningful reminiscence. Our phenomenological investigation of the place of collective memory must thus proceed by clarifying the relation between personal memory and collective forms of remembrance conveyed by means of symbols. To present an initial phenomenological elucidation of the relation between personal memory and symbolically elaborated collective remembrance, let us draw on an example that seems particularly appropriate for this task: the famous speech of Martin Luther King Jr. known as "I Have a Dream."

We recall that Martin Luther King Jr. presented this speech on August 28, 1963, during a March on Washington that rallied nearly 250,000 participants. The demonstration was called in the name of the civil rights movement, which protested against the conditions of political and social inequality to which black Americans were subjected. This event also marked a commemoration: with the marchers assembled before the Lincoln Memorial, it was held during the centenary of the famous Emancipation Proclamation by which President Abraham Lincoln, in the midst of the American Civil War, proclaimed the liberation of slaves in the Confederate states. King called attention to this commemoration in his speech, and also reminded his hearers that the promise of equality made by Lincoln had never been kept.

The evocative power of King's speech stems, however, not only from the fact that he reminded his hearers of this unkept promise. At another level, the Protestant pastor recalled something else, which stood at the heart of Lincoln's most famous speech, the Gettysburg Address: the idea of equality upon which the American nation, beginning with the Declaration of Independence of 1776, had been founded. We can read in this document the words, "We hold these truths to be self-evident, that all men are created equal"—words cited by Lincoln and evoked once again by King. More important still, the Founding Fathers did not limit themselves to a purely *political* legitimation of this principle of equality; they grounded it in what they considered to be divine sanction. If Lincoln did not hesitate to refer to this religious foundation of the principle of equality, Martin Luther King Jr. recalled, with singular eloquence, its profound eschatological source. After envisioning an end to racial inequality in America, and the possibility that black and white children might walk peacefully hand in hand, the Protestant pastor evoked prophetic vision—drawing on the New Testament's Gospel of Saint Luke, which explicitly recalled the Old Testament words of the prophet Isaiah: "the glory of the Lord shall be revealed, and all flesh shall see it together."[12]

This example permits us to establish an important distinction, which is necessary for the elucidation of the phenomenon of collective memory. At one level of our analysis, we can elicit the collective memory retained by those who listened to the speech on August 28, 1963. As a young schoolboy, I recall how vividly this address moved me as I watched it on television. I remember the tense context in which it was presented in the year 1963 which, less than three months later, would witness the assassination of President John F. Kennedy. With this example in mind, we may identify as a first "place" of collective memory the recollection of shared experience that a group retains. The demonstrators in Washington who witnessed King's speech on this day of August 28, 1963, the schoolboy who viewed it on television, and the contemporaries who learned of the event through the printed media, all remember it, albeit in different ways and at various points of distance from the event itself. Maurice Halbwachs, in his pioneering works *Les cadres sociaux de la mémoire* and *La mémoire collective*, defined the phenomenon of collective memory in similar terms, as the experience that a group shares and retains. For Halbwachs, collective memory lasts only as long as the group that remembers the shared experience, and disappears as soon as its members passed away.

At this point, collective memory gives way to historiography and to its quest for traces of a past that living individuals no longer retain.[13]

When defined in these terms, however, the phenomenon of collective memory still remains at a preliminary level of analysis. It would have been possible, indeed, to listen to King's speech without comprehending its significance. One might have failed to pay attention to its words, as many often do while listening to political utterances that are for them a source of infinite boredom. One might in such a case recall ancillary or even trivial phenomena—the beautiful sun that illuminated the August sky, the unusually large number of police forces called in for the occasion, or the tension that could everywhere be felt on this momentous occasion. To my mind, it is essential to distinguish between the direct recall of an event and another moment with which it is often confused: its *symbolic embodiment.* Symbolic embodiment as a collective phenomenon precedes and distinguishes itself from historical narrative, which seeks to grasp the event following the disappearance of all living memory. In its fluidity and immediacy it also differs from what we commonly refer to as *tradition*, with which it is often confused. If imagination accompanies the activity of remembrance (it would reach beyond my present analysis to examine this in detail), it is *a fortiori* an essential moment in the symbolic embodiment of collective memory. For this reason, symbolic embodiment may very well arise in the direct experience of the event, forming the core of subsequent recollection: contemporaries who appreciated the contribution of Martin Luther King Jr. and the theologico-political depth of his speech initially grasped the importance of the event, which is today the object of official commemoration on a national scale. This is not to deny the existence of different and even contradictory manners of symbolically embodying an event: Southerners hostile to the message of the black pastor, or the head of the FBI at the time, J. Edgar Hoover, who evinced an implacable hostility toward Martin Luther King Jr. and toward his cause, accorded a very different symbolic significance to the event than did King's supporters. In this sense, collective memory is, from the very point of its genesis, fragmented memory.[14] At the same time, it is in each case the symbolic force that permits collective memory to constitute a source of temporal continuity of group identities, which, as collective memory is codified, lends itself to the formation of what we normally call tradition.

Here we draw a distinction that is essential to our discussion. We distinguish between the multitude of perspectives retained by personal memories of a collectively experienced event and the symbolic embodiment of memory, constituting a collectively identifiable locus for past experience.

And the point that we seek to make is that "collective memory" can neither be reduced to one or the other of these moments, but gravitates between them as modes of recall of the remembered past. At one extremity we find the singularity of perspective that roots all collectively significant experience in the web of personal remembrance; at the other extremity, symbolic embodiment raises remembrance beyond personal experience to confer upon it significance and communicability in the collective sphere. At one extremity, it is possible to limit remembrance so completely to the realm of personal experience that its collective significance is blurred ("the beautiful sun that illuminated the August sky, the unusually large number of police forces called in for the occasion, the tension that could everywhere be felt on this momentous occasion"); at the other extremity, even after all personal, living recollection of the event has vanished, its symbolic embodiment can be recalled and reenacted to lend significance to later collective experience ("I have a dream"). It is in the thickness of its many stratifications that symbolic embodiment confers on collective memory a perdurability extending well beyond the lives of those who directly experience a moment in its ongoing and changing articulation. And this perdurability, amid profound shifts and discontinuities, indicates a dimension of symbolic embodiment of language and bodily gesture that constitutes a metapersonal fount of personal and interpersonal interaction.

III

If we examine the concept of memory elaborated by Paul Ricoeur in light of the above reflection, it appears to me that the emphasis he places on categories of analysis extrapolated from the sphere of personal experience risks obscuring the phenomenon of collective memory in its full depth. This tendency becomes evident, to my mind, above all when he indifferently applies categories of the "debt" or the "psychological traumatism" to individual and community. Of course, I do not deny the possibility of holding a community responsible for collective acts, nor do I seek to minimize the effect upon larger groups of traumatic experiences; on the contrary, such categories seem to me highly pertinent in dealing with collective experience. And if I readily acknowledge the originality of Ricoeur's analysis in *Memory, History, Forgetting* of the notion of collective moral debt and of collective traumatism, the terms of his analysis lead me to raise the question whether such categories indeed help us to reveal what we designate as "collective memory."

To return to the example of Martin Luther King Jr., it is certainly possible to characterize his movement in psychological terms and to emphasize in this respect the traumatic experiences to which black Americans were subjected after they were torn from their African homelands and enslaved over a period of centuries in what became the southern United States. Following their liberation they were victims of a century of injustice and discrimination. Changes in American legislation that confirmed their political rights, due in important measure to the nonviolent tactics of the civil rights movement, have far from entirely erased conditions of inequality. In view of the traumatic experiences to which black Americans were subjected, it would indeed be possible to interpret the relation between American society as a whole and black Americans as a situation of indebtedness, given the fact that the promise of equality has still not been fulfilled. King himself, indeed, initially affirmed in "I Have a Dream" that he had come to Washington to "cash a check," and this situation of indebtedness might still be taken quite literally. Conversely, on the basis of efforts already expended on behalf of black Americans that have established their equal rights as citizens, one might be tempted to characterize as an "abuse" of memory the continuing claims of black rights groups whose central aim might be interpreted as an attempt to convert an initial situation of injustice into the new privileged status of the creditor. Is it not then particularly advantageous to "adopt the pose of the victim" (*s'installer dans la posture de la victime*)[15] in order to demand other forms of repayment? As Tzvetan Todorov writes, in applying the psychological categories of family therapy to the political sphere, "To have been a victim gives you the right to complain, to protest, and to make demands."[16] In adopting a similar psychological perspective in *Memory, History, Forgetting*, Ricoeur, while indicating that he does not wish to overstate this point, in no way questions Todorov's idea, quoted in this context, that the pose of the victim "creates an exorbitant privilege, which places the rest of the world in the situation of indebtedness to a creditor."[17] And this leads him to abandon the idea of a "duty to remember" (*devoir de mémoire*), for which he substitutes, according to the Freudian terminology he applies to this theme, the "work of memory" (*travail de mémoire*) in relation to past traumatic experience.[18]

Nonetheless, by setting aside the symbolic force of Martin Luther King Jr.'s speech, or by reducing it to a psychological manifestation of resentment or anger—even if legitimate resentment or anger—one would seem to level it down to a simple claim advanced by a pressure group. In either case such categories of analysis fail to account for the symbolic force that nourishes collective memory by conferring upon it a meaning that, if is to be comprehended, must be situated at a metapersonal level of experience. For this reason, the method that attempts to explain collective remembrance through an analogy with the psychic processes of individuals or with principles drawn from the sphere of personal conduct risks obscuring the symbolic depth and the capacity of long perdurability of experience that is specific to political communities and appears only in the space between personal reminiscence and its symbolic incorporation.

This brings me to the example that most directly concerns Ricoeur and Todorov, the genocides of the twentieth century, above all the Nazi extermination of European Jewish communities during the Second World War. Here too the categories of the debt and of the duty to remember, as well as of the work of memory, do not touch on the essential problem. Beyond the reality of the physical disappearance of these vast communities, it is essential to identify a radical break in continuity of the European world itself, in terms of which any attempt at symbolic expression can only remain silent. What is essential here absolutely escapes the categories of quantification in terms of psychic processes or of individual morality applied to collectivities, in other words, in regard to groups that face each other in the form of "debtors" and "creditors" or of "patients" and "therapists." The true problem concerns less a carrying out of the "work" of memory in order to remedy the excess of memory or of forgetting, than the general awakening of comprehension that this radical break touches the vibrant fiber of a Europe stemming from antiquity, which the genocides of the twentieth century have irrevocably denatured.

In *Memory, History, Forgetting* there is a surprising absence of analysis of the symbol in relation to collective memory, above all given the fact that in his book *Freud and Philosophy*, Ricoeur devotes an important examination to the limits of psychoanalytic interpretation of the symbol. In this work he convincingly argues that while symbols can indeed represent symptoms of neurotic illnesses, an essential part of their meaning may be lost when they are examined exclusively in this light. The symbol may be a sign of regression and a symptom of illness but, according to Ricoeur's terminology, it may also convey a progressive significance, serving as a source of inspiration, as in the case of a work of art, a religious doctrine, or a political foundation.[19]

Ricoeur's earlier interpretation stands in closer proximity to what I understand to be symbolic incorporation, since it indicates a plenitude of the symbol that cannot be reduced to simply psychological categories. At a metapersonal level, it is the force of symbolic incorporation that, withstanding its transformations and meanders, accounts for the persistence of collective memory at its profoundest levels.

Refiguring Virtue

BOYD BLUNDELL

By Paul Ricoeur's own account, the dynamic of detour and return is the central motif of his philosophy. As he said to Charles Reagan: "Detour/return is the rhythm of my philosophical respiration."[1] The pattern is so pervasive that it shaped the trajectory of his entire career: a philosophy of the will that *detours* through analyses of sign, symbol, metaphor, and narrative, *returning* to a richer account of personal identity in his hermeneutics of the self.[2] But Ricoeur's endlessly dialogical mode of thinking not only leads him to take many detours; it also makes his work suitable to be used as a detour for the projects of others. In this paper, I will examine James Keenan's proposal to "update" the classical virtues in order to reflect developments in contemporary anthropology, specifically the notion that the human creature is constitutively *relational.* I will then turn to Ricoeur's relational anthropology as it comes to fruition in the seventh study of *Oneself as Another* to provide a concrete anthropological vision for Keenan's project. Finally I will reassess Keenan's proposal, and suggest possible directions in which these relational virtues might be developed.

The 1981 publication of Alisdair MacIntyre's *After Virtue* was a watershed moment in the shift of ethical analysis away from the act and back to the person. The classical virtues were reintroduced to the discussion, but it remained unclear what anyone was to do with them. This has resulted in a wide range of "virtue" discussions—there are literally dozens of "virtue ethics" books in print—but most are concerned with the reintroduction of the classical virtues into contemporary discourse. Anthropology has changed drastically since the times of Aristotle, Cicero, and Aquinas, to name the most prominent exponents of the classical virtues.

Keenan begins with a defense of virtue ethics, using a reflection on an ethical dilemma he was presented with in a graduate school classroom.[3] It was the famous case of Mrs. Bergmeier, an unjustly imprisoned woman who can only return to care for her ailing family by committing adultery and becoming pregnant. Keenan's interest in the case is purely methodological: he is less interested in the conclusions reached by his classmates than he is by the manner in which they argue their point. What Keenan finds notable is that in the course of the discussion, no one considered how Mrs. Bergmeier would be affected by her own actions, and asks whether she should be at the center of the discussion. This leads to the retrieval of an alternative method, virtue ethics, which is distinguished by "[p]lacing the moral agent and not moral action or its consequences at the center of moral reflection."[4]

With the moral agent at the center of the inquiry virtue ethics turns to the consideration of what the moral agent should look like. This is broken down into three basic questions: identity (who am I?), call (who ought I to become?), and strategy (how ought I to get there?). Thus the task of virtue comes to be defined as "the acquisition and development of practices that perfect the agent into becoming a moral person while acting morally well."[5] This leads to the further question of which practices actually do perfect the agent, and here the virtue ethicist runs up against two obstacles: cultural diversity and individual uniqueness. MacIntyre calls into question any attempt to enumerate virtues that should be cultivated in any human being, anywhere, at any time. He puts great stress on the diversity of cultures, noting that the model of the "excellent" person varies widely, both geographically and temporally. Owen Flanagan attenuates this concern, noting that even *within* a shared cultural framework there are a virtually unlimited number of ways to achieve moral excellence. The immense complexity of the individual forbids any attempt to box moral excellence into a single set of virtues. So the virtue ethicist, chastened by these criticisms, proceeds more cautiously, leaving aside the issue of moral excellence. Keenan argues that the most the virtue ethicist can hope to do is provide the "bare essentials," sketching the "minimal conditions that must be met to call any person virtuous."[6] But if that is the most that can be done, it is also the least that must be done.

The cardinal virtues, most famously articulated by Thomas Aquinas, divide the moral fiber of the human person into four basic parts, each with a governing virtue: practical reason, with the virtue of prudence; the will, with the virtue of justice; irascible appetites, with the virtue of courage; and concupiscible appetites, with the virtue of temperance. The virtues themselves are not supposed to come into conflict, since the four components are discrete. Even if there were to be conflict, the virtues themselves are hierarchically ordered:

> Temperance and fortitude are predominantly at the service of justice. Prudence determines the right choice of means for each of the virtues, but it especially looks to recommend the just action, since justice governs all exterior principles. In a manner of speaking, the anthropological identity of the virtuous person is the just one.[7]

Justice takes precedence over fortitude and temperance, and prudence orders the latter two toward the former.

Keenan identifies a number of difficulties with any attempt to apply these virtues directly to our contemporary situation. The first inadequacy lies in the lack of conflict in Aquinas's model. Returning to the Bergmeier case, he argues that there is "something deeply disturbing about the inadequacy" of considering Mrs. Bergmeier in terms of prudence ordering temperance and fortitude towards justice. It certainly resolves the tensions, but at the expense of leaving too many questions unanswered. By treating Mrs. Bergmeier as an "object" and not an "agent"—in Ricoeur's terms, a "what" (*idem*) instead of a "who" (*ipse*)—an uncritical application of Aquinas's model does violence to the dignity and freedom of Mrs. Bergmeier herself. We cannot avoid the fact that our dilemmas arise not from "the simple opposition of good and evil but, more frequently, the clash of goods."[8]

There is an emerging consensus in theological ethics on a relational model of anthropology, with virtues being proposed to address it. Keenan cites Ricoeur, particularly for his essay "Love and Justice,"[9] as an instance of one of the many contemporary thinkers who acknowledge the tensions in ethical living.[10] From this, Keenan concludes that the "anthropology that underlies the cardinal virtues" needs to be reconsidered. As noted above, central to this reconsideration is the move from the human as "object" to the human as "agent," with the agent construed as intrinsically relational:

> Thus virtues do not perfect what we have or what we do; rather they perfect who we are in the mode of our being, which is as being in relationships. Virtues do not perfect powers or "things" inside of us, but rather ways that we are.[11]

It is with this in mind that Keenan proposes to update the cardinal virtues, presenting a new list that takes into account the relationality of the human agent.

The New Virtues

Keenan generates his views from a simple assessment of the ways in which we are relational, each with a corresponding virtue. One's general relationships are perfected by the virtue of justice, one's special relationships by the virtue of fidelity, and one's unique relationship to oneself by the virtue of self-care. Prudence remains as the fourth cardinal virtue, determining "what constitutes the just, faithful, and self-caring life for an individual."[12]

In keeping with his virtue approach to ethics, Keenan is careful not to become mired in the millennia-old discussion of *justice* as a principle. He follows Ricoeur in noting that from Aristotle to Rawls, justice is intertwined with a notion of equality.[13] But Keenan's virtue approach goes a step beyond this to make justice an interior quality. Citing Bernard Williams's work on this virtue, he places the emphasis on the formation of our dispositions rather than on our external acts alone.

Of the four virtues in the proposal, *fidelity* is the most discontinuous with the classical cardinal virtues. It is also the most interesting of the four proposed virtues, mainly because of its immediate application to lacunae in social reflection. Fidelity is a virtue of partiality and particularity, and completely at odds with the rhetoric of our culture, clashing with both self-centeredness and social justice. It points outward and considers the welfare of particular others ahead of one's own personal welfare, but in this outward orientation, it is appallingly unfair in its discrimination between those who really matter to one and those who don't. It is fidelity that best manifests the relational nature of this revision of the virtues. The classical virtues are incommensurable (at least ideally). One could not judge temperance by the criteria of courage, because they dealt with completely different areas of the person. But fidelity's failure to conform to the demands of justice demonstrates both that the virtue of fidelity is categorically different from the virtue of justice, and that it is still related to the virtue of justice. Fidelity fails by the criteria of justice because of its difference, but it is only because of its relatedness to justice that it can be judged by the criteria of justice at all.

In a relational anthropology, there is room for only one inwardly directed virtue, *self-care*. It takes the virtues of temperance and fortitude, combines them into a single virtue, and then adds more. Keenan opts for the term *self-care* over *self-love* to steer clear of the ambiguity surrounding the word *love*. He also relegates another popular term, *self-esteem*, to a subsidiary position under self-care. One's esteem for oneself is but one of the many aspects of what it means to be virtuous in one's treatment of oneself. But it cannot be inferred that because there is now only one inwardly directed cardinal virtue, the care of self has thus diminished in importance. On the contrary, care of self has increased in importance because it is *not* ordered toward the external virtues, but rather exists on an equal footing with them.

Keenan rightly points out that prudence is not, and has never been, that "tepid little virtue" of cautious behavior, but rather a master virtue that "looks forward to the overall end of life and sets the agenda for attaining that end and all intermediate ends."As Aquinas himself said, the "whole matter of moral virtues falls under the one rule of prudence." One can refer to prudence as a "governing" or a "strategic" virtue, but the precise role of prudence proves elusive. It is everywhere and nowhere at the same time.

Whatever the final working role of prudence might be, it appears in a markedly different category than the other three proposed virtues. It is not an inherently relational virtue. The other three virtues involve a number of questions that need to be asked in an ethical decision process, while prudence is the virtue of being good at asking those questions, thinking such questions are worth asking, and judging between the respective claims of the other virtues. The mode of thinking at work in proposing new cardinal virtues is itself an exercise in prudence, in that the classical virtues are judged to be ineffective in light of a new anthropology.

Even in light of the above, there is still some reason to consider how prudence now functions with respect to the other virtues. The primary way that prudence has been changed is that it is necessarily a more "hands-on" virtue, if it is in a set with other virtues that can conflict. Rather than seeking the mean between recklessness and cowardice in the irascible appetites, the prudent person must now make phronetic evaluations of the relative strength of the claim by each of the other three virtues *considered together*. While refiguring prudence is not the primary thrust of Keenan's proposal, prudence does not survive the process unchanged. If we take prudence to be a "governing" virtue, the inherent instability of having competing "governed" virtues requires a stronger government. But in order to govern well, one must understand the governed. What kind of person is it that embodies these virtues? A relational person, for sure, but why relational in precisely this way? To further pursue these questions, we must come to some understanding of precisely what *kind* of relational anthropology is operational.

Paul Ricoeur's Relational Anthropology

To help flesh out an anthropology that might give further substance to these virtues, we turn to the hermeneutical philosophy of Paul Ricoeur. Ricoeur, along with Hans-Georg Gadamer, is the leading voice in the hermeneutical tradition that stems from Martin Heidegger and Wilhelm Dilthey. He has combined this hermeneutical interest with the "existentialist" approach of Gabriel Marcel and Karl Jaspers, and also has some affinity for the critique of ideology that is espoused by Jürgen Habermas. We can see in this that Ricoeur is a disciple of no one, but rather an original thinker of his own. He is better identified by his method, which explores the dialectic between critique and conviction. Rather than submit conviction to the judgment of critique (as with Habermas) or vice versa (as with Gadamer), Ricoeur prefers what he calls the "hermeneutical detour," which moves from understanding to understanding by way of explanation (or from conviction to conviction by way of critique).

If the hermeneutical detour defines the shape of Ricoeur's thinking, then personal identity has been the origin and goal of his reflection. He himself describes his philosophy as a "philosophical anthropology."[14] His first major project was a projected three-volume opus entitled *Philosophy of the Will.* This project was eventually abandoned after the second volume, as Ricoeur came to realize that his method was too direct. It was here that he took his hermeneutical turn, realizing that any phenomenology of the will had to be mediated by the signs and structures within which human beings live their lives. The next fifteen years of his life were dedicated to generating a theory of signs, beginning with *Freud and Philosophy* and culminating in his three-volume magnum opus, *Time and Narrative.* This detour, which took Ricoeur through psychoanalysis, linguistics, structuralism, metaphor, symbol, and finally narrative, may in itself prove to be Ricoeur's most lasting contribution to the philosophical conversation, and prepared Ricoeur for his return move to personal identity, which he undertook in *Oneself as Another.*

Oneself as Another

Oneself as Another represents Ricoeur's latest foray into the problem of personal identity. This time, however, he has several new tools with which to work the problem. He begins the book with a reflection on the state of the cogito, which was posited in Descartes and shattered in Nietzsche. The subject is "exalted" in Descartes and "humiliated" in Nietzsche, and Ricoeur attempts throughout the book to position himself between the two, with a "wounded" cogito. This attempt began with Ricoeur's delivery of the 1986 Gifford Lectures at the University of Edinburgh, which explored the theme of the "capable person." A person can speak, can act, can tell stories, and can make promises and decisions, and it is these capabilities that organize Ricoeur's reflection on the self. In each case, he asks who it is that has these capabilities.

Four years after these lectures, Ricoeur wrote for the book a further three chapters that constitute what he modestly calls his "little ethics."[15] It is these three chapters that are Ricoeur's major contribution to the field of ethics. The first chapter has an Aristotelian focus, asking what is meant when one speaks of the "pursuit of the good life." The second chapter takes a more Kantian approach, asking what it is to do one's duty. The third chapter asks a question that breaks out of the context of a teleological/deontological discussion: "What is it to resolve an entirely novel ethico-practical problem?" Ricoeur is keenly aware that his discussion of ethical aims and moral duty puts him in the middle of a long-standing debate. He explicitly rejects any concern with "Aristotelian or Kantian orthodoxy," although he takes freely from both. It is the first, teleologically oriented chapter that concerns us here, but it must be emphasized that this chapter does not stand alone.

Ricoeur's "Little Ethics"

Study	*Self*	*Other*	*Each One*	*Mode*
7. Ethical Aim	Self-Esteem	Solicitude	Sense of Justice	Optative
8. Moral Norm	Autonomy	Respect	Principles of Justice	Imperative
9. Practical Wisdom	Dependent Autonomy	Critical Solicitude	Domesticated Sittlichkeit	Attesting

The Self and the Ethical Aim

The study on the ethical aim comes first because Ricoeur argues for "the primacy of ethics over morality—that is, of the aim over the norm."[16] In the second study he will argue for the indispensability of moral norms as a necessary "sieve" through which ethics must pass, but in the third, he reiterates that it is ethics to which morality must ultimately have recourse when confronted with limit cases. In this, Ricoeur again retraces on a micro level the journey of his philosophy as a whole. The move from the ethical aim (conviction, understanding) through moral norms (critique, explanation) and back to the ethical aim mirrors the move from the self to the self by way of the study of signs. With this in mind, we can turn to Ricoeur's working definition of intention: "aiming at the 'good life' with and for others, in just institutions."[17] He develops in turn each of the three natural divisions in the definition.

"aiming at the 'good life' . . ."

In Ricoeur's definition, the phrase *good life* is enclosed in scare quotes, implying that he is aware that there is something troubling about the phrase. What is troubling in this case is the difficulty encountered in filling it with any content. But Ricoeur is comfortable in restricting himself to the formal level: "Whatever the image that each of us has of a full life, this apex is the ultimate end of our action." This is the Aristotelian "good-for-us" that we aim at, not the Platonic Good. Ricoeur argues that the formal nature of the claim is not to be confused with a *vague* claim; this is avoided by the Aristotelian grounding of the good life in praxis.

The consideration of praxis leads Ricoeur into a dialogue with MacIntyre and his notion of "standards of excellence," which are, as Ricoeur describes them,

> rules of comparison applied to different accomplishments, in relation to ideals of perfection shared by a given community of practitioners and internalized by the masters and virtuosi of the practice considered.[18]

This communitarian approach to what constitutes the good life is not as stifling as it might seem at first glance. One is not hopelessly stuck within the traditions of the community, although one must in fact live within those traditions, which are the social fabric that forms our context. This does not quell, but rather *enables* controversy and growth. A new virtuoso who does things that have never been done before is recognized *as* a virtuoso precisely because she is still recognized as excellent according to the standards already in place.

The discussion of "standards of excellence" applies to the ethical aim in two ways, which are again the two movements that we see everywhere in Ricoeur. We formulate our "life plans" with reference to these standards that *precede* us and enable us to speak of the "internal goods" of a practice. That a doctor works to heal a wounded person is an *internal* good to being a doctor, in that a doctor who does such can appraise himself as in some way being a *good* doctor. The practices of working to heal will inevitably be codified in rules and regulations, for both evaluative and pedagogical reasons. But the second application comes when the doctor is faced with limit situations. In these cases, the rules cannot stand on their own, but must have recourse to the *internal goods* that generated them. Thus, a "life plan" is a continuous process:

> moving back and forth between far-off ideals, which have to be made more precise, and the weighing of the advantages and disadvantages of the choice of a given life plan on the level of practice.[19]

This process of weighing is not a deductive process, but rather an interpretive one. Ricoeur invites us to view our actions as texts to be interpreted, for two reasons: 1) our important decisions and our life plan are understood in terms of each other, in the same way that part of a text and its whole are understood in terms of each other; and 2) interpreting an action as text enables us to consider the action's meaning *for us,* rather than its meaning in general. Searching for adequation between our life plan and our concrete decisions becomes an act of self-interpretation, which requires practical wisdom, or *phronesis*:

> the search for adequation between our life ideals and our decisions, themselves vital ones, is not open to the sort of verification expected in the sciences of observation.[20]

This interpretive task offers no didactic certainty, but rather can aspire at most to a "plausibility" in the eyes of the community. The reflexive moment of such a task, when one has judged oneself to have provisionally achieved such an adequation, is manifested in *self-esteem.* To better understand the role that self-esteem plays in this process, we must move to the second grammatical person, the "thou."

". . . with and for others . . ."

It is, of course, intrinsic to any relational anthropology that the "other" somehow be involved in the study of the self. In Keenan's proposal, this appeared under the virtue of fidelity. In Ricoeur, this relational moment falls under the heading of *solicitude,* which "is not something added on to self-esteem from outside," but instead "unfolds the dialogic dimension of self-esteem."[21] It turns out that self-esteem is a complex, multistage task, one that cannot be realized alone:

> if one asks by what right the self is declared to be worthy of esteem, it must be answered that it is not principally by reason of its accomplishments but fundamentally by reason of its capacities. . . . The

question is then whether the mediation of the other is not required along the route from capacity to realization.[22]

Ricoeur answers this last question emphatically in the affirmative, and he asserts (following Charles Taylor) that understanding this is the only way to strike at the root of pernicious political atomism, where the subject is first and foremost a subject of law, prior to any social relationships.

The role of solicitude in realizing self-esteem is a delicate one, and needs to be elucidated carefully. Drawing heavily on Aristotle's analysis of friendship in the *Nicomachean Ethics*, Ricoeur argues that friendship is not simply a psychology of cathectation but belongs rather to an ethics of reciprocity. Reciprocity can be broken down into three fundamental elements: reversibility, nonsubstitutability, and similitude. *Reversibility* refers to the nature of person-to-person designation, where every statement can be meaningfully turned around. We see this in the grammatical context when it is shown that when one says "you" to another, that person understands that as an "I" for themselves, and vice versa. *Nonsubstitutability* refers to the unique status of each person in the I-Thou relationship. The other is valued, or esteemed by the self, and is not replaceable in that valuation and esteem, and the esteem that the other holds for the self is similarly irreplaceable. *Similitude*, which transcends the first two terms, refers to the fundamental recognition of likeness in the other, in spite of unavoidable discrepancies in the "equality" that is necessary for true friendship. It is only at this point that solicitude and self-esteem can finally emerge as a dialogical pairing. Ricoeur describes similitude as "the fruit of the exchange between esteem for oneself and solicitude for others."[23] It is the recognition that the other is a *self* and calls to be esteemed as such, as a self who also generates life plans, makes decisions, and esteems others. More particularly, that other has an irreplaceable esteem for one's own self. Through this extension of solicitude one can now take the final step in the realization of self-esteem, which recognizes the equivalency of "the esteem of the *other as a oneself* and the esteem of *oneself as another*."[24]

Solicitude gives voice to a fundamental lack in the self; we need to have others in order to be a self at all. There is in fact *no* self prior to this process, because the self is not posited, but is rather implied reflexively in the relationship. But just as that reflexive implication forces us to contextualize our reflection on the self, so too does the fact that all interpersonal relationships happen in a wider social setting force us to widen the scope even further to the question of *just institutions*.

". . . in just institutions."

The third section of the chapter is entitled ". . . in Just Institutions," which will obviously map onto Keenan's virtue of justice. In our syntactical model, we've moved from considering the first-person "I" through the second-person "thou," and have now arrived at the third person, the "each one." Ricoeur's reflection on justice is founded on two basic premises: 1) that living well (self-care) extends beyond interpersonal relations (fidelity) to the realm of *institutions*; and 2) the measure of these institutions is *justice*, which is of a different ethical order than the solicitude of interpersonal relationships.

Institution is central to Ricoeur's notion of third-person relations. While interpersonal relationships can be governed by the free give-and-take of solicitude, these wider relationships require something more structured. Ricoeur defines the institution as "the structure of *living together* as this belongs to a historical community," whose fundamental characteristic is "the bond of common mores and not that of constraining rules."[25] The legitimacy of seeing institutions as enabling relationships rather than constraining them is found in Hannah Arendt's distinction between "power in common" and "domination." In contrast to the more pessimistic view of Max Weber, who necessarily sees domination and violence as intrinsic to political institutions, Arendt stresses the concertedness of human action that is embodied in institutions.

Recalling the reversibility of the I-thou relationship, we can now add to reversibility *plurality*, which acknowledges that each such relationship exists in a wider network of other such relationships, faceless people for whom we are also faceless. Just as a relationship to the other is necessary for me to realize myself, the consideration of these faceless others is necessary for me to have such relationships, and vice versa. The desire to act in concert on this project of enabling human relationships, and to give it a permanence over time, can only be actualized in the structure of the institution.

The success of an institution's enabling of concerted action, or its corresponding failure to do so by degenerating into sheer domination, is governed by the virtue of *justice*. Ricoeur defends his treatment of justice in the ethical rather than the moral section of his analysis by pointing out that even the arch-deontologist John Rawls opens with a teleological moment, a characterization of justice as "the first virtue of social institutions." Ricoeur also distinguishes between two facets of justice: that which addresses the *good*, and that which addresses the *legal*.

Ricoeur's ethical analysis deals only with the "good" facet of justice, and relies heavily on Aristotle's account in the *Nicomachean Ethics*. The most interesting part of the analysis is Ricoeur's insistence that Aristotle's limiting of the field of justice to *distributive* matters must be construed in the broadest possible sense. What is being distributed is not merely material goods and benefits, but also shares in participation and responsibility. The *justice* of this distribution is evaluated with respect to *equality (isotes)*, which is not a brute arithmetic equality, but is rather a *proportionate equality*, which addresses both person and merit. The intricacies of this interaction fall outside the scope of this analysis; here we are concerned primarily with the fact that there is an inevitable relationship between justice and equality, however the latter is defined.

Recalling Ricoeur's definition of the ethical perspective as *aiming at the good life with and for others in just institutions*, we can now see how the components of that definition fit together. One's aim for the good life is not a solitary project. Others do not constitute an intrusion into the project, but are in fact intrinsic to its success. Solicitude is the name given to this extension of esteem toward the other, which recognizes the other's esteem for oneself and makes possible one's ability to realize self-esteem. Justice is the virtue governing the realization of some form of equality, which, according to Ricoeur, "is to life in institutions what solicitude is to interpersonal relations."[26] A just institution enables interpersonal relations to flourish, both by providing a stable forum in which those relations can take place, and by providing avenues of concerted action.

Reevaluating the Virtues

In examining Keenan's proposal of new cardinal virtues and Ricoeur's analysis of the ethical perspective, one cannot help but notice a number of striking similarities. There is an obvious correspondence between Keenan's three relational virtues and Ricoeur's three-part definition, each of which address the first, second, and third grammatical persons (I, thou, each one). The question is then whether Ricoeur's philosophical anthropology is one that meshes well with Keenan's proposal.

In the case of the first-person perspective, the "self-esteem" approach of Ricoeur fits nicely into Keenan's virtue of self-care. As we noted above, Keenan has a place for self-esteem, but one that does not exhaust the definition of self-care. Whether Ricoeur's definition of self-esteem is broader than Keenan's is ultimately not a decisive issue, for self-care is a *virtue*, not simply a measuring principle. In fact, Ricoeur's analysis of self-esteem and its relation to the good life adds a great deal of positive philosophical weight to self-care.

With respect to the second person, Ricoeur's deep analysis of solicitude also blends well with Keenan's virtue of fidelity. There is an *internal* demand of solicitude, however, that goes beyond Keenan's rather sketchy presentation of fidelity. In Keenan's presentation, fidelity seems designed to offset the relentlessly equalizing demands of justice, making a space for the "overvaluing" of personal relations, for *discrimination* in the positive sense. Fidelity functions well in its capacity to make space for the increased claim of our personal relationships, enabling us to come to terms with the fact that we should not be out working in the homeless shelter if we have failed to take care of our own families. This is very important, but ultimately too limited in scope. It deals too obviously with relationships that *already exist*, and does not capture the openness to new claims that are made on us. There are those with whom we deal regularly but toward whom we have no formal responsibilities, and fidelity has little to say to how these relationships should be ordered. I would instead propose the use of *availability* (Gabriel Marcel's *disponibilité*) as the virtue of the second person. Marcel's famous assertion that "all commitment is a response" is used by Ricoeur to introduce the notion of *disponibilité*,[27] which is "the key that opens self-constancy to the dialogic structure established by the Golden Rule."[28] I do this for reasons similar to those Keenan offers for the use of the idea of self-care over self-esteem. Availability opens up more space for the perfection of the power to relate face-to-face, and offers a richer field to cultivate. There are those who are on the periphery of our lives, as well as those who have yet to enter. The cultivation of availability would enable us to be more open to these new claims. Fidelity will not disappear, but will be incorporated into availability, in much the same way that self-esteem is part of self-care.

As both authors use the term *justice* with respect to the third person, there is no quibbling over terms. What Ricoeur contributes is a more thorough philosophical explication of what is involved in justice, which supplements Keenan's brief account. Ricoeur outlines the inherently institutional nature of justice, and provides the criteria of *equality* and *concerted action* to determine whether an institution is just. To this, Keenan adds the theologian's perspective of considering justice not merely as a principle, but as a virtue. We can cultivate our attitudes toward the structures with which we live, and develop a sensitivity for the unequal distribution of shares (broadly construed). If we are in a position to cultivate healthy and rewarding relationships, but only at the expense of others being denied such opportunities, cultivating the virtue of justice will prevent us from being satisfied with such an unjust situation.

As was adverted to above, prudence does not survive this refiguring process unaltered. In fact, prudence changes so fundamentally that it almost warrants a new word, so I will revert to the translation of *phronesis* that bypasses the Latin *prudentia*: practical wisdom. We can still say that practical wisdom looks to find the golden mean, but we can no longer picture this mean as a linear midpoint between two vices. Instead we have a planar mean, best pictured as the center of an equilateral triangle (see Figure 11.1). The points of the triangle represent the claims of self-care, fidelity, and justice. Achieving the mean involves balancing the competing claims perfectly, and settling in the center of the triangle.

To illustrate this, we must become more specific, and return to the explicitly theological model that Keenan uses. In such an approach to virtue, the "good" and the "right" are not distinguished as philosophers distinguish them, as in Ricoeur's distinction between the ethical aim and the moral norm. The theological virtue ethicist defines the "good" in terms of the theological virtue of charity, and the "right" in terms of being well ordered, as expressed through the virtues. Self-care is then the rightly ordered love of self, availability the rightly ordered love of others, and justice the rightly ordered love of those with whom we have no contact.

Too much self-care can result in pure selfishness (1), a narcissism that ignores the claims of availability and justice. An excess of the virtue of justice can lead to a bloodless idealism (2), as could be characterized in social activists who pour themselves into their cause, caring neither for themselves nor for those who surround them, and thus burn out quickly. An excess of availability leads to an identity absorbed into a local community or family, best represented by the mafioso (3) who subordinates his own needs to those of "the Family" and also cares nothing for those beyond "the Family." The added difficulty is that while one can still have too much of a virtue, there are *several* ways to have not enough of that virtue. The bourgeois (4) realizes, albeit imperfectly, the virtues of self-care and availability to one's friends and family, but shows a lack of regard for the injustice of the institutions that make one's relationships possible.

Figure 11.1

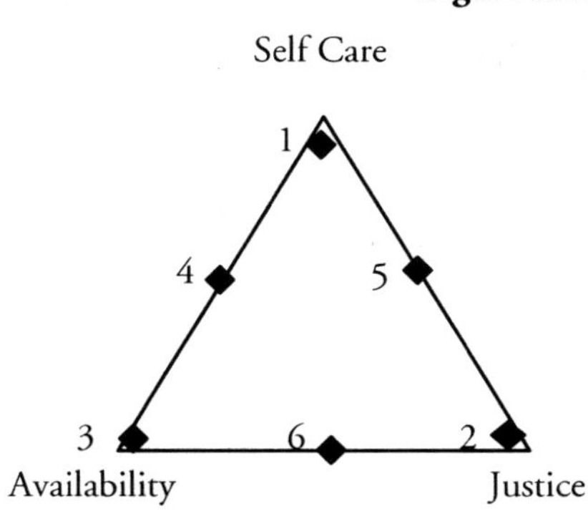

1. Narcissist
2. Pure Idealist
3. Mafioso
4. Bourgeois
5. Individualist Idealist
6. Supermom

The individualist idealist (5) both exercises good self-care and is keenly aware of the demands of justice, but is not available for personal relationships. The "supermom" (6) gives of herself to her family and to many causes without any self-care, a self-negating service characterized in many dramas. There is, of course, a final option not displayed by the figure: a lack in all three virtues. This self-abnegating nihilism is where the lack of self-care, availability, and justice is sufficiently clear that it warrants the psychological diagnosis of depression.

The burden on practical wisdom is very heavy, for it must operate without clear guidance. Keenan makes the point that justice took precedence over the other classical virtues, which preserved the lack of conflict between the other virtues. Prudence ordered temperance and fortitude toward justice, but now practical wisdom must not only order the competing virtues of self-care, availability, and justice, but it must do so without a virtue toward which to order them. In the structure of Ricoeur's little ethics we find one tool to help navigate the competing claims. Beginning with the *ethical aim* to live well with and for others in just institutions, and passing through the universalizing *moral norms* of autonomy, respect, and principled justice, we return to a *practical wisdom* that operates in a mode of *attestation*. In Keenan's theological language, the competing claims are navigated by a liberated sinner (dependent autonomy) who is known by his love of neighbor and self (critical solicitude) in a community bound together by the Spirit (domesticated *Sittlichkeit*). This provides a structure through which to think virtue ethics, and lends it the appropriate humility.

If Ricoeur's little ethics gives us tools for navigation, his work on the integration of identity in narrative gives virtue its orientation. We have already seen how his exposition of self-esteem, solicitude, and justice harmonize as much as they compete, which sets a horizon for the work of virtue. We cannot achieve self-esteem without relationships of solicitude, which in turn cannot be realized without institutions that enable concerted action and create space for those relationships. Thus a fully integrated identity would remain forever out of our reach, for we could not be fully integrated so long as others were not. But even in our above account of the failure to be virtuous, the terms such as *mafioso* or *bourgeois* serve to call up more fully fleshed-out narratives that help to shape our culture. Just as Aristotle advised that in order to understand virtue we must look to the virtuous person, so too we need to look for, or produce, narratives that embody the wise ordering of self-care, availability, and justice.

Emplotting Virtue

Narrative and the Good Life

BRIAN TREANOR

> The cultivation of virtues depends on narratives, vision, and the power of examples.
>
> **Louke van Wensveen, *Dirty Virtues***

> How many a man has dated a new era in his life from the reading of a book?
>
> **Henry David Thoreau, *Walden***

Paul Ricoeur's work remains lamentably underappreciated a few years after this death. Several factors contribute to the relative neglect of his thought. First, Ricoeur is fastidious to a fault in acknowledging his intellectual debts, which can, deceptively, make his thought appear derivative. Second, the pattern of "detour and return" that characterizes his thinking can make it difficult to keep up with him. Following Ricoeur takes one through the diverse fields of existentialism, structuralism, psychoanalysis, and analytic philosophy, to name only a few of his better-known detours. How many philosophers read both Derrida and Parfit? Heidegger and Searle? Nevertheless, those willing to invest a bit of effort and attention will find that Ricoeur's thought is both startlingly original and carefully argued, and that he deserves to be considered alongside the greatest philosophers of the twentieth century.

One of Ricoeur's major contributions to philosophy can be found in the "little ethics" of *Oneself as Another*, in which he ingeniously interweaves Kantian deontology and Aristotelian virtue ethics.[1] According to

Ricoeur, the ethical aim of the good life (i.e., the *telos* of "aiming at the good life with and for others") must pass through the sieve of moral norms (e.g., deontology and the categorical imperative). When moral norms fail us, however—as they inevitably do in the complex and messy world in which we live and act—we resolve the *aporia* through recourse to the overarching ethical aim (via *phronesis*). Because of the primacy of the ethical aim in this account, it is clear that despite the symbiosis between moral norms and the ethical aim, Ricoeur's own emphasis is squarely on the virtue ethics component of this alliance.

Without critiquing Ricoeur's own approach—a full-blown ethics will need certain deontological principles to supplement the teleological aim of the good life—I want to suggest that there are untapped resources in the virtue theory component of ethics, particularly as viewed through the lens of Ricoeur's work on narrative and identity. As such, this chapter represents an attempt to make what Henry Venema and I called in the introduction a "productive appropriation" of Ricoeur's work. The focus on narrative helps to clarify both the necessary passing of the ethical aim through the sieve of moral norms and the ultimate primacy of the ethical aim with respect to those moral norms. A "narrative virtue ethics" avoids several problems associated with virtue ethics *simpliciter*. Moreover, in the contemporary context, narrative supplements virtue ethics in a way that makes the overall account stronger and more convincing.[2]

Classical Virtue Ethics

Most accounts of virtue ethics—at least those operating on an Aristotelian, eudaimonistic model—take it for granted that each virtuous individual exhibits differently the character traits that contribute to human flourishing. Virtues are universal in theory, in the sense that everyone should be, for example, courageous. Individual idiosyncrasies, however, insure that each person is unique in ethically significant ways, which means that each person exhibits or manifests the virtue of courage differently. This means that there is not a single "right thing to do" in any situation; indeed, we cannot even say "what the virtuous person would do," because people are virtuous in different ways, and, therefore, there are multiple different possible virtuous responses to any situation.[3]

This position is further complicated by the fact that, according to Aristotle, the virtues cannot be exactly prescribed—although we can say they are "destroyed by excess or defect, and preserved by the mean."[4] This ambiguity makes it difficult to ascertain whether or not one has hit the mean. The virtuous person must do more than accomplish the right act;

she must do the right thing, in the right way, at the right time, with the right motive, feeling the right emotion with respect to the right objects, and so forth.[5] "Wherefore goodness is both rare and laudable and noble,"[6] said Aristotle. Because virtue is a mean of both action and emotion, it is difficult, if not impossible, to determine with certainty whether or not another person has acted virtuously. Indeed, because we are not always transparent to ourselves, we can doubt whether we acted with the proper emotion or whether we took pleasure in the virtuous act. Given these challenges, even if we are attentive to the specificity of the situation and the unique character of the agent, talk about virtue will tend to be general rather than specific. One gets the feeling that accounts of virtue will look more like an heirloom cooking recipe given a personal flourish—a dash more garlic, a splash more wine—and less like the precise, standardized, and impersonal formula of a nutritionist or pharmacist. A bit more of the art of the cook and a bit less of the science of the chemist, so to speak. Indeed, Aristotle warns us that the discussion of virtue is necessarily imprecise:

> Our discussion will be adequate if it has as much clearness as the subject-matter admits of, for precision is not to be sought for alike in all discussions. . . . We must be content, then, in speaking of such subjects and with such premises to indicate the truth roughly and in outline, and in speaking about things which are only for the most part true, and with premises of the same kind, to reach conclusions that are no better.[7]

These characteristics, however—the individual application of the virtues, ambiguous definitions, vague criteria, and so forth—inevitably raise the specter of relativism. How are we to characterize flourishing (i.e., the *telos*, or goal, of human life)? What virtues are constitutive of flourishing? How shall we cultivate the virtues ourselves? These questions are made more challenging by the very flexibility that makes virtue ethics attractive. If there is no universal or objective criterion to which virtuous actions must conform, can *any* decision, act, or lifestyle "count" as appropriately virtuous merely because the agent in question feels she is acting virtuously? This seems a bit like having the fox guard the henhouse. It is not too difficult to imagine a spendthrift exerting a very minor degree of restraint and claiming that she is acting with virtuous economy simply because she genuinely feels that she is hitting the mean between profligacy and miserliness.

Aristotle, of course, is aware of these problems, and addresses them in several ways. His most direct safeguard is perhaps his reference to and faith in the *phronimos*, the man or woman of practical wisdom (*phronesis*). He states that that "virtue . . . is a state of character concerned with choice, lying in a mean, i.e., a mean relative to us," but qualifies this flexibility by asserting that the mean is to be "determined by a *rational principle* . . . by that principle by which the man of practical wisdom [*phronimos*] would determine it."[8] So, while virtue is contextual, it is prevented from sliding into full-blown relativism by the requirement that it conform to a "rational principle" as determined by the *phronimos*. This solution no doubt seemed reasonable to both Aristotle and his contemporaries, who had the good fortune of having (or believing they had) *phronimoi* in the community to whom they could point. In fact, Aristotle often begins by citing examples from his community. He notes the "general agreement" about the importance of *eudaimonia* and concludes, "we must consider happiness [*eudaimonia*] in the light not only of our conclusion and our premises, but also in light of what is commonly said about it."[9] Having come to some preliminary conclusions about virtue, he pauses to consider his view in light of the wisdom of his tradition. "Now some of these views have been held by many men and men of old, others by a few eminent persons; and it is not probable that either of these should be entirely mistaken, but rather that they should be right in at least some one respect, or even in most respects."[10] This pattern of turning to examples and beliefs in the community is repeated in the attempt to circumscribe *phronesis*: "Regarding practical wisdom [*phronesis*] we shall get at the truth by considering who are the persons we credit with it [i.e., the *phronimoi* in the community]."[11]

Virtue Ethics in a Paralogical Age

In the contemporary cultural landscape, however, I don't believe any virtue ethics can seriously adopt the notion of the *phronimos* as envisioned by Aristotle, and therefore relativism remains a serious problem for any virtue ethicist in our "postmodern" age. Indeed, while certainly not without historical precedent, the lure of relativism is perhaps symptomatic of our time. In the global marketplace of ideas, different, even contradictory, conceptions of the "good life" come into contact. So-called grand narratives (or metanarratives)—the overarching systems that give meaning to our world—are called into question by other, competing grand narratives. A Christian, for example, sees the world in terms of the Christian narrative, and her beliefs, convictions, and assumptions with respect to the good, the true, and the real reflect this perspective. The existence, however, of other metanarratives in close proximity—real and virtual—held by other intelligent and sincere people, inevitably leads a thoughtful person to realize that her perspective, her metanarrative, is shot through with contingencies. If she had been born elsewhere or otherwise, she would very likely see the world in terms of a different metanarrative, say Hindu or Muslim, and her beliefs, convictions, and assumptions would reflect that perspective.

In his famous "report on knowledge," Jean-Francois Lyotard defined the postmodern condition as one characterized by "incredulity toward metanarratives."[12] This, predictably, leads to crises of identity and legitimation when one's faith in one's metanarrative—indeed, in the very possibility of a metanarrative—begins to erode. Jack Caputo points out that this situation presents a serious problem for Aristotelian virtue ethics. *Phronesis*, he points out, was a virtue of the "homogeneous, top down, aristocratic, rigidly closed little society" that was Aristotle's Athens; it assumes an agreement regarding ethical schemata and a univocal view of the right way to live that are simply lacking in the postmodern milieu.[13] "Aristotle had a more settled view of things than [we do today]. Aristotle thought the main problem facing ethical judgment lay in the movement from the general schema to the concrete situation, but he did not think there was a crisis in the schemata."[14]Aristotle assumed, with justification, a high degree of correspondence between his own ideas about virtue and the ideas of his students and readers. If asked, they would praise the same virtues and, indeed, would likely come up with very similar "short lists" when discussing the identity of the *phronimos*. Today, however, "even Aristotle . . . would have a tough time telling us who the *phronimos* is."[15]

So it seems that standard challenges to virtue ethics—how to identify the operative model of flourishing, how to identify the virtues that constitute that model, and how to cultivate those virtues in oneself—are exacerbated in the postmodern milieu. This situation seems to leave us abandoned in the wilderness, without a map, without even landmarks with which to orient ourselves. Thrown and lost, we nevertheless must act, choose a direction, and begin walking (choosing to remain put, if that were an option, would still be an act, a choice for the particular perspective or micronarrative into which we have been thrown). We do not have any objective, unbiased confirmation that our choice is the correct one; we cannot escape the hermeneutic circle. But postmodern philosophies of paralogy are making an even stronger claim: there is no perspective that could offer such a confirmation. As Caputo points out, there is no "privileged access to The Secret [that is, an 'objective' meta-perspective, a transparent *arche*, or an ultimate *telos*]."[16] Indeed, "the secret is, there is no Secret."[17] Which narrative shall we embrace? In our world, characterized more by heterogeneity than homogeneity, there is much less agreement about the good life and how to achieve it. We must choose among a bewildering array of perspectives, in a situation in which there is no broad agreement about the schema for the good life or the *phronimos* who embodies it.

A *Narrative* Virtue Ethics

One promising response to the problems that confront virtue ethics in the postmodern context can be found in Ricoeur's hermeneutic philosophy, especially his work on narrative identity. Ricoeur's concern is with identity as a practical rather than theoretical category. Viewed in this way, it is clear that there is a narrative aspect to identity, evident in the answer to any question of *who*. "*Who* did that?" "*Who* are you?" Such questions are answered with narratives that tell, in greater or lesser detail, the story of the agent.

> The fragile offshoot issuing from the union of history and fiction is the assignment to an individual or a community of a specific identity that we can call their narrative identity. Here "identity" is taken in the sense of a practical category. To state the identity of an individual or a community is to answer the question, "Who did this?" "Who is the agent or author?" . . . To answer the question "Who?" as Hannah Arendt has so forcefully put it, is to tell the story of a life. The story tells us about the action of the "who." And the identity of this "who" therefore itself must be a narrative identity.[18]

Ricoeur does not ignore the unchanging aspects of identity that carry the sense of "unchanged over time" or "the quality of being identical." According to Ricoeur, human identity is constituted by both *idem*-identity (sameness over time) and *ipse*-identity (selfhood, self-sameness, self-constancy).[19] The former primarily indicates sameness as permanence over time, the quality of a thing being identical with itself (as it was at a former time), which applies to both human and nonhuman beings. The latter sort of identity, however, is not static, but includes change over time. If *idem* addresses the "what" of a person, *ipse* addresses the "who."

The dialectic between *idem* and *ipse* is evident when a person considers whether or not she is the "same" person she was ten, twenty, or thirty years ago. The answer, clearly, is both yes and no. One's DNA remains the same, identifying one as the same biological organism over time. Everyone understands, however, more or less intuitively, that people change over time. While we always remain *what* we are, *who* we are changes throughout our lives.

> Unlike the abstract identity of the Same . . . narrative identity, constitutive of self-constancy, can include change, mutability, within the cohesion of one lifetime. The subject then appears both the reader and the writer of its own life, as Proust would have it. As the literary analysis of autobiography confirms, the story of a life continues to be refigured by all the truthful or fictive stories a subject tells about himself or herself. This refiguration makes this life a cloth woven of stories told.[20]

It is this "refiguration" of a life that constitutes narrative's special usefulness for any postmodern (i.e., contemporary) virtue ethics. Ricoeur's understanding of identity recognizes narrative's power: narrative does not merely recount stories; rather it both *describes* and *prescribes.* Indeed, Ricoeur claims that narrative constitutes the "natural transition between description and prescription," which clearly suggests narrative's usefulness for self-cultivation and virtue ethics.[21] His formula is "describe, narrate, prescribe—each moment of [this] triad implying a specific relation between the constitution of action and the constitution of the self."[22] How exactly does this work?

Ricoeur describes metaphor and narrative in terms of *mimesis,* which he views through an Aristotelian rather than Platonic lens—that is, in terms of imitating *action* rather than imitating *nature.* His understanding of *mimesis* follows a tripartite model. First, in order to comprehend any narrative, we must have a preliminary understanding of human action. Ricoeur calls this prefigurative understanding "*mimesis*$_1$" and describes it as having three main components: structural, symbolic, and temporal. We approach any narrative with an understanding of structure that allows us to make sense of the "what," "why," "who," "how," "with whom," and "against whom" of any action, and to link these categories to one another.[23] Thus, we can grasp, for example, that "Ahab pursues Moby Dick to avenge the loss of his leg," and that "Thoreau went to the woods in order to live deliberately and to learn what life had to teach." We also have a symbolic preunderstanding of narrative that confers the "initial readability of an action"—that, for example, a raised hand is hailing a taxi as opposed to voting or greeting someone (each of these actions using the same movement of the hand).[24] In addition to the descriptive aspect of symbolic preunderstanding—and of the greatest importance for narrative's application to virtue ethics—there is a normative aspect of symbolic understanding that allows us to attribute *value* to actions and to agents, pointing towards the implicit ethical quality of any narrative. Ricoeur goes so far as to say that "there is no action that does not give rise to approbation or reprobation, to however small a degree, as a function of a hierarchy of values for which goodness and wickedness are the poles."[25] Finally, we have a temporal preunderstanding that, among other things, helps us to understand the role of temporality in action. We can grasp the temporal development of an action—how actions unfold over time as related to other events—and understand, for example, that John Muir left his job and home after nearly losing his eye in an accident.

Mimesis$_2$, in turn, is the configuration or "emplotment" of the narrative. This includes: 1) the "organization of the events," not as a series of sequential events, but into an intelligible whole that "transforms the events into a story" with meaning or purpose; 2) bringing together heterogeneous elements such as "agents, goals, means, interactions, circumstances, and unexpected results"; and 3) mediating the temporal characteristics that allow the aforementioned synthesis of the heterogeneous.[26] The result is that the reader does the work of emplotting the narrative. The heterogeneous elements of the narrative must be organized by the reader so that they make sense as a narrative.

> It is the reader who completes the work [of emplotment]. . . . [The written word] consists of holes, lacunae, zones of indetermination, which, as in Joyce's *Ulysses*, challenge the reader's capacity to configure what the author seems to take malign delight in defiguring. In such an extreme case, it is the reader, almost abandoned by the work, who carries the burden of emplotment.[27]

Rather than finding the narrative "whole cloth" in the words of the text, the elements of the narrative must be organized and connected by the reader (indeed, in some sense the author herself is merely the "first reader" of her narrative).

Finally, *mimesis*$_3$ is the "intersection of the world of the text and the world of the hearer or reader"; it is in the reader or hearer that the narrative reaches its fulfillment.[28] Herein lies the real power of narrative for our purposes: the power to refigure our lives. Reading stories is more than (just) an exercise in historical curiosity or whimsical fantasy. Narratives allow us to see things from a different perspective. When we read stories we enter new worlds and try out new identities—worlds and identities that may, and in some sense always do, reshape the world and the identity with which we began the story. Through narrative we can gain a sort of "virtual" or "as if" experience. Richard Kearney goes so far as to suggest that although such "experience is vicarious—i.e. unreal on the face of it—it is experience nonetheless; and one more real sometimes than that permitted in so-called reality."[29] Kearney continues, citing Dermot Healy: "I can still remember the liquid feel of . . . words for rain. How the beads were blown against the windowpane, and glistened there and ran. The words for rain were better than the rain itself."[30] In a letter to his father, Ernest Hemingway wrote, "I'm trying in all my stories to get the feeling of the actual life across—not to just depict life—or criticize it—but to actually make it alive. So that when you have read something by me you actually experience the thing."[31]

On the face of it, however, the idea that narrative actually represents reality seems like a stretch. Isn't any story detached, by its very nature, from the reality it is trying to represent, victim to its own kind of abstraction?[32] Implying that narrative can connect us to reality as a substitute for gross contact smacks of naïve posturing. It reminds me of the astonishment (and, frankly, disgust) I felt when, after the release of *Saving Private Ryan*, I heard more than one person comment, "It's just like being on the beaches of Normandy," and found out that post-traumatic stress disorder hotlines were set up (perhaps as a marketing tool?) for viewers "traumatized" by the opening fifteen minutes. It may be true that, to understand something about courage, we tell the story of Achilles—or, perhaps, some other modern virtuoso of courage—but reading about the siege of Troy or the slaughter on Omaha Beach and *Pointe du Hoc* is a far cry from actually experiencing either battle. This is why, unlike the repetition of actual virtuous acts prescribed by Aristotle, no amount of reading about courage will fully succeed in making someone courageous. The "as if" experience of narrative differs from the visceral experience of lived reality in important ways. As Kearney himself points out, in reference to the obscenity trial surrounding Joyce's *Ulysses*, "no one was ever raped by a book."[33] Nevertheless, one can genuinely learn something of courage (what courageous actions are like, how to recognize courage) from hearing and reading about courage, and we should not discount this fact. It is because of the ability of narrative to facilitate the refiguration of our lives that a text can actually teach us something beyond "facts" of the persons, places, and events of the story. Good narratives—good in both senses: virtuous and well constructed—call us to be better people and, moreover, they can help us to effect this change.

What are we to make of this situation? How could the words for rain be "better," as Healy claimed, than real rain? Ricoeur points out, correctly in my view, that we end up refiguring our lives as the result of the narratives we emplot; the stories we hear and tell shape the persons we are and the way we are in the world. Sometimes the refiguration of a life is dramatic, as when a life is changed by the reading of a book; more often, however, the refigurative changes are subtler in character. It's hard to say what exactly gives a narrative the power to fundamentally reshape a life—it took three readings over fifteen years before *Walden* became one of the books that changed my life. While a precise formula for narrative power is not possible, we can say that the impact of a narrative is the result of the interaction between 1) the text itself (its structure, its content, etc.) and 2) the reader of the text (the manner in which she emplots the narrative, the timing of her encounter with it, her existing library of narratives, her prefigurative *ipse*-identity, etc.).

Whatever the specific nature of this interaction, the fact is that stories can and do change people's lives. Epiphanies are no doubt often the result of "real" experience; however, narratives can also bring about these radical transformations, and indeed have a particular facility for doing so. The imaginative play of narrative and the "synthesis of the heterogeneous" that are part of emplotment are capable of highlighting paradoxes, emphasizing essential truths, and revealing hidden mysteries that can be overlooked in the hustle and bustle of actual experience. Simply put, narrative can help us to focus on things we would ordinarily overlook by transforming the "simple contingencies of everyday life . . . into narrative epiphanies."[34] Returning to Dermot Healy's claim, we might say that the *words for rain* are "better" than the *rain itself* insofar as the words, the story or narrative, can be, at least in some cases, more effective at bringing about the life-altering insights that drive personal transformation. The words for rain are better at transmuting the simple contingencies of everyday life into narrative epiphanies. Rain simply falls; it doesn't *mean* anything. It takes narrative to suggest that rain is good or bad, that it quenches the thirst of the Earth, that "rain is grace,"[35] or that rain "speaks" and is "joyful."[36] It is precisely because narrative gives meaning to facts that Jack Turner argues, "Old ways of seeing do not change because of evidence, they change because a new language captures the imagination."[37]

Relativism and Narrative

How might the configuration (*mimesis*$_2$) of stories work to refigure (*mimesis*$_3$) our lives in ways that encourage and support flourishing? I'll briefly enumerate a variety of ways in which I think an emphasis on narrative might be useful for virtue ethics—without pausing here to argue thoroughly for each one—before turning my attention to the specter of relativism raised above.

The clearest use of narrative is in the realm of moral education. Narratives can *inspire* us (i.e., arouse in a person the desire to be virtuous) and *motivate* us (i.e., to persevere in the cultivation of virtue). In addition to this exhortative function, narratives can help in the actual *transmission* of the virtues. Ricoeur calls narrative an "ethical laboratory."[38] We use narratives to *experiment* with possibilities, exploring different situations and different ethical responses. We project ourselves into stories and make judgments about the actions of characters. Such experiments serve several useful functions. First, narrative experiments help us to cultivate the habit of ethical *discernment*, differentiating between different ethical schemas, dispositions, responses, and so forth. Second, these experiments help us to *understand* virtue (and flourishing), including which virtues "succeed" and which ones "fail." Because of this, narrative does more than merely illustrate virtue. It is one of the important ways in which we grasp what "works" in terms of flourishing. Therefore, narratives often help us to *identify* good role models and the virtues that make them role models; they actually help us to *determine* what we view as flourishing and what we take to be virtuous and vicious; they *persuade* us to consider, and perhaps adopt, an alternative perspective. Moreover, narratives are frequently the method (or at least a central part of the method) by which we *apply* and *cultivate* virtues in our own lives. Because narratives provide us with a sort of "as if" experience, they often constitute the first step, as it were, on the road to actually developing a particular virtue.

Arguing for most of these salutary aspects of narrative will have to wait for another time. Here I want to address directly the specter of relativism raised by the postmodern condition. Relativism can mean many different things. Some stripes of relativism are less problematic than others; indeed, some sorts of relativism are not problematic at all. Few people, for example, bother to argue seriously about the objectively best cuisine—*de gustibus non est disputandum*. Therefore, we have to be clear about 1) which sort of relativism or relativisms present a temptation that is problematic or dangerous, and 2) what, if anything, narrative has to say about the matter.

On one level, relativism may be a merely descriptive claim about the way things are. As we saw above, conceptions of virtue differ from culture to culture. Some versions of relativism, however, take this a step further by making normative claims, denying absolute truth and asserting that moral claims are only true in the context of a particular framework, situation, tradition, or culture. Thus, what courage *is* (or was) in feudal Japan is fundamentally different from what courage *is* in contemporary France.

Postmodern undecidability implies, I take it, both descriptive and normative relativism, as when Caputo denies that there is a "Secret" metaperspective from which we might compare incommensurable perspectives.

Normative ethical relativism can itself take several forms. A very strong sort of relativism, exaggerated I would argue, becomes subjectivism, the claim that moral judgments (in this case, judgments about virtue) are absolutely relative, differing from individual to individual with no external basis for approbation or reprobation. Subjectivism bleeds into, or at least courts, nihilism—because there is no larger truth, no action is better than any other action, all things are equally (un)true. As the Cheshire Cat quips to Alice, "if you don't know where you're going, any road will take you there." A somewhat less radical position, which we might call contextualism, argues that such judgments differ from culture to culture, context to context. No action is demonstrably good in a way independent of its context; the goodness of any good action is relative to the context in which it is performed.

There is a thriving literature related to the challenge of relativism;[39] rather than reviewing that material at length, however, I want to point out some specifically narrative rejoinders to the challenge of relativism. What can narrative contribute to this discussion? First, a narrative approach suggests that descriptive relativism is not so obvious as it seems. There are, in fact, some more or less universal narratives. Take, for example, the "golden rule," which, in addition to being found in Ricoeur's work, can be found in (at least) Christianity, Judaism, Islam, Greek thought, Buddhism, Confucianism, and Hinduism. Moreover, certain narratives certainly seem to have very broad cross-cultural, if not universal, appeal—*King Lear*, the *Odyssey*, and the *Bhagavad-Gita*, for example.

Second, while normative relativism of the "exaggerated" sort is thought to be self-refuting because of its absolute claim that there are no absolutes, objections from several sides make radical normative relativism less plausible: Aristotle's teleological biology; Ronald Sandler's insistence that virtue is intimately connected to the "type of being [we] are"; and Rosalind Hursthouse's emphasis on our rational nature.[40] In addition, the narrative objection to descriptive relativism would also imply that radical normative relativism is wrong, insofar as certain narratives do appear cross-culturally, suggesting that certain narratives articulate virtues in the context of the broadly human, rather than the specifically Japanese or French, situation.

Moreover, an emphasis on narrative tends to make radical normative relativism much less attractive. Why? Recall again the ethical judgment solicited by narrative. "There is no action that does not give rise to approbation or reprobation, to however small a degree, as a function of a hierarchy of values for which goodness and wickedness are the poles."[41] Action, and thus narrative, "can never be ethically neutral."[42] Emphasizing the role of narrative downplays (without refuting) a relativistic perspective; we judge acts that are narratively recounted to be good or bad, suggesting that all responses are not equal (as exaggerated relativism suggests). The approbation and reprobation called for by every narrative imply—even when such judgments are tentative or uncertain—that some actions are better than others, some visions of the good life are better than others, and, thus, that some perspectives are more true than others. As Kearney notes, the "concreteness" of fictive examples fleshes things out in a way that the cold detachment of pure theory does not. Narratives put a *face* to ethical questions.[43] It is one thing to entertain, intellectually, the possibility of the cold indifference of the stars[44]; it is another to assert that it does not matter whether or not this particular and unique person here before us is raped or murdered. This is why Camus's stranger is not heroic, but inhuman. No person being victimized thinks, "My attacker's interpretation of this situation is not congenial to mine!" Victims of injustice cry out, and ought to cry out, against injustice.[45] Radical normative relativism is something that one can entertain in the abstract, but in concrete (or narrative) situations it seems less plausible and is much less palatable.

If these narrative insights suggest that descriptive ethical relativism is only true within certain limits and that an exaggerated type of normative ethical relativism is nothing more than a bogeyman, then what virtue ethics really has to come to terms with is a less radical relativism, a "contextualism" that insists that we cannot speak clearly about virtue and vice abstracted from concrete situations. Here again, however, narrative has something to say about the limits of contextual relativism. At the risk of pedantry, we could point again to the quasi-universal narratives that seem to undermine an overly broad affirmation of descriptive relativism. No doubt these narratives are ubiquitous in part because of the common human condition—a universal human context—to which they respond, which is perhaps another way of getting to the commonalities implied by Sandler's attention to the "type of being" that we are. The analysis of narrative suggests that virtue, while contextual and therefore pluralistic, is not relative in the strong sense. Such a pluralistic perspective can be clarified through a mathematical analogy. On a number line, there are an infinite number of points between four and five; nevertheless, we know that three, six, and so forth are not included in this range. Similarly, while there is an infinite diversity of ways in which to be virtuous—narratives about virtue are structurally open ended—some things are right out.

Conclusions

A narrative approach to virtue ethics offers a rich landscape for philosophical reflection, and here I can only venture a sketch of a few conclusions I think we can draw from an analysis of the chiasmi between virtue ethics and narrative. The first thing we ought to notice is that virtue ethics is fundamentally narrative. Narrative is not a creative spin on virtue ethics; rather, virtue ethics is an *essentially* narrative enterprise. This is evident, on a basic level, in the omnipresence of examples in virtue theory. Ricoeur's work illustrates the way in which narratives serve a constructive function with respect to character formation. Narratives help to shape our self-understanding, and their inescapably ethical nature shapes our understanding of virtue, vice, and human flourishing. Encountering a narrative always changes us, sometimes imperceptibly, but sometimes in profound and dramatic ways. As Henry David Thoreau notes in the epigraph above, "How many a man has dated a new era in his life from the reading of a book?"

In an age in which many people find it difficult to locate models of flourishing, virtue, or practical wisdom in their immediate communities, narratives can acquaint us with virtuous models. Such models can teach us something about virtue, and can inspire us to pursue virtue in our own lives. Recall, for example, the story of Victorinus, which inspired St. Augustine and persuaded him that his own conversion was a real possibility. "When Simplicanus, your servant, related to me [the story of] Victorinus, I was on fire to imitate him, and it was for this reason that he had told it to me."[46] Such inspiration and instruction is far from trivial. Assuming a person is not yet virtuous, she needs some way of beginning to walk the path. In any of its various forms, virtue ethics requires a model of some sort in order to help us identify the virtues, inspire us to pursue them, and guide us in doing so. Narratives can offer us such models; indeed, the number of such narrative models far exceeds the number of actual virtuous persons.

In addition, in the course of reading or hearing narratives, we project ourselves into the story; narratives give us a sort of "as if" experience in which we can imaginatively inhabit other lives, actions, perspectives, and virtues. In this vein, Ricoeur calls narrative an "ethical laboratory."[47] Richard Kearney elaborates, asserting that narratives allow us to explore, to "try out" as it were, other possibilities: "To understand what courage means, we tell the story of Achilles; to understand what wisdom means, we tell the story of Socrates; to understand what *caritas* means, we tell the story of St. Francis of Assisi."[48] Such a view is essentially Aristotelian, insofar as it suggests that narrative can teach us and help us to understand universal aspects of the human condition. "The validity of Ricoeur's observation can be seen in the simple fact that while ethics often speaks generally of the relation between virtue and the pursuit of happiness, fiction fleshes it out with experiential images and examples—that is, with particular stories."[49] It is narrative that allows us to imagine ourselves otherwise, which is essential for facilitating the conversion necessary to move from one "view" of flourishing and its constitutive virtues to another.

Indeed, upon reflection, the narrative structure of the acquisition of virtues applies much more broadly than the hearing of stories and the reading of texts. Take, for example, the situation of someone who, happily, finds herself in close association with a *phronimos*. How does such a person become virtuous herself? Aristotle makes it very clear that moral virtues cannot be taught, so the aspiring virtuous person cannot simply study at the foot of the *phronimos* as an apprentice studies at the foot of the master craftsman. One might think that the process is more akin to imitating the *phronimos*, carefully copying her actions as a novice martial artist copies her *sensei*. This, however, is also impossible with respect to moral virtues. The "student" cannot *copy* the master, for the master is a different person, with different skills and abilities, in a different situation. The master's courageous action may well be rash and foolhardy if undertaken by the student. So neither simple instruction nor faithful mimicry will work for cultivating virtues. Cultivating a virtue is less like the mimicry associated with apprenticeship in a craft and more like the experience of reading of a good story. As Emerson notes, good books are for inspiration rather than imitation; they inspire us to better ourselves.[50]

The *phronimos*—actual or narrative—is not someone to be imitated in the sense of *copying*, but someone who inspires those who are not yet virtuous to attempt to act virtuously themselves, and, indirectly, guides them in doing so. The proper question for the moral/ethical aspirant is not, "What would the *phronimos* do?" The *phronimos* is a different person, with different skills, a different background, different relationships, and so forth; therefore, the entire context is different. If the novice soldier attempts to *copy* the veteran, he will very likely be acting too rashly (and will, perhaps, bring about an abrupt and early end to his aspiration to virtue). The proper question is, "What would I do if I were like the *phronimos*? (i.e., if I had the virtue in question, which the *phronimos* does). Asking this latter question is more akin to the "as if" experience of hearing a story and imaginatively projecting oneself into the narrative than it is like the imitation associated with learning a craft. Thus, even when the cultivation of a given virtue does take place under the guidance of a figure like the *phronimos*, the experience is much more like narrative refiguration (*mimesis*$_3$) than is generally supposed. Thus, 1) narrative is often how we come to identify virtues, because narratives expose us to a wide variety of ethical situations; and 2) narrative is always, because of the imaginative "as if" world or ethical laboratory that it opens up, central to the way in which we cultivate those virtues in ourselves (though, of course, habituation is still necessary). While narrative cannot provide us with step-by-step instructions for virtue, neither can a *phronimos*.[51]

Finally, recall that narrative's contribution to virtue theory—the essential "fleshing out" of ethical theory with narrative examples—is the very thing that allows a virtue ethics to pass between the Scylla of absolutism and the Charybdis of relativism.[52] Although there are absolutist narratives and relativist narratives, the productive friction between narratives in a "narrative virtue ethics" promotes a healthy pluralism that steers clear of both absolutism and the worst excesses of relativism.

It should be fairly clear that virtue ethics, even in its classical formulations, is allergic to any sort of simple absolutism. Virtue, Aristotle asserts, lies in a mean that is "relative to us," that is relative to the agent. Generally speaking, there are no "one-size-fits-all" answers to ethical questions. A narrative approach to virtue ethics reinforces this aversion to dogmatism, easy answers, closure, or smug certainty regarding virtue. Both ongoing, open-ended interpretation *within* a narrative tradition and the encounters and exchanges *between* narrative traditions foster a "productive friction" that introduces alternative perspectives (and thus critique) into one's thinking about virtue, preventing ossification or dogmatic narrow-mindedness. Because there are always other interpretations, narratives help us to develop the habit of, as well as skill in, discrimination. It is in this vein that Miguel de Unamuno claims, "the more books one reads the less harm they do."[53] More narratives—especially different narratives—give us more perspectives and, thus, more insight. As we saw above, however, an aversion to dogmatism and closed systems does not mean that a narrative virtue ethics must embrace a robust form of relativism. Indeed, because all stories solicit ethical judgment, focusing on narratives actually reinforces the idea that there are right things to do and wrong things to do, even if one is currently uncertain of how to act. This distaste for strong forms of relativism is further strengthened by what we might call the concreteness of narrative virtue ethics. Using this approach, questions of virtue and vice are not asked in a sterile and theoretical vacuum; rather, such questions are asked in context—fictive or historical—in such a way that we are forced to confront the faces of the others implicated in our ethical or unethical conduct. Narrative virtue ethics succeeds in preserving the flexibility that makes virtue theory so intuitive and attractive, while offering a rejoinder of sorts to the types of postmodern relativism that threaten to push that flexibility to the point of incoherence.

Preserving the Eidetic Moment

Reflections on the Work of Paul Ricoeur

DAVID RASMUSSEN

I

My original encounter with the person and the work of Paul Ricoeur began with an attempt to appropriate his thought for the retrieval of the symbolic. This led to a concern with what I called *mythic-symbolic* language correlated with anthropological considerations about the nature of the human, subjectivity, the self—stemming from his *Philosophy of the Will.* At that time I had been meeting once a week with the Romanian phenomenologist of religion Mircea Eliade to discuss his work in general, which I wanted to write about. I had told Eliade that I was not particularly interested in his classes; what I was really interested in was the philosophical meaning of his books. He took this seriously, and for about a year we met to discuss what it was that his work was about. I realize now that Eliade was a Nietzschean, and that his program in the phenomenology of religion had really followed Nietzsche's own desire to uncover the archaic dimension of history and experience, and to use that knowledge to affect contemporary culture. Hence, Eliade's *The Myth of the Eternal Return* had its real origins in Nietzsche's *The Birth of Tragedy.* Looking back, Eliade's concern for the recovery of the archaic shaped my encounter with Ricoeur, who had come to the University of Chicago to give some lectures. Before I actually met Ricoeur, I had read the essay translated as "The Symbol Invites Thought" and was swept away by it. The essay seemed to do the philosophical work necessary to carry on my developing desire to retrieve the symbolic in the context of what I then considered to be an abomination, namely, the rage for demythologization that was rampant on the campus of the University of Chicago at the time. I should add parenthetically that I became, in a rebellion against my Danish Grundtvigian heritage, a rabid Kierkegaardian as an undergraduate. Ricoeur's idea of going beyond the pale of ordinary language to a kind of second, indirect discourse seemed like a good idea.

Before coming under the spell of Eliade I had considered myself to have been a Whiteheadian, until I realized that Whitehead's metaphysics was based on mathematics and to do it effectively I would have to become something of a mathematician, a task for which I was neither motivated nor equipped. These shifts from a kind of abstract rationalism to a committed existentialism can be expected of a student. Unfortunately, shifts like these have tended to characterize my entire intellectual life. In any case, this is how I came to be entranced by Ricoeur's *Philosophy of the Will.* Simultaneously, I discovered phenomenology, which I experienced as a liberation from the pragmatism I had been studying. Of course, I would come back to that, too, in another form.

Ricoeur's methodological transition from eidetic to hermeneutic phenomenology fascinated me. The shift paved the way for a special orientation toward the philosophy of language that would be distinctive among continental philosophers. Now we can see that Ricoeur was at the beginning of a long road that would take him from symbol and myth to metaphor and narrative, always with a passion for the nature of the self, the subject, personal identity—in phenomenological terms, subjectivity. When I first wrote on Ricoeur I did not see that. What I saw and wrote about was shaped only by Ricoeur's movement from the eidetic to the hermeneutic. (I was so fascinated by the hermeneutic approach that I went on to found the journal *Cultural Hermeneutics.* Ricoeur happily joined as an editorial board member.)

Ricoeur's particular redemption of myth and symbol allowed me to pursue what I would characterize now as a more or less Nietzschean project, namely, the retrieval of the archaic as a form of language. Hence, the final chapter of my book on Ricoeur is entitled "Toward a Working Theory of Language Correlated with a Philosophical Anthropology."[1] My overall point was that a hermeneutics of symbol and myth could be conducted without recourse to reductionism. At that point I had absorbed Nietzsche only from working on Eliade's thought; I did not go on to make sense of the famous claim, "for it is only as an aesthetic phenomenon that existence and the world are eternally justified."[2] Instead, I argued Ricoeur's point that we can only get to a certain understanding of the human through an act of interpretation of a symbolic form. Ricoeur, I believe, had a slightly different agenda. After all, anyone who chooses the philosophy of the will as a topic and comes from a rigorous Protestant upbringing will possibly be preoccupied with the bondage of the will and its great Western tradition, from St. Paul to Augustine, through Calvin and Luther, to Kant. The problem of the freedom of the will was one, as he once told me, that he had been preoccupied with since childhood. The surd of the will, the involuntary, would not only find its expression in the bodily involuntary, but in the hermeneutics of evil—the self embroiled in its own inarticulate articulation, expressed in the symbols of stain, sin, and guilt. Here, in language, Ricoeur finds a kind of archaism, not the archaism of ritual as in Nietzsche, but the archaism of singular expression. Hence, Ricoeur in his linguistic turn would construct a path that was unique among his fellow practitioners of the philosophy of language: at the heart of language he would find something like subjectivity—the triumph of singular expression, the language of avowal. This would mean that although he would make the move to language, he would always retain subjectivity as a theme, both consciously and unconsciously, and although it might be more appropriate to eidetic phenomenology, this theme would find expression throughout his linguistic and hermeneutic turn. Ricoeur's uniqueness was that he would always retain a kind of Husserlian preoccupation with subjectivity, immediacy, time, and temporality, even though he had made the move to language. Hence, the dilemma of the subject in the *Philosophy of the Will* as the dialectic between the voluntary and the involuntary, between freedom and nature, would find expression throughout his work, even to the end. "*Whose* memory is it?"[3]

II

Shortly after my first grand encounter with the work of Paul Ricoeur, I turned, for better or worse, to political philosophy and a tradition with which I think Ricoeur was always somewhat uncomfortable, namely, the Hegelian tradition. Recently, I saw that discomfort again when I wrote the foreword to the new edition of his *History and Truth*. Quoting from my foreword,

> This book bears witness to Ricoeur's belief that the distinction between reflection and action is in some sense a false distinction because reflection is a way of acting. Hence the opposition between theory and praxis is, as he reminds us in the introduction, a false opposition. It follows that any reflection about the truth is about

making the truth. For Ricoeur, philosophy was always an act of personal attestation.[4]

I go on to suggest that one finds here the trace of Ricoeur's ethical philosophy, which bore fruit in his later reflections regarding justice, politics, and even recognition (more about this later). What I mean, however, when I point to Ricoeur's discomfort with the Hegelian tradition is that Hegel was willing to collapse self and other. (When Kant speaks of *Würde*—respect—he deliberately distinguishes it from the terminology of exchange, in order to preserve its uniqueness. Hegel deliberately uses the language of exchange when he uses *Würde* in his doctrine of right.) Hence, in the move from autonomy (Kant) to intersubjectivity (Hegel), the uniqueness of the self is reduced to an identity with others, something Ricoeur would later call "sameness." One of the consequences, whether it be in the development of Critical Theory and its claim about intersubjectivity, or in the philosophy of language and its discourse on representation, is that the uniqueness of self-identity is lost. In my view, Ricoeur addresses both traditions, perhaps inadvertently, in his monumental book *Oneself as Another*.

As Ricoeur later told me, his argument with regard to the philosophy of language fell on deaf ears. No one in the analytic camp responded to it. In my view, however, it is a brilliant argument. In *Oneself as* Another Ricoeur developed a strategy for reflecting on the process of identification by attending to the basic analytic transitions from the kind of philosophy of language that bases itself on semantics to its pragmatic turn, while keeping in mind the relationship of the problem of identity to self-identity. Ricoeur develops a four-step argument that I can only allude to here. The first part of the argument suggests that theories of reference and reflexivity under the rubric of semantics can conceive of identity only on the basis of a conception of self as *idem*, or sameness. Pragmatics (speech-act theory) that attempts to move beyond semantics tries to get beyond the question of identity to self-identity through a theory of interlocution. Ricoeur argues that similar theories based on semantics (so-called pragmatic theories) are also limited by being able to consider identity only on the basis of sameness. Ricoeur's project would be to work out a theory of interlocution based on what he calls *ipséité*, that is, the self-as-sameness related to the self-as-situated-in-time. The narrative theory of identity is thus able to overcome the dilemma of identity that has been present in the philosophy of language, with its preoccupation with the universality of signs, and even in its pragmatic form that is concerned with interlocution. At the same time, the narrative theory of identity is able to speak to the intersubjectivist tradition following from Hegel's critique of Kant's notion of autonomy. Ricoeur's theory sustains the uniqueness of subjectivity, while at the same time affirming the continuity of identity through a conception of narrative identity. For me, the issue became central when both traditions, the Hegelian legacy on the one hand, and the philosophy of language on the other, were summed up in a form of Critical Theory that incorporates speech-act theory.

Having made the shift to political philosophy in general, and Critical Theory in particular, I would find in Ricoeur's reflections an aid to my personal development. What I realize now is that Ricoeur, who made the transition to the philosophy of language, would also find a way of preserving the eidetic moment within that transition. To put it more concretely, he would find a way of preserving subjectivity, or the subjective experience of the self, temporality, within language. That may be his peculiar legacy in philosophy. I have argued elsewhere that through narrative identity Ricoeur has found, on the level of language, a way to preserve the distance between self and other that is reflected in the famous fifth meditation of Husserl's *Cartesian Meditations*.[5] For those who practiced Critical Theory as I did, Husserl's fifth meditation presented a kind of dilemma where it was acknowledged that the phenomenological ego could not constitute the other in the same way that it constituted itself. Husserl, through the use of apperception, appresentation, and paring, attempted to find ways through which the other could be constituted by analogy to the self. In the end his analysis posed an epistemological problem. Critics would point out that one could never know the other in the same way that one could know the self, and as such, the specter of solipsism seemed to haunt Husserl's philosophy. In retrospect, however, Husserl may have had a point. Perhaps there is a sense in which the other can never be known by the self in the same sense that the self can know itself. Ricoeur would take this view a step further, finding duality and difference at the very heart of *self*-identity. Narrative identity could preserve the continuity of the subject with its own past, while at the same time sustaining transformation and change. A narrative can link the past with the future by giving a sense of continuity to an ever-changing story of the self. Because narrative has this potential, it is uniquely qualified to express the ongoing dialectic of selfhood and sameness, while at the same time trying to rethink the meaning of subjectivity.

We can now return to Kant's attempt to preserve the uniqueness of autonomy through his notion of respect and Hegel's critique of Kant through his theory of intersubjectivity. The critique is probably correct, but it is bought at a very high price. The price was identity philosophy.

One might say that this problem occurs in a different way in the philosophy of language. The overcoming of the philosophy of the subject by the philosophy of language certainly amounts to a significant achievement, but in certain instances, at least, it is achieved at the cost of the experience of the temporality of the subject. Ricoeur's critique of both the semantic theory of representation and the pragmatic theory of interlocution preserves the temporality of the subject within a philosophy of language. In this sense, the concept of narrative identity has been able to overcome the dilemma that was at the heart of a theory of interlocution. Ricoeur's critique of a theory of interlocution was not intended to merely undercut that theory, however—the critique also has a positive outcome. If every speech-act commits the speaker, it does so in time. In this sense assertions are not mere empty identities; rather, they have a temporal context, which presumes sincerity. When we conceive of a promise or a commitment in time, clearly it will have the implication that one will be bound to it. Obligation in the present leads to obligation for or toward the future. The result, from the point of view of interpretation, is that narrative identity when written into a theory of interlocution becomes fraught with ethical obligation. How close we seem still to the *Philosophy of the Will*!

III

As the issue of global and cosmopolitan justice has come to the fore in recent years, I have had one more occasion to return to the work of Paul Ricoeur. Of course, along with Kant, I find cosmopolitanism almost infectious. Yet, there is a tendency for much of cosmopolitan discourse to be overly abstract, a bit ethnocentric, and reductive. Cautioned by my recent experience with the later Rawls and his somewhat less than enthusiastic rejection of cosmopolitanism in his *Law of Peoples*, yet instructed by the recent writings of Jürgen Habermas to see the development of justice from the point of view of developments within international law, I have found myself on the horns of a dilemma to which Ricoeur's thought has been something of an antidote. Two problems emerge: 1) diversity of cultures and nations requires sensitivity to difference on a global scale; and 2) given the necessity for universal human rights, it is imperative that everyone be treated equally. We might call this the "paradox of global justice." How is it possible to acknowledge the distinctiveness of other political cultures while at the same time granting legitimacy and validity to individual claims for rights? This dilemma is made more complex when, as we move beyond the confines of the nation-state, the rights of individuals somehow transcend nationality.[6]

The concept of narrative identity developed in *Oneself as Another* preserves the nonidentical relation between self and self, and between self and other. One need say only that such a concept or model enables an encounter with non-Western or nondemocratic cultures that allows for sufficient difference so that the identity of the other is not reduced to the identity of the self. The result would be the preservation of a certain asymmetry of interpretation. In Ricoeur's book *The Just*, narrative identity has precisely this function. As such, narrative identity can play a constructive role that, instead of reducing other cultures to our own, enriches the overall significance of the story in which the cultures of the world play the part of the protagonists. However, that very narrative identity that can account for difference, given its temporal exposition as theory of interlocution, requires a certain respect for the other. And in the respect for the other, one acknowledges both the rule of sincerity and the capacity to fulfill it. In this sense, the universality of human rights is acknowledged. That means that the acknowledgment of diversity simultaneously involves the attribution of human rights.

To sum up, what I find distinctive and unique about Ricoeur is his way of sustaining that eidetic moment, subjectivity, through the various stages of his hermeneutic philosophy of language. In my judgment, no one else has been able to do that with his freshness and originality. Of course, in the shadow of that stalwart defense of subjectivity and temporality lies the idea that never left him, the philosophy of the will.

Notes

Introduction: How Much More Than the Possible?
Brian Treanor and Henry Isaac Venema

1. Paul Ricoeur, "Emmanuel Mounier: A Personalist Philosopher," in *Truth and History,* trans. Charles A. Kelbley, 2d. ed. (Evanston, Ill.: Northwestern University Press, 1965), 133. On a similar theme, see Paul Ricoeur, *Living Up to Death*, trans. David Pellauer (Chicago: University of Chicago Press, 2009), 59–61.

2. David Pellauer, "Remembering Paul Ricoeur," *Philosophy Today* 51, SPEP Supplement 2007, 9. This article is reprinted in this volume under the same title.

3. At last count, 3,051 items were listed on the Ricoeur bibliographic database at the library of St. Paul's University, in Ottawa, Canada, but the database doesn't include anything published after 2002. See also the archive *Fonds Ricoeur*, www.fondsricoeur.fr.

4. Cf. Paul Ricoeur, "Intellectual Autobiography," in *The Philosophy of Paul Ricoeur,* ed. Lewis Edwin Hahn (Chicago: Open Court, 1995), 3–53. See also Paul Ricoeur, *Critique and Conviction: Conversations with François Azouvi and Marc de Launay,* trans. Kathleen Blamey (New York: Columbia University Press, 1998).

5. Charles E. Reagan, *Paul Ricoeur: His Life and His Works* (Chicago: University of Chicago Press, 1996), 1.

6. Paul Ricoeur, "Freedom in the Light of Hope," in *The Conflict of Interpretations,* ed. Don Ihde (Evanston, Ill.: Northwestern University Press, 1974), 407–10. Also see "Love and Justice," in *Figuring the Sacred: Religion, Narrative, and Imagination,* trans. David Pellauer, ed. Mark I. Wallace (Minneapolis: Fortress Press, 1995), 324–29.

7. Richard Kearney, "Capable Man, Capable God," in this volume, 58.

8. Kearney, "Capable Man, Capable God," in this volume, 57.

9. Paul Ricoeur, *Memory, History, Forgetting,* trans. Kathleen Blamey and David Pellauer (Chicago: University of Chicago Press, 2004), 493.

10. See Paul Ricoeur, "Religious Belief: The Difficult Path of the Religious," in this volume, 35.

11. Paul Ricoeur, *The Symbolism of Evil,* trans. Emerson Buchanan (Boston: Beacon Press, 1967), 151–57.

12. Paul Ricoeur, "Religion and Symbolic Violence," in *Contagion* 6 (spring 1999): 8.

13. In "Christianity and the Meaning of History," an essay dating from 1951, Ricoeur tells us that meaning, both personal and historical, can be expressed in religious terms, and in this case Christian terms. While it is true that Ricoeur's religious thought has evolved over the course of his life, such that he would express his ideas differently by the late 1990s (see *Critique and Conviction*), this 1951 essay is particularly revealing of how Ricoeur has understood the relation between meaning and Christian faith:

> Meaning: there is a unity of meaning; it is the fundamental source of the courage to live in history. Mystery: but this meaning is hidden; no one can *say* it, rely upon it, or draw an assurance from it which would be a counter-assurance against the dangers of history. One must risk it on signs. . . . What authorizes the Christian to speak of meaning when he takes shelter in mystery? What authorizes him to transcend this schema of ambiguity in which history may turn for the worse or for the better, in which rising and falling civilizations may weave their way into the fabric of progress? Does all of this have a total meaning?
>
> For the Christian, faith in the Lordship of God dominates his entire vision of history. If God is the Lord of individual lives he is also Lord of history: God directs this uncertain, noble, and guilty history toward Himself. To be more precise, I think that this Lordship constitutes a "meaning" and not a supreme farce, a prodigious caprice, or a last "absurdity," because the great events that I recognize as Revelation have a certain pattern, constitute a global form, and are not given as pure discontinuity. *Revelation* has a kind of bearing which is not an absurdity for us, for we may discern in it a certain *pedagogical* plan in going from the Old Testament to the New Testament. The great Christian events—death and resurrection—constitute an order open to what St. Paul calls "the understanding of faith.

"Christianity and the Meaning of History," in *History and Truth,* trans. Charles A. Kelbley, 2d. ed. (Evanston: Northwestern University Press, 1965), 93.

14. Ricoeur, "Religious Belief," 29.

15. Ricoeur, *Memory, History, Forgetting,* 485.

16. Ricoeur, *Memory, History, Forgetting,* 457. For further analysis and development of Ricoeur's understanding of forgiveness, see Gaëlle Fiasse, "The

Golden Rule and Forgiveness," and Henry Isaac Venema, "The Source of Ricoeur's Double Allegiance," included in this volume of essays.

17. In "Freedom in the Light of Hope"(404), Ricoeur uses Jürgen Moltman's *The Theology of Hope* to distinguish these two logics of the cross and resurrection. This difference between these two kinds of possibility is remarkably similar to the distinction made by Jacques Derrida between the possible, as the programmable, and the event of "the impossible," which arrives beyond all means of calculation and programmability. Derrida writes that the "event" is,

> in the face of questions like *hospitality* (*invitation/visitation*, and a whole chain of associated topics: the *promise, testimony,* the *gift, forgiveness*, etc.), also capable of withstanding [*à l'épreuve de*] an impossible that would not be negative. Such a test implies another thinking of the event, of the *avoir-lieu:* only the impossible takes place. The deployment of a potentiality or a possibility that is already there will never make an event or an invention. What is true of the event is also true of the decision, therefore of responsibility: a decision that I *am able* to make, the decision that is *in my power* and that indicates the passage to the act or the deployment of what is *already possible* for me, the actualization of my possible, a decision that only depends on me: would this still be a decision? Whence the paradox without paradox that I am trying to accept: the responsible decision must be this impossible possibility of a "passive" decision, a decision of the other-in-me who will not acquit me [*qui ne m'exonère*] of any freedom or any responsibility.

Jacques Derrida, "As If It Were Possible, 'Within Such Limits . . .'" in *Negotiations: Interventions and Interviews, 1971–2001*, ed., trans., and with an introduction by Elizabeth Rottenberg (Stanford, Calif.: Stanford University Press, 2002), 357.

18. Paul Ricoeur, "Experience and Language in Religious Discourse," in *Phenomenology and the Theological Turn: The French Debate,* ed. Dominique Janicaud (New York: Fordham University Press, 2000), 145.

19. Ricoeur, "Experience and Language in Religious Discourse," 145.

20. Paul Ricoeur, *Oneself as Another,* trans. Kathleen Blamey (Chicago: University of Chicago Press, 1992), 24.

21. During a roundtable discussion at the conference, Ricoeur said:

> I am ready to put aside the strategy of merely being a university professor. For when I was still teaching, it was a permanent requirement to be recognized as a philosopher because I was under the pressure of the atheistic trend of French philosophy. I had permanently to justify my existence saying that I was not a "crypto-theologian." But the problem is whether I am not a "crypto-philosopher" in theology; this is the other side of the coin. I put that aside because I am no longer part of the Establishment. I am beyond that. I do not have to justify myself, in order to remain in that position. Secondly, I have proposed a further solution—if not a solution

> at least the prolegomenon of a solution—by distinguishing "motivation" from "argumentation." I am ready to agree that there is a strong religions motivation even in my philosophical work. It is not by chance that I was interested in narrative, because of the role of narrative in the bible. This is the key as you suggested: my fight against the Cartesian tradition is surely motivated by religious and Christian presuppositions that the ego and even the self is not the last word. So there is a sacrifice of the claim to be the master of meaning, as I used to say a few years ago.

"Roundtable Discussion," in *Memory, Narrativity, Self and the Challenge to Think God: The Reception within Theology of the Recent Work of Paul Ricoeur,* ed. Maureen Junker-Kenny and Peter Kenny (Münster: LIT Verlag, 2004), 203. This remarkable claim of religious motivation as central to Ricoeur's philosophical argumentation brushes aside his claims of philosophical agnosticism. This is a criticism already made by Henry Isaac Venema, *Identifying Selfhood: Imagination, Narrative, and Hermeneutics in the Thought of Paul Ricoeur* (Albany: SUNY Press, 2000), 161–63. See also Venema, "The Source of Ricoeur's Double Allegiance," in this volume.

22. Paul Ricoeur, *Living Up to Death*, trans. David Pellauer (Chicago: University of Chicago Press, 2009), 69–70.

23. Ricoeur, "Religious Belief," 29. In the essay "Religion and Symbolic Violence" (2), Ricoeur gives a slightly different version this conviction: "at the very basis of my conviction, of my own confession, I recognize a reality which I do not control as my own. I discern at the base of my position a source of inspiration, which exceeds my capacity of reception and comprehension by reason of its demand on thought, its power of practical motivation, and its emotional dynamic" (2).

24. Ricoeur, "Religious Belief," in this volume, 36.

25. Ricoeur, *Oneself as Another*, 172.

26. See Richard Kearney's essay in this volume for a development of the idea of a "capable God."

27. Paul Ricoeur, *Freedom and Nature: The Voluntary and the Involuntary*, trans. and with introduction by Erazim V. Kohak (Evanston, Ill: Northwestern University Press, 1965).

28. Paul Ricoeur, *Fallible Man,* trans. Charles Kelbley (Chicago: Henry Regnery, 1965).

29. Paul Ricoeur, "Asserting Personal Capacities and Pleading for Mutual Recognition," in this volume, 22.

30. Kaplan lists nine features implied in Ricoeur phenomenology of the capable man that are "both the starting point and destination of philosophical analysis." See "Paul Ricoeur and Development Ethics" in this volume.

31. Ricoeur, *Fallible Man*, 223.

32. Ricoeur, *Fallible Man*, 224.

33. Ricoeur, "Asserting Personal Capacities," in this volume, 22.

34. Ricoeur, *Fallible Man*, xix.
35. Ricoeur, *Fallible Man*, 3.
36. Ricoeur, "Asserting Personal Capacities," 22.
37. Ricoeur, "Asserting Personal Capacities," 23.
38. Ricoeur, "Religion and Symbolic Violence," 1.
39. Ricoeur, "Religion and Symbolic Violence," 2, 10.
40. Ricoeur, "Religion and Symbolic Violence," 8.
41. Ricoeur, *Fallible Man*, 223.
42. Ricoeur, *Fallible Man*, xx.
43. Paul Ricoeur, "A Response by Paul Ricoeur," trans. David Pellauer, in *Paul Ricoeur and Narrative: Context and Contestation*, ed. Morny Joy (Calgary: University of Calgary Press, 1997), xxxix.
44. Ricoeur, *Fallible Man*, 207.
45. Ricoeur, "Religion and Symbolic Violence," 3, 6. Emphasis mine.
46. Ricoeur, "Religious Belief," in this volume, 27.
47. Ricoeur, "Religious Belief," 28.
48. "However *radical* evil may be, it cannot be as *primordial* as goodness" (Ricoeur, *The Symbolism of Evil*, 156).
49. Ricoeur, "Religious Belief," 30. In an interview with Brother Roger of the Taizé Community in France, Ricoeur, when asked "What do I come looking for in Taizé?" responds as follows:

> I would say to experience in some way what I believe most deeply, namely that what is generally called "religion" has to do with goodness. To some extent the traditions of Christianity have forgotten this. There has been a kind of narrowing, an exclusive focus on guilt and evil. Not that I underestimate that problem, which was a great concern of mine for several decades. But what I need to verify is that however radical evil may be, it is not as deep as goodness. And if religion, if religions have a meaning, it is to liberate that core of goodness in human beings, to go looking for it where it has been completely buried. Now here in Taizé I see goodness breaking through, in the community life of the brothers, in their calm and discreet hospitality, and in the prayer. I see thousands of young people who do not express a conceptual articulation of good and evil, of God, of grace, of Jesus Christ, but who have a fundamental tropism towards goodness."

Taizé website, http://www.taize.fr/en_article102.html.
50. Ricoeur, "Religious Belief," 34.
51. Ricoeur, "Religious Belief," 35.
52. Ricoeur, "Religious Belief," 36.
53. See Paul Ricoeur, "Love and Justice," in *Figuring the Sacred*, 315–29.
54. See "Experience and Language in Religious Discourse," where Ricoeur writes: "This restoration, the regeneration, this rebirth of the capable self, stands in close relation to the economy of the gift which I celebrate in the study 'Amour et justice' " (146).

55. Ricoeur, "Religious Belief," 37.

56. Ricoeur, "Naming God," in *Figuring the Sacred,* 217–35.

57. Ricoeur, *Oneself as Another,* 19.

58. Paul Ricoeur, "The Self in the Mirror of the Scriptures," in *The Whole and Divided Self,* ed. David E. Aune and John McCarthy (New York: Crossroad Publishing, 1997), 211.

59. Ricoeur, "The Self in the Mirror of the Scriptures," 213.

60. Ricoeur, "The Self in the Mirror of the Scriptures," 219.

61. The figure of the desert is ambiguous. Ricoeur's often-quoted statement, "Beyond the desert of criticism we wish to be called again" (Ricoeur, *The Symbolism of Evil,* 349), has led many to assume that Ricoeur has pointed the way through the desert, if not the actual passage beyond the desert itself. Rather, the desert figure serves Ricoeur as an eschatological call for departure within the desert. This is a journey set out in hope that follows the morning star, but never claims that the dawn has arrived. The desert is a historical space, "an open-ended, incomplete, imperfect mediation, namely, the network of interweaving perspectives of the expectation of the future, the reception of the past, and the experience of the present, with no *Aufhenbung* into a totality where reason in history and in reality would coincide" (Paul Ricoeur, *Time and Narrative,* trans. Kathleen Blamey and David Pellauer [Chicago: University of Chicago Press, 1998], 3:207). Continually open for the arrival of what is to come, this space is in process of being formed in and through a promise that the desert will one day become a fertile field and begin to bloom. While the desert is the place where all life wanders, it is not a symbol of Derridian "destinerrance." For Ricoeur the desert is not barren desolation without the possibility of the arrival of the kingdom to come; rather, Ricoeur's hope is rooted in the promise of a possibility previously thought impossible that has been made possible in the incarnation. Therefore, when St. Paul says that "Christ is the mystery that has been hidden since the foundation," this counters the endless impossible messianic future with the promise that the future will bring the same quality of light as that revealed by the "bright Morning Star." While Derrida's formulation of khoral spacing and différance is close to Ricoeur's formulation of disproportion, much closer than many scholars are willing to concede, Ricoeur's confession of Christian faith does not let him claim disproportionate space as neutral or barren. Ricoeur has wagered in faith that existence is indeed the good gift of God, and as such, the meaning of the disproportion of finite capacity and infinite excess is best understood as a loving space interpreted through the religious symbols of the crucifixion and resurrection of Christ.

62. Kearney, "Capable Man, Capable God," in this volume, 58.

63. The self that responds to the Prophetic call, the self that conforms to the Christ figure, the self that responds to the inner teacher, and the self summoned within conscience, are all treated as various fruits hanging from the same tree: "the summoned subject." See Paul Ricoeur, "The Summoned Subject," in *Figuring the Sacred,* 263. Also see his "Experience and Language in Religious Discourse," 144–46.

64. Ricoeur, "Experience and Language in Religious Discourse," 145.

65. Ricoeur, "Experience and Language in Religious Discourse," 142–43.

66. Ricoeur, "The Self in the Mirror of the Scriptures," 219.

67. Ricoeur, "Religious Belief," in this volume, 39.

68. Paul Ricoeur, "Phenomenology and Hermeneutics," in *Hermeneutics and the Human Sciences: Essays on Language, Action, and Interpretation,* ed. and trans. John B. Thompson (Cambridge: Cambridge University Press, 1981), 113.

69. Jean Greisch's essay in this volume, "Towards Which Recognition?" offers an alternative but similar narrative configuration of Ricoeur's work, taking "attestation as the secret password of all the hermeneutics of self."

70. Ricoeur, "Experience and Language in Religious Discourse," 145. Emphasis mine.

71. "As long as one remains within the circle of sameness-identity, the otherness of the other than self offers nothing original. . . . A kind of otherness that is not (or not merely) the result of comparison is suggested by our title, otherness of a kind that can be constitutive of selfhood as such. *Oneself as Another* suggests from the outset that the selfhood of oneself implies otherness to such an intimate degree that one cannot be thought of without the other, that instead one passes into the other, as we might say in Hegelian terms. To 'as' I should like to attach a strong meaning, not only that of a comparison (oneself similar to another) but indeed that of an implication (oneself inasmuch as being other)" (Ricoeur, *Oneself as Another,* 3).

72. Ricoeur, *Freedom and Nature*, 353.

Remembering Paul Ricoeur
David Pellauer

1. Paul Ricoeur, "Preface to the First Edition (1955)," *History and Truth*, trans. Charles A. Kelbley (Evanston, Ill.: Northwestern University Press, 1965), 5.

2. Paul Ricoeur, *Memory, History, Forgetting*, trans. Kathleen Blamey and David Pellauer (Chicago: University of Chicago Press, 2004).

3. Paul Ricoeur, "The Fragility of Political Language," trans. David Pellauer, *Philosophy Today* 31 (spring 1987): 35–44.

4. "Les historiens et le travail de mémoire," *Esprit* (August–September 2000); "La pensée Ricoeur," special issue of *Esprit* (March–April, 2006); Bertrand Müller, ed., *L'histoire entre mémoire et épistemologie* (Lausanne: Éditions Payot , 2005); Olivier Abel, Enrico Castelli-Gattinnara, Sabinna Loriga, and Isabell Ullern-Weité, eds., *La juste mémoire: Lectures autour de Paul Ricoeur* (Geneva : Labor et Fides, 2006); Maureen Junker-Kenny and Peter Kenny, eds., *Memory, Narrativity, Self and the Challenge to Think God: The Reception within Theology of the Recent Work of Paul Ricoeur* (Münster: LitVerlag, 2004). See also François Dosse, *Paul Ricoeur, Michel Certeau. L'histoire: Entre le dire et le faire* (Paris: L'Herne, 2006).

5. See Paul Ricoeur, *Oneself as Another*, trans. Kathleen Blamey (Chicago: University of Chicago Press, 1992), 4–16.

6. This concern for embodied consciousness is already evident in Ricoeur's earlier work, *Freedom and Nature: The Voluntary and the Involuntary*, trans. Erazim V. Kohák (Evanston, Ill.: Northwestern University Press, 1966). Indeed he is already looking for a way to get beyond the Cartesian model there, having recognized that neither Jaspers nor Marcel really succeed in their own attempts to deal with it.

7. That is, if we read Descartes' model to really involve the following structure: *ego cogito cogitatum*.

8. Paul Ricoeur, "Structure and Hermeneutics," in *The Conflict of Interpretations* (Evanston, Ill.: Northwestern University Press, 1974), 33.

9. The "celebrated Cartesian cogito, which grasps itself directly in the experience of doubt, is a truth as vain as it is invincible. I do not deny that it is a truth; it is a truth that posits itself, and as such it can be neither verified nor deduced. It posits at once a being and an act, an existence and an operation of thought: I am, I think; to exist, for me is to think; I exist insofar as I think. But this truth is a vain truth; it is like a first step which cannot be followed by any other, so long as the ego of the ego cogito has not been recaptured in the mirror of its objects, of its works, and, finally, of its acts" ("Existence and Hermeneutics," in *The Conflict of Interpretations*, 17).

10. For Ricoeur's final word on this topic, see *The Course of Recognition*, trans. David Pellauer (Cambridge, Mass.: Harvard University Press, 2005), 260–63.

11. This is one reason why, when he does speak of ontology, Ricoeur likes to repeat with Aristotle that being can be said in many ways.

12. Jean-Pierre Changeux and Paul Ricoeur, *What Makes Us Think? A Neuroscientist and a Philosopher Argue about Ethics, Human Nature, and the Brain*, trans. M. B. DeBevoise (Princeton, N. J.: Princeton University Press, 2000), 25–29. See also "The Problem of Double Meaning as Hermeneutic Problem and as Semantic Problem," in Ricoeur, *The Conflict of Interpretations*, 63.

13. See Ricoeur, *The Course of Recognition,* 55–61.

Capable Man, Capable God
Richard Kearney

1. Paul Ricoeur, *Vivant jusqu'à la mort; suivi de Fragments* (Paris: Editions du Seuil, 2007), 130. Ricoeur is responding here to my notion of divine *posse* as developed in several works, notably, Richard Kearney, *Poétique du possible: Vers une herméneutique phénoménologique de la figuration* (Paris: Beauchesne, 2004), *The God Who May Be: A Hermeneutics of Religion* (Bloomington: Indiana University Press, 2002), and "Enabling God," in *After God: Richard Kearney and the Religious Turn in Continental Philosophy*, ed. John Manoussakis (New York: Fordham University Press, 2005).

2. Paul Ricoeur, "The Power of the Possible," reprinted in Richard Kearney, *Debates in Continental Philosophy: Conversations with Contemporary Thinkers* (New York: Fordham University Press, 2004), 42–46. For a more elaborate version of this exchange see *"A colloquio con Ricoeur"* in Fabrizio Turoldo, *Verita de*

metodo: Indagini su Paul Ricoeur (Padova: Il Poligrafo, 2000), 241–91. See also my first dialogue with Ricoeur on this subject in 1978, "Myth as the Bearer of Possible Worlds," *The Crane Bag Journal* 2, nos. 1–2 (1978), reprinted in Kearney, *Debates in Continental Philosophy*, 117–25.

3. Ricoeur, *Colloquio*, 277–78.

4. Ricoeur, *Colloquio*, 278.

5. Ricoeur, *Colloquio*, 278.

6. Ricoeur, *Colloquio*, 280.

7. Ricoeur, *Colloquio*, 279.

8. Ricoeur, *Colloquio*, 278–79.

9. Ricoeur, *Colloquio*, 278. This useful remark is from Fabrizio Turoldo.

10. Ricoeur, *Colloquio*, 279. For a more detailed development of this theme of attestation see Ricoeur, *Oneself as Another* (Chicago: University of Chicago Press, 1992), and "Attestation: Entre phénoménologie et ontologie," in *Métamorphoses de la raison herméneutique*, ed. Jean Greisch and Richard Kearney (Paris: Cerf, 1991), 381–403.

11. Ricoeur, *Colloquio,* 260.

12. Ricoeur, "Imagination in Discourse and Action," in *From Text to Action: Essays in Hermeneutics, II* (Evanston, Ill.: Northwestern University Press, 1991), 177.

13. Ricoeur, "Imagination in Discourse and Action," 177.

14. Ricoeur, "Imagination in Discourse and Action," 177. Ricoeur goes on as follows: "Imagination offers the common space for the comparison and mediation of terms as heterogeneous as the force that pushes as if from behind, the attraction that seduces as if from in front, and the reasons that legitimate and form a ground as if from beneath. It is in a form of the imaginary that the common 'dispositional' element is able to be represented in practical terms, allowing us to distinguish, on the one hand, between a physically compelling cause and a motive and, on the other hand, between a motive and a logically compelling reason. This form of the practical imaginary finds its linguistic equivalent in expressions such as 'I would do this or that, if I wanted to.'"

15. Ricoeur, "Imagination in Discourse and Action," 178.

16. Ricoeur, "Imagination in Discourse and Action," 177–78.

17. Paul Ricoeur, *Time and Narrative* (Chicago: University of Chicago Press, 1990), 3:216. See also 3:227, 3:219, and 3:240.

18. Ricoeur, *Time and Narrative,* 3:331.

19. Ricoeur in conversation with David Carr and Charles Taylor, "Discussion: Ricoeur on Narrative," in *On Paul Ricoeur: Narrative and Interpretation*, ed. David Wood (London: Routledge, 1991), 187. On the question of this retrieval and exchange of memories see also Ricoeur, "Reflections on a New Ethos for Europe," in *Paul Ricoeur: The Hermeneutics of Action*, ed. Richard Kearney (London: Sage, 1996), 5–9.

20. Paul Ricoeur, "Epilogue: Difficult Forgiveness," in *Memory, History, Forgetting* (Chicago: University of Chicago Press, 2004), 459.

21. Ricoeur, "Epilogue,"490.

22. Ricoeur, "Epilogue,"491. Emphasis mine.

23. Ricoeur, "Epilogue," 491.

24. Ricoeur, "Epilogue," 491.

25. Ricoeur, "Epilogue," 492.

26. Ricoeur, "Epilogue," 493.

27. Ricoeur, "From Interpretation to Translation." in *Thinking Biblically* (Chicago: University of Chicago Press, 1998), 331ff. See also Ricoeur, "La croyance religieuse: Le difficile chemin du religieux," CNAM (Paris: Odile Jacob, 2000), especially the section entitled "L"homme capable, destinataire du religieux," 207 et seq.

28. Ricoeur, *Colloquio*, 254.

29. Ricoeur, "The Poetics of Language and Myth," in Kearney, ed., *Debates in Continental Philosophy,* 99 et seq.

30. Ricoeur, *Colloquio,* 255.

31. Ricoeur, *Colloquio,* 255.

32. Ricoeur, "The Nuptial Metaphor," in *Thinking Biblically,* 265ff.

33. Paul Ricoeur, *Vivant jusqu'à la mort*, 45.

34. Ricoeur, *Vivant jusqu'à la mort*, 45.

35. Ricoeur, *Vivant jusqu'à la mort*, 47.

36. Ricoeur, *Vivant jusqu'à la mort*, 76.

37. Ricoeur, *Vivant jusqu'à la mort*, 90.

38. Ricoeur, *Vivant jusqu'à la mort*, 91.

39. Paul Ricoeur, "The Critique of Religion," in *The Philosophy of Paul Ricoeur*, ed. Charles Regan and David Stuart (Boston: Beacon, 1978), 213ff. Ricoeur talks about the related notion of returning to a second naïveté of authentic faith after the dogmatisms and prejudices of one's first naïveté have been deconstructed and purged. To which critical act of purgation and return one might add his more recent notions of "linguistic hospitality" and "eucharistic hospitality." See Ricoeur, *On Translation* (New York: Routledge, 2006), 23–24: "Bringing the reader to the author, bringing the author to the reader, at the risk of serving and of betraying two masters: this is to practice what I like to call linguistic hospitality. It is this which serves as a model for other forms of hospitality that I think resemble it: confessions, religions, are they not like languages that are foreign to one another, with their lexicon, their grammar, their rhetoric, their stylistics which we must learn in order to make our way into them? And is Eucharistic hospitality not to be taken up with the same risks of translation-betrayal, but also with the same renunciation of the perfect translation?" See also in this connection L-M. Chauvet, *Sign and Sacrament: A Sacramental Reinterpretation of Christian Experience* (Collegeville, Minn.: The Liturgical Press, 1995). See for example p. 503, where Chauvet describes how the self is only rediscovered through deconstructive exposure to the other: "It is 'I' which is possible only in its relationship with what is most different, the YOU (the reverse of 'I'); and it is precisely from this tear of otherness, impossible to mend, that the likeness and the reciprocity permitting communication are born."

40. See Ricoeur's final reference to my notion of divine *posse* in one of the last "Fragments" of *Vivant jusqu'à la mort,* 129–30. This occurs in the context of Ricoeur's discussion of Marc Philonenko's reading of the "Our Father." Remarking that we are concerned in this prayer less with a statement about God's being (the fact that God *is*) than an invocation to action and doing, Ricoeur sees here a movement beyond a traditional ontology of being to an eschatology of "possibilisation." "Une invocation s'addresse à *un Dieu qui peut ce qu'il fait*" [my italics]. Dans les demandes en tu, il est demandé à Dieu de *faire* qu'il règne. . . . Peut-être un Dieu du *posse* (Richard Kearney). La vision eschatologique est celle d'une complétude de l'*Agir*" (129–30). Returning to his oft-repeated desire for a hermeneutical rereading of Aristotle's dialectic of possibility and actuality, Ricoeur notes that Christ's appeal to the Father takes the form not just of wish but of expectancy, an act of trust in the accomplishment of action (*agir*). Here Ricoeur sees a "coupling" of capacities, human and divine, seeking to be realized in a "coupling" of actions. "Forgive us as we forgive others," etc. "Le *comme* opère verbalement ce que la symétrie inégale des deux agir opère effectivement" (130). Ricoeur concludes with an eschatological reinterpretation of Aristotle's ontology of potency and act, involving a new hermeneutic "coupling," with its own radical charge of semantic interanimation and innovation: "Telle serait la possibilisation d'une énonciation en terme d'agir. Non grec. Mais possibilité d'une réecriture du verbe être à la façon d'Aristote. Etre comme *dunamis-energeia.* L'agir rend *possible* cette réecriture de l'être grec. Comme déjà Exode 3, 14–15. Voir *Penser le Bible* sur 'Je suis qui je serai'" (131–32). In this final reflection on the eschatological "capacity" for pardon, Ricoeur appears to reconcile his ontological and theological insights into the transformative power of the "possible."

The Source of Ricoeur's Double Allegiance
Henry Isaac Venema

1. Paul Ricoeur, *Critique and Conviction: Conversations with François Azouvi and Marc de Launay,* trans. Kathleen Blamey (New York: Columbia University Press, 1998), 2, 6.

2. Paul Ricoeur, *Living Up to Death,* trans. David Pellauer (Chicago: University of Chicago Press, 2009), 70.

3. Ricoeur explains that "when I was still teaching, it was a permanent requirement to be recognized as a philosopher because I was under the pressure of the atheistic trend of French philosophy. I had permanently to justify my existence saying that I was not a 'crypto-theologian.' But the problem is whether I am not a 'crypto-philosopher' in theology; this is the other side of the coin. I put that aside because I am no longer part of the Establishment. I am beyond that. I do not have to justify myself, in order to remain in that position." Paul Ricoeur, "Roundtable Discussion," in *Memory, Narrativity, Self and the Challenge to Think God: The Reception within Theology of the Recent Work of Paul Ricoeur,* ed. Maureen Junker-Kenny and Peter Kenny (Münster: LIT Verlag, 2004), 203.

4. I take the "deliberately pejorative" meaning of the term *Christian philosopher* to be someone who has accepted a sedimentation of philosophical categories

and/or structures as closed off to innovation because the truth of the Christian faith has been revealed within a particular philosophical paradigm, assumed to be universally true, and therefore deemed appropriate to be repeated endlessly as the Truth.

5. Ricoeur, *Living Up to Death*, 69–70.

6. Paul Ricoeur, *Oneself as Another*, trans. Kathleen Blamey (Chicago and London: University of Chicago Press, 1992), 24.

7. See Ricoeur, "Roundtable Discussion," 203; *Critique and Conviction*, 139–70; and *Living Up to Death*, 69–70.

8. Ricoeur, *Living Up to Death*, 64–65.

9. Is Christ an example of the Essential, or vice versa? Derrida raises this issue in an interesting way in "The Villanova Roundtable: A Conversation with Jacques Derrida," in *Deconstruction in a Nutshell*, ed. with a commentary by John D. Caputo (New York: Fordham University Press, 1997), 20–25.

10. Ricoeur, *Living Up to Death*, 52–54.

11. Ricoeur, *Living Up to Death*, 14–16.

12. Ricoeur, *Critique and Conviction*, 157.

13. Ricoeur, *Living Up to Death*, 42.

14. Paul Ricoeur, *Memory, History, Forgetting*, trans. Kathleen Blamey and David Pellauer (Chicago and London: University of Chicago Press, 2004), 457–93.

15. Ricoeur, *Critique and Conviction*, 158.

16. Paul Ricoeur, "Religious Belief: The Difficult Path of the Religious," published in this volume, 35.

17. Ricoeur, *Critique and Conviction*, 144.

18. Ricoeur, *Critique and Conviction*, 144–45.

19. Ricoeur, *Oneself as Another*, 19.

20. Ricoeur, *Critique and Conviction*, 144, 146.

21. Ricoeur, "Religious Belief," in this volume, 35.

22. Ricoeur, *Oneself as Another*, 22–23.

23. Ricoeur, *Critique and Conviction*, 143.

24. Ricoeur, *Oneself as Another*, 355.

25. Charles E. Reagan, *Paul Ricoeur: His Life and His Work* (Chicago and London: University of Chicago Press, 1996), 125.

26. Ricoeur, *Oneself as Another*, 315.

27. Ricoeur, *Living Up to Death*, 83.

28. Ricoeur, "Religious Belief," in this volume, 35.

29. Paul Ricoeur, *Memory, History, Forgetting*.

30. Richard Kearney, *Debates in Continental Philosophy: Conversations with Contemporary Thinkers* (New York: Fordham University Press, 2004), 42.

31. Ricoeur, *Memory, History, Forgetting*, 457.

32. Ricoeur, *Memory, History, Forgetting*, 490.

33. Ricoeur, *Memory, History, Forgetting*, 457.

34. Ricoeur, *Memory, History, Forgetting*, 458.

35. Ricoeur, *Memory, History, Forgetting*, 459.
36. Ricoeur, *Memory, History, Forgetting*, 467.
37. Ricoeur, *Memory, History, Forgetting*, 468.
38. Ricoeur, *Memory, History, Forgetting*, 460.
39. Ricoeur, *Memory, History, Forgetting*, 460.
40. Ricoeur, *Memory, History, Forgetting*, 460.
41. Ricoeur, *Memory, History, Forgetting*, 466.
42. Ricoeur, *Memory, History, Forgetting*, 462.
43. The nature of primordial desire provides Ricoeur with an important point of connection with the work of René Girard, allowing Ricoeur to explain religious violence as mimetic desire transformed into a desire for domination and control of the "groundless ground" of finite existence. See Ricoeur, "Religious Belief," in this volume, and "Religion and Symbolic Violence," *Contagion* 6 (spring 1999).
44. Ricoeur, *Memory, History, Forgetting*, 462.
45. Paul Ricoeur, *The Rule of Metaphor: Multi-Disciplinary Studies of the Creation of Meaning in Language*, trans. Robert Czerny with Kathleen McLaughlin and John Costello, (Toronto: University of Toronto Press, 1977), 255.
46. Ricoeur, *Memory, History, Forgetting*, 462–63.
47. Interestingly, this can also be linked to Ricoeur's claim in *The Symbolism of Evil* (Boston: Beacon Press, 1986) that no matter how "*radical* evil may be, it cannot be as *primordial* as goodness" (p. 156). And it can be further linked to one of his earliest essays, dating from 1956, called "Negativity and Primary Affirmation," where he argues that although the original or "primary affirmation is, through my own fault, primordially lost . . . [nevertheless,] under the pressure of the negative, of negative experiences, we must re-achieve a notion of being which is *act* rather than *form*, living affirmation, the power of existing and making exist." Paul Ricoeur, *History and Truth*, trans. Charles A. Kelbley (Evanston, Ill.: Northwestern University Press, 1965), 327–28.
48. Ricoeur, *Memory, History, Forgetting*, 464.
49. Ricoeur, *Memory, History, Forgetting*, 466.
50. Ricoeur, *Memory, History, Forgetting*, 483.
51. Ricoeur, *Memory, History, Forgetting*, 486.
52. Ricoeur, *Memory, History, Forgetting*, 485.
53. Ricoeur, *Memory, History, Forgetting*, 485.
54. Ricoeur, *Memory, History, Forgetting*, 490.
55. Ricoeur, *Memory, History, Forgetting*, 490. Emphasis mine.
56. Ricoeur, *Memory, History, Forgetting*, 491.
57. Ricoeur, *Memory, History, Forgetting*, 490.
58. Ricoeur, *Oneself as Another*, 315.
59. Ricoeur, *Memory, History, Forgetting*, 492.
60. Ricoeur, *Memory, History, Forgetting*, 493.
61. Ricoeur, *Memory, History, Forgetting*, 490. Emphasis mine.
62. Ricoeur, *Memory, History, Forgetting*, 493.

63. Kearney, *Debates in Continental Philosophy*, 44.

64. Kearney, *Debates in Continental Philosophy*, 43.

65. Kearney, *Debates in Continental Philosophy*, 45.

66. Cf. Richard Kearney, "Capable Man, Capable God," published in this volume, 58.

67. Ricoeur, *Memory, History, Forgetting,* 485.

68. Paul Ricoeur, "The Logic of Jesus, the Logic of God," *Criterion* 18, no. 2 (summer 1979): 5.

69. Ricoeur, *Living Up to Death*, 69.

70. Romans 5:9–11

71. Ricoeur, *Living Up to Death*, 70.

72. Ricoeur, *Living Up to Death*, 48.

73. Ricoeur, *Critique and Conviction*, 148. Here we find a deep connection between Ricoeur's understanding of narrative selfhood and the narrative of scriptures, and an ontology and anthropology of capability.

The Golden Rule and Forgiveness
Gaëlle Fiasse

1. Ricoeur's reading of Levinas has been the subject of several writings. The Levinasian author Richard A. Cohen has strongly criticized Ricoeur's interpretation of Levinas. Patrick L. Bourgeois has been more sensitive to the intention of both authors. One should indeed be aware of just how much respect Ricoeur also pays to Levinas throughout his work. My only concern is to emphasize the important role Ricoeur attributes to friendship in his own ethics, to insist on the mutuality. See Patrick L. Bourgeois, "Ricoeur and Levinas: Solicitude in Reciprocity and Solitude in Existence," in *Ricoeur as Another: The Ethics of Subjectivity*, ed. R. A. Cohen and J. I. Marsh (New York: State University of New York Press, 2002), 109–26, and Richard A. Cohen, "Moral Selfhood: A Levinasian Response to Ricoeur on Levinas," in *Ricoeur as Another*, 127–60.

2. Paul Ricoeur, "Responsibility and Fragility: An Ethical Reflection," *Journal of the Faculty of Religious Studies* 21:7–10, and Paul Ricoeur, *Oneself as Another*, trans. K. Blamey (Chicago: University of Chicago Press, 1992), 168.

3. Ricoeur, *Oneself as Another*, 22: "If one admits that the problematic of acting constitutes the analogical unity within which all of these investigations are grouped, attestation can be defined as the *assurance of being oneself acting and suffering*." See also Ricoeur, *Oneself as Another*, 190.

4. Ricoeur, *Oneself as Another*, 170.

5. Immanuel Kant, *Groundwork for the Metaphysics of Morals*, trans. J. W. Ellington (Indianapolis: Hackett Publishing, 1994), 4:429

6. Luke 6:31. Quoted by Ricoeur in "Ethical and Theological Considerations on the Golden Rule," in *Figuring the Sacred: Religion, Narrative, and Imagination*, ed. M. I. Wallace, trans. D. Pellauer (Minneapolis: Fortress Press, 1995), 294, 324, 328.

7. John Stuart Mill, *Utilitarianism* (Malden–Oxford: Blackwell, 2003), 194.

8. See Marcel Hénaff, "Remarques sur la Règle d'Or: Ricoeur et la question de la réciprocité," in *L'Herne: Paul Ricoeur* (Paris: Éditions de l'Herne, 2004), 335–36. His insistance on mutual recognition in the Golden Rule misses this asymmetry.

9. Ricoeur, *Oneself as Another*, 180–81: "We have continually been speaking of esteem of the self and not esteem of myself. *To say self is not to say myself.* . . . Under what condition is this other not just a reduplication of myself—another myself, an alter ego—, but genuinely an other, other than myself?" (italics in original).

10. This precision can help to clarify the debates on the Christian Golden Rule. See Alan Kirk, "'Love your Enemies': The Golden Rule, and Ancient Reciprocity (Luke 6:27–35)," *Journal of Biblical Literature* 122, no. 4 (2003): 667–86.

11. Ricoeur, *Oneself as Another*, 183. Contrary to translator Kathleen Blamey, I prefer to render the French *égologique* as *egological*, instead of *egoistic*. This neologism, in French and in English, respects the Ricoeurian principle of taking his distance from the "egologies," the philosophies of the subject, such as that of Husserl, which are unable to really consider otherness and mutuality.

12. Ricoeur, *Oneself as Another*, 219: "The most remarkable element in the formulation of this rule lies in the fact that this demanded reciprocity *emerges from the backdrop* [*se détache sur le fond*] of the presupposition of an initial dissymmetry between the protagonists of action." The expression *se détacher sur le fond de* is difficult to express in English. Kathleen Blamey has chosen *stands out against*, but this expression loses the backcloth of the canvas, which dwells as the foundation. This notion of asymmetry is fundamental to understanding Ricoeur's point of view. See Ricoeur, "Ethical and Theological Considerations on the Golden Rule," 294.

13. Ricoeur, *Oneself as Another*, 225

14. Paul Ricoeur, *Parcours de la reconnaissance: Trois etudes* (Paris: Stock, 2004), 376–77.

15. Ricoeur, *Oneself as Another*, 223. We translate the French *égaliser* by *balance*.

16. Ricoeur, *Oneself as Another*, 202. See W. David Hall, "The Economy of the Gift: Paul Ricoeur's Poetic Redescription of Reality," *Literature and Theology* 20, no. 2 (June 2006): 1–16: "It is at least difficult to think the ideas of 'economy' and 'gift' together." We may also notice that in French the word *économie* can be used as a synonym for the English term *logic* (as in "*l'économie* d'une loi," "*l'économie* du corps humain"), whose meaning does not fit into the English term *economy*.

17. Ricoeur, "Ethical and Theological Considerations on the Golden Rule," 301.

18. Ricoeur, "Ethical and Theological Considerations on the Golden Rule," 300.

19. Paul Ricoeur, "Love and Justice," in *Radical Pluralism and Truth: David Tracy and the Hermeneutics of Religion*, ed. W. G. Jeanrond and J. L. Rike (New York: Crossroad, 1991), 189–90.

20. Franz Rosenzweig, *The Star of Redemption*, trans. B. E. Galli (Madison: University of Wisconsin Press, 2005), 220.

21. Ricoeur, "Ethical and Theological Considerations on the Golden Rule," 299: "No one can take my life from me, but I lay down my life in order to take it up again (John 10:18)."

22. In this sense, the article by W. David Hall highlights the dichotomy between economic rationality based on a calculation of returns and the supramoral gift of existence made by God. Our answer to this dichotomy lies in the gift as a call for love, which can neither be reduced to an economic exchange, nor to a gift without possibility of return. See Hall, "The Economy of the Gift," 196.

23. Paul Ricoeur, "The Difficulty to Forgive," in *Memory, Narrativity, Self and the Challenge to Think God: The Reception within Theology of the Recent Work of Paul Ricoeur*, ed. M. Junker-Kenny and P. Kenny (Münster: LIT Verlag, 2004), 11.

24. Hanna Arendt, *The Human Condition* (Chicago: University of Chicago Press, 1998).

25. Paul Ricoeur, "The Difficulty to Forgive," 15.

26. Paul Ricoeur, "The Difficulty to Forgive," 6: "This hymn to forgiveness is akin to the similar hymn dedicated to love and joy. Listening to that voice, I have to confess that forgiving may be impossible, and yet, *there is* forgiveness."

27. Paul Ricoeur, *Memory, History, Forgetting*, trans. K. Blamey and D. Pellauer (Chicago: University of Chicago Press, 2004), 478.

28. Ricoeur, *Memory, History, Forgetting*, 482.

29. Ricoeur, *Oneself as Another*, 21.

30. Ricoeur, *Memory, History, Forgetting*, 490.

31. Ricoeur, *Memory, History, Forgetting*, 466.

32. Ricoeur, *Memory, History, Forgetting*, 490.

33. Klaus M. Kodalle, *Verzeihung nach Wendezeiten?* Conférences inaugurales données à l'université Friedrich-Schiller de Iéna, 2 juin 1994 (Erlangen et Iéna: Palm et Enke, 1994).

34. Paul Ricoeur, "Responsabilité: Limitée ou illimitée?" in *Le crime contre l'humanité mesure de la responsabilité?* Actes du cycle des conférences "Droit, Liberté et Foi," Juin 1997, 23–30 (Paris: CERP, 1998), 29.

35. Ricoeur, "Ethical and Theological Considerations on the Golden Rule," 299.

Toward Which Recognition?
Jean Greisch

1. Paul Ricoeur, *The Course of Recognition*, trans. D. Pellauer (Cambridge, Mass.: Harvard University Press, 2005).

2. Ricoeur, *The Course of Recognition*, 247.

3. Ricoeur, *The Course of Recognition*, x.

4. Ricoeur, *The Course of Recognition*, 16–17.

5. Ricoeur, *The Course of Recognition*, 80.

6. Translation of P. Boutang's French translation of *Symposium* 191, 5–7, to preserve the use of the word *symbole*. Benjamin Jowett's translation from the Greek reads: "Each of us when separated, having one side only, like a flat fish, is but the indenture of a man, and he is always looking for his other half."

7. *Nicomachean Ethics* VI, 12, 1143a25–b13.

8. Paul Ricoeur, *Oneself as Another*, trans. K. Blamey (Chicago: University of Chicago Press, 1992), 290.

9. Ricoeur, *Oneself as Another*, 169.

10. Ricoeur, *Oneself as Another*, 317.

11. Ricoeur, *Oneself as Another*, 291.

12. Ricoeur, *Oneself as Another*, 292.

13. Ricoeur, *Oneself as Another*, 295.

14. Ricoeur, *Oneself as Another*, 296.

15. Ricoeur, *The Course of Recognition*, x.

16. Ricoeur, *The Course of Recognition*, 17.

17. Ricoeur, *The Course of Recognition*, 21.

18. G. F. W. Hegel, *Phenomenology of Spirit*, §175.

19. Hegel, *Phenomenology of Spirit*, §177.

20. Hegel, *Phenomenology of Spirit*, §177.

21. Hegel, *Phenomenology of Spirit*, §178.

22. Ricoeur, *The Course of Recognition*, 35.

23. Ricoeur, *The Course of Recognition*, 53.

24. Ricoeur, *The Course of Recognition*, 37.

25. Ricoeur, *The Course of Recognition*, 55.

26. Ricoeur, *The Course of Recognition*, 43.

27. Ricoeur, *The Course of Recognition*, 55.

28. Ricoeur, *The Course of Recognition*, 56.

29. Ricoeur, *The Course of Recognition*, 58.

30. Ricoeur, *The Course of Recognition*, 59.

31. Ricoeur, *The Course of Recognition*, 65.

32. Ricoeur, *The Course of Recognition*, 67.

33. Paul Ricoeur, *From Text to Action: Essays in Hermeneutics, II*, trans. K. Blamey and J. Thompson (Evanston, Ill.: Northwestern University Press, 1991), 88.

34. Ricoeur, *The Course of Recognition*, 68.

35. Rémi Brague, *Aristote et la question du monde* (Paris: PUF, 1988), 13.

36. Ricoeur, *The Course of Recognition*, 73.

37. Ricoeur, *The Course of Recognition*, 77.

38. Ricoeur, *The Course of Recognition*, 77.

39. One might wonder if the title "wisdom of uncertainty," used by Kundera to describe the art of the novelist, does not equally suit Ricoeur's idea of practical

wisdom. For more on this see my study, "Paul Ricoeur: La sagesse de l'incertitude," in *Transversalité: Revue de l'Institut Catholique de Paris,* 94 (April–June 2005): 11–32.

40. Ricoeur, *The Course of Recognition*, 89.
41. Ricoeur, *Oneself as Another*, 21–23.
42. Ricoeur, *The Course of Recognition*, 94.
43. Ricoeur, *The Course of Recognition*, 109.
44. Ricoeur, *The Course of Recognition*, 110.
45. Ricoeur, *The Course of Recognition*, 110.
46. Ricoeur, *The Course of Recognition*, 151.
47. Ricoeur, *The Course of Recognition*, 140.
48. Ricoeur, *The Course of Recognition*, 150.
49. Ricoeur, *The Course of Recognition*, 152.
50. Ricoeur, *The Course of Recognition*, 156.
51. Ricoeur, *The Course of Recognition*, 161.
52. Ricoeur, *The Course of Recognition*, 257.
53. Ricoeur, *The Course of Recognition*, 24, note 31.
54. Ricoeur, *The Course of Recognition*, 181.
55. Ricoeur, *The Course of Recognition*, 187.
56. Ricoeur, *The Course of Recognition*, 191.
57. Ricoeur, *The Course of Recognition*, 192.
58. Ricoeur, *The Course of Recognition*, 194.
59. Ricoeur, *The Course of Recognition*, 196.
60. Ricoeur, *The Course of Recognition*, 278, note 25.
61. Ricoeur, *The Course of Recognition*, 200.
62. Ricoeur, *The Course of Recognition*, 200.
63. Ricoeur, *The Course of Recognition*, 210.
64. See in particular Paul Ricoeur, "L'usure de la tolérance et la résistance de l'intolérable," *Diogène* 176 (October–December 1996): 166–76; and "Tolérance, intolérance, intolerable," in *Lectures 1* (Paris: Editions du Seuil, 1991), 294–311.
65. Ricoeur, *The Course of Recognition*, 217.
66. Ricoeur, *The Course of Recognition*, 319.
67. Ricoeur, *The Course of Recognition*, 326.
68. Ricoeur, *The Course of Recognition*, 153.
69. Ricoeur, *The Course of Recognition*, 209.

Paul Ricoeur and Development Ethics
David M. Kaplan

1. Amartya Sen, *Development as Freedom* (New York: Knopf, 1999).
2. Paul Ricoeur, *The Course of Recognition*, trans. David Pellauer (Chicago: University of Chicago Press, 2005).
3. Paul Ricoeur, "Ethics and Human Capability: A Response," in *Paul Ricoeur and Contemporary Moral Thought*, ed. John Wall, William Schweiker, and W. David Hall (New York: Routledge, 2002), 280.

4. Sen, *Development as Freedom*, 75.

5. Sen, *Development as Freedom*, 75.

6. Martha Nussbaum, *Women and Human Development: The Capabilities Approach* (Cambridge: Cambridge University Press, 2001).

7. Ricoeur, *The Course of Recognition*, 143.

8. Ricoeur, *The Course of Recognition*, 12.

9. Ricoeur, *The Course of Recognition*, xi.

10. Paul Ricoeur, *The Rule of Metaphor: Multi-Disciplinary Studies in the Creation of Meaning in Language*, trans. Robert Czerny, with Kathleen McLaughlin and John Costello, S. J. (London: Routledge and Kegan Paul, 1978).

11. Paul Ricoeur, *Time and Narrative*, 3 vols., trans. Kathleen McLaughlin and David Pellauer (Chicago: University of Chicago Press, 1984, 1985, 1988).

12. Paul Ricoeur, *From Text to Action: Essays in Hermeneutics, II*, trans. Kathleen Blamey and John B. Thompson (Evanston, Ill.: Northwestern University Press, 1991), 177.

13. Ricoeur, *From Text to Action*, 177.

14. Cornelius Castoriadis, *The Imaginary Institution of Society*, trans. Kathleen Blamey (Cambridge, Mass.: MIT Press, 1998).

15. Paul Ricoeur, *Lectures on Ideology and Utopia*, ed. George Taylor (New York: Columbia University Press, 1986).

16. Nussbaum, *Women and Human Development*, 41.

17. Martha Nussbaum, *Cultivating Humanity: A Classical Defense of Reform of Liberal Education* (Cambridge, Mass.: Harvard University Press, 1998).

18. Paul Ricoeur, "Reflections on a New Ethos for Europe," *Philosophy and Social Criticism* 21, no. 5/6 (1995).

19. Ricoeur, "Reflections on a New Ethos for Europe,"12.

20. Nussbaum, *Cultivating Humanity*, 97.

21. Paul Ricoeur, *Oneself as Another*, trans. Kathleen Blamey (Chicago: University of Chicago Press, 1992), 190.

22. Paul Ricoeur, "Autonomy and Vulnerability," in *Reflections on the Just*, trans. David Pellauer (Chicago: University of Chicago Press, 2007), 73.

23. Paul Ricoeur, *Fallible Man*, trans. with an introduction by Walter J. Lowe (New York: Fordham University Press, 1986).

24. Paul Ricoeur, *Freud and Philosophy: An Essay on Interpretation*, trans. Denis Savage (New Haven: Yale University Press, 1970).

25. Ricoeur, *Reflections on the Just*, 40.

26. Paul Ricoeur, "Interview with Charles Reagan," in Charles E. Reagan, *Paul Ricoeur: His Life and His Work* (Chicago: University of Chicago Press, 1996), 113.

27. Paul Ricoeur, "The Fragility of Political Language," *Philosophy Today* 31, no. 1 (spring 1987): 35–44.

28. Ricoeur, "The Fragility of Political Language," 43.

29. For more on the connection between Ricoeur's philosophical anthropology and his political philosophy, see Bernard P. Dauenhauer, *Paul*

Ricoeur: The Promise and Risk of Politics (Lanham, Md.: Roman and Littlefield, 1998).

30. Paul Ricoeur, "Fragility and Responsibility," in *Philosophy and Social Criticism* 21, no. 5/6 (1995): 21.

Narrative Matters among the Mlabri: Interpretive Anthropology in International Development
Ellen A. Herda

Parts of this essay were drawn from a paper delivered at the Language and Nationhood Conference in Kuala Lumpur, Malaysia, May 2007.

1. See Ellen Herda, *Research Conversations and Narrative: A Critical Hermeneutic Orientation in Participatory Inquiry* (London: Praeger, 1999); Ellen Herda, "Advocacy in Development: Identity and the World of Work among the Mlabri of Northern Thailand"; Ellen Herda, "Nation Vanishing: Horizons of Social Imagery in Development," *The Applied Anthropologist* (spring 2007).

2. Hugo Bernatzik, *The Spirit of the Yellow Leaves* (London: Robert Hale, 1951); Jan J. Boeles, "Second Expedition to the Mrabri of North Thailand ('Khon Pa')," *Journal of Siam Studies* 51, no. 2 (1963): 133–60; and Surin Pookajorn et al., *The Phi Tong Luang (Mlabri): A Hunter-Gatherer Group in Thailand* (Bangkok: Silpakorn University, 1992).

3. Bernatzik, *The Spirit of the Yellow Leaves,* and Boeles, "Second Expedition to the Mrabri."

4. Erik Seidenfaden, "Further Notes about Chaubun," *Journal of Siam Studies* 13, no. 3 (1919): 47–53, and Arthur Francis George Kerr, "The Kha Tawang Luang," *Journal of the Siam Society* 18(2): 142–4.

5. H. Oota, B. Pakendorf, G. Weiss, A. von Haeseler, S. Pookajorn et al., "Recent Origin and Cultural Reversion of a Hunter–Gatherer Group," *PLoS Biol* 3(3): e71. doi:10.1371/journal.pbio.0030071 (2005).

6. Pookajorn et al., *The Phi Tong Luang (Mlabri).*

7. Additional information may be found, however, in Herda, "Power and Place: A Hermeneutic Orientation in Development and Education Among the Mlabri of Northeast Thailand," *High Plains Applied Anthropologist* 22, no.1 (2002): 101–9; Herda, "Identity and Development: Learning, Language and Policy Implications," *The Applied Anthropologist* 27, no. 1 (2007): 4–21; Anna Quirk, "Conversations of Change: Graphic, Musical, and Dialogical Texts in Malbri Life," *High Plains Applied Anthropologist* 24, no.1 (2004): 1–10.

8. Arturo Escobar, *Encountering Development: The Making and Unmaking of the Third World* (Princeton, N. J.: Princeton University Press, 1995), 22.

9. Amartya Sen, interview with Nermeen Shaikh, in Nermeen Shaikh, *The Present as History: Critical Perspectives on Global Economy* (New York: Columbia University Press, 2007), 3.

10. William Easterly, *The Elusive Quest for Growth: Economists' Adventures and Misadventures in the Tropics* (Cambridge, Mass.: MIT Press, 2001); William Easterly, *The White Man's Burden: Why the West's Efforts to Aid the Rest Have*

Done So Much Ill and So Little Good (New York: Penguin, 2006); Joseph E. Stiglitz, *Globalization and Its Discontents* (New York: Norton, 2003).

11. Bill Cooke and Uma Kothari, *Participation: The New Tyranny* (London: Zed, 2000); Uma Kothari and Martin Minogue, eds., *Development Theory and Practice: Critical Perspectives* (London: Palgrave, 2002); Ronaldo Munck and Denis O'Hearn, eds., *Critical Development Theory: Contributions to a New Paradigm* (London and New York: Zed, 1999); David Gow, "Anthropology and Development: Evil Twin or Moral Narrative?" *Human Organization* 61, no. 4 (2002): 299–313.

12. Amartya Sen and Jean Dreze, *The Amartya Sen and Jean Dreze Omnibus. India: Economic Development and Social Opportunity* (New Delhi: Oxford University Press, 1999); Mozzafar Qizilbash, "Ethical Development," *World Development* 24 (1996): 1209–21; Martha Nussbaum, *Women and Human Development: The Capabilities Approach* (Cambridge and New York: Cambridge University Press, 2000).

13. The phrase *living text* was coined by Kelly Carey, "Emerging from Isolationism: Slovenia in Conversation," *The Applied Anthropologist* 27, no. 1 (2007): 22–30.

14. Paul Ricoeur, *Oneself as Another,* trans. Kathleen Blamey (Chicago: University of Chicago Press, 1992), 180.

15. Hans-Georg Gadamer, *Truth and Method* (New York: Seabury Press, 1988).

16. Jürgen Habermas, *Communication and the Evolution of Society*, trans. Thomas McCarthy (Boston: Beacon Press, 1979), 97–98.

17. Richard Kearney, "Narrative and the Ethics of Remembrance," in *Questioning Ethics: Contemporary Debates in Philosophy*, Richard Kearney and Mark Dooley, eds. (London and New York: Routledge, 1999), 27.

18. Paul Ricoeur, *Memory, History, Forgetting*, trans. Kathleen Blamey and David Pellauer (Chicago: University of Chicago Press, 2004), 559.

19. Ricoeur, *Memory, History, Forgetting,* 559.

20. Ricoeur, *Memory, History, Forgetting*, 559.

21. Ricoeur, *Memory, History, Forgetting*, 559.

22. Paul Ricoeur, *Time and Narrative,* trans. Kathleen Blamey and David Pellauer (Chicago: University of Chicago Press, 1988), 3:249; 3:248.

23. Ricoeur, *Time and Narrative,* 3:248.

24. Ricoeur, *Time and Narrative,* 3:248.

25. Ricoeur, *Time and Narrative*, 3:249.

26. Ricoeur, *Time and Narrative*, 3:249.

27. Ricoeur, *Time and Narrative*, 3:249.

28. Ricoeur, *Time and Narrative*, 3:249.

29. Ricoeur, *Time and Narrative*, 3:249.

30. Valerie Dzubur, "Primary Healthcare in Laos: Fragility and Responsibility," *The Applied Anthropologist* (2007).

31. Ricoeur, *Oneself as Another*, 165–66.

32. Richard Kearney, *On Stories* (London and New York: Routledge, 2002), 25.

33. Ricoeur, *Oneself as Another*, 172.

34. Paul Ricoeur, *The Course of Recognition*, trans. David Pellauer (Cambridge, Mass.: Harvard University Press, 2005), 103.

The Place of Remembrance: Reflections on Paul Ricoeur's Theory of Collective Memory
Jeffrey Andrew Barash

1. Paul Ricoeur, *La mémoire, l'histoire, l'oubli* (Paris: Seuil, 2000), 1. Unless otherwise stated, all translations are my own.

2. John Locke, *An Essay on Human Understanding*, book 2, ch. 27 (London: Penguin, 1997), 302.

3. Locke, *An Essay on Human Understanding,* 302; Ricoeur, *La mémoire, l'histoire, l'oubli*, 23–131.

4. Ricoeur, *La mémoire, l'histoire, l'oubli*, 149.

5. It is perhaps Marcel Proust who best illustrates that in the final analysis, memory depends upon the attention the individual pays to an experience and upon the importance he or she accords to it. "Even when endowed with an equal capacity to remember," he writes, "two people never remember the same things. One will pay scant attention to a fact which, for another, will be a source of profound remorse." Marcel Proust, *À la recherche du temps perdu*, vol. 3, *Le temps retrouvé* (Paris: Gallimard, édition de la Pléiade, 1954), 971.

6. Edmund Husserl, *Cartesian Meditations: An Introduction to Phenomenology*, trans. Dorian Cairns (The Hague: Martinus Nijhoff, 1977), 128–29.

7. Ricoeur, *La mémoire, l'histoire, l'oubli*, 143.

8. Paul Ricoeur, *De l'interprétation: Essai sur Freud* (Paris: Seuil, 1965), 425; Paul Ricoeur, *Soi-même comme un autre* (Paris: Seuil, 1990), 22–27.

9. Ricoeur, *La mémoire, l'histoire, l'oubli*, 145.

10. "Hic vero, cum animus sit etiam ipsa memoria"; "interiore loco, non loco." St. Augustine, *Confessions*, vol. 2, bk. 10, Loeb Classical Library 27 (Cambridge, Mass.: Harvard University Press, 1988), 111, 101.

11. In this study my use of the term *phenomenology* is more directly inspired by Charles Sanders Peirce than by Husserl, above all in view of Peirce's pioneering investigation of the dynamic aspects of the symbol. I do not, any more than Peirce, take the symbol to be a historically reified, immutable essence, but understand it, in his terms, to be a "regularity of the indefinite future." C. S. Peirce, "Logic as Semiotic: The Theory of Signs," in *The Philosophy of Peirce: Selected Writings,* ed. Julius Buchler (London: Routledge, 2001), 112. It would reach beyond the scope of the present paper to deal in detail with this theme, which will be the topic of investigation in my forthcoming book entitled *What is Collective Memory?*

12. Martin Luther King Jr., "I Have a Dream," in *Autobiography* (New York: Warner Books, 1998), 226.

13. Maurice Halbwachs, *La mémoire collective* (Paris: Albin Michel, 1997), 97–142.

14. On this topic see Doron Mendels, *Memory in Jewish, Pagan and Christian Societies of the Graeco-Roman World* (London and New York : Clark International, 2004), 30–47.

15. Ricoeur, *La mémoire, l'histoire, l'oubli,* 104.

16. "Avoir été victime vous donne le droit de vous plaindre, de protester, et de réclamer." Tzvetan Todorov, *Les abus de la mémoire* (Paris: Arléa, 1995), 56.

17. "Engendre un privilège exorbitant, qui met le reste du monde en position de débiteur de créances." Ricoeur, *La mémoire, l'histoire, l'oubli,* 104.

18. Ricoeur, *La mémoire, l'histoire, l'oubli,* 104; Ricoeur, "L'écriture de l'histoire et la représentation du passé," *Le Monde,* June 15, 2000. For a critical examination of Ricoeur on this point see Rainer Rochlitz, "La mémoire privatisée," *Le Monde,* June 26, 2000, as well as Sarah Gensburger and Marie-Claude Lavabre, "Entre 'devoir de mémoire' et 'abus de mémoire': La sociologie de la mémoire collective comme tierce position," in *L'Histoire, entre mémoire et épistémologie: Autour de Paul Ricoeur,* Bertrand Müller, ed. (Dijon-Quetigny: Éditions Payot Lausanne, 2000), 75–98.

19. Ricoeur, *De l'interprétation,* 514–43.

Refiguring Virtue
Boyd Blundell

1. Charles E. Reagan, *Paul Ricoeur: His Life and His Work* (Chicago: University of Chicago Press, 1996), 91.

2. See Yvanka Raynova, "All That Gives Us to Think: Conversations with Paul Ricoeur," in *Between Suspicion and Sympathy: Paul Ricoeur's Unstable Equilibrium,* ed. Andrzej Wiercinski (Toronto: Hermeneutic Press, 2003), 671.

3. J. F. Keenan, S. J., "Proposing Cardinal Virtues," *Theological Studies* 56 (1995): 709–29.

4. Keenan, "Proposing Cardinal Virtues," 710.

5. Keenan, "Proposing Cardinal Virtues," 711.

6. Keenan, "Proposing Cardinal Virtues," 713.

7. J. F. Keenan, "Virtue and Identity," in *Creating Identity,* ed. H. Häring, M. Junker-Kenny, and D. Mieth (London: SCM Press, 2000), 73.

8. Keenan, "Virtue and Identity," 74.

9. Paul Ricoeur, "Love and Justice," in *Figuring the Sacred: Religion, Narrative, and Imagination,* trans. David Pellauer, ed. Mark Wallace (Minneapolis, Minn.: Fortress Press, 1995), 315–29.

10. Among the theological ethicists Keenan enlists are Margaret Farley, Daniel Maguire, William Werpehowski, Reinhold Niebuhr, Fred Kammer, Walter Burghardt, William Spohn, William Frankena, Tom Beauchamp, and James Childress. See Keenan, "Proposing Cardinal Virtues," 721–22, notes 54–62.

11. Keenan, "Proposing Cardinal Virtues," 723.

12. Keenan, "Virtue and Identity," 74.

13. Keenan, "Proposing Cardinal Virtues," 724.

14. Reagan, *Paul Ricoeur*, 118.

15. Ricoeur, *Critique and Conviction: Conversations with Francois Azouvi and Marc de Launay* (New York: Columbia University Press, 1998), 92.

16. Ricoeur, *Oneself as Another*, trans. K. Blamey (Chicago: University of Chicago Press, 1992), 171.

17. Ricoeur, *Oneself as Another*, 172.

18. Ricoeur, *Oneself as Another*, 176.

19. Ricoeur, *Oneself as Another*, 177.

20. Ricoeur, *Oneself as Another*, 180.

21. Ricoeur, *Oneself as Another*, 180.

22. Ricoeur, *Oneself as Another*, 182.

23. Ricoeur, *Oneself as Another*, 193.

24. Ricoeur, *Oneself as Another*, 194.

25. Ricoeur, *Oneself as Another*, 194.

26. Ricoeur, *Oneself as Another*, 202.

27. Marcel, *Being and Having*, 46.

28. Ricoeur, *Oneself as Another*, 268.

Emplotting Virtue: Narrative and the Good Life
Brian Treanor

1. Paul Ricoeur, *Oneself as Another*, trans. Kathleen Blamey (Chicago: University of Chicago Press, 1992), 169–296 (studies 7, 8, and 9).

2. After centuries of relative neglect, virtue ethics has seen something of a renaissance in the past several decades (MacIntyre, Foot, Nussbaum, etc.). In addition to theoretical developments introducing novel ways to think of virtue, virtue theory as been applied in several regions where one might not intuitively think it to be particularly useful; among these is the development of the nascent field of environmental virtue ethics (Van Wensveen, Cafaro, Sandler). However, virtue ethics continues to be beset by significant challenges, some of which are exacerbated by our contemporary, "postmodern" milieu.

3. Ronald Sandler, *Character and Environment: A Virtue-Oriented Approach to Environmental Ethics* (New York: Columbia University Press, 2007); see especially chapter 4.

4. Aristotle, *The Nicomachean Ethics*, trans. David Ross (Oxford: Oxford University Press, 1980), 31.

5. See, for example, Aristotle, *Nicomachean Ethics*, 38 and 45.

6. Aristotle, *Nicomachean Ethics*, 45.

7. Aristotle, *Nicomachean Ethics*, 3. "We must be content, then, in speaking of such subjects and with such premises to indicate the truth roughly and in outline, and in speaking about things which are only for the most part true, and with premises of the same kind, to reach conclusions that are no better" (*Nicomachean Ethics*, 3).

8. Aristotle, *Nicomachean Ethics*, 39. Emphasis mine.

9. Aristotle, *Nicomachean Ethics*, 5 and 15, respectively.

10. Aristotle, *Nicomachean Ethics*, 15–16. He also asserts the importance of having been brought up well, which certainly includes, among other things, being a free citizen of Athens (*Nicomachean Ethics*, 5).

11. Aristotle, *Nicomachean Ethics*, 142.

12. Jean-Francois Lyotard, *The Postmodern Condition: A Report on Knowledge*, trans. Geoff Bennington and Brian Massumi (Minneapolis: University of Minnesota Press, 1984), xxiv–xxv.

13. Jack Caputo, *More Radical Hermeneutics* (Bloomington and Indianapolis: Indiana University Press, 2000), 182.

14. Caputo, *More Radical Hermeneutics,* 182.

15. Caputo, *More Radical Hermeneutics,* 182.

16. Caputo, *More Radical Hermeneutics,* 1. Note, however, that one can maintain that the hermeneutic circle is inescapable while asserting that there is truth. See, among other examples, the work or Merold Westphal. In an interview with B. Keith Putt, Westphal is asked whether there "*is* a metanarrative." He responds, "Yes. There is truth with a capital 'T,' but our truth is truth with a small 't.'" For Westphal, this is because "the world *is* a system for God, but not for us" ("Talking to Balaam's Ass: A Concluding Conversation," in *Gazing Through a Prism Darkly: Reflections on Merold Westphal's Hermeneutical Epistemology*, ed. B. Keith Putt [New York: Fordham University Press, 2009]).

17. Caputo, *More Radical Hermeneutics*, 1.

18. Paul Ricoeur, *Time and Narrative*, trans. Kathleen Blamey and David Pellauer (Chicago: University of Chicago Press, 1990), 3:246. Richard Kearney, Ricoeur's student and friend, puts it this way: "Telling stories is as basic to human beings as eating. More so, in fact, for while food makes us live, stories are what make our lives worth living. They are what make our condition *human*" (Richard Kearney, *On Stories* [London: Routledge, 2002], 3). Kearney goes on to point out that stories make reality shareable—implying that they are therefore essentially ethically loaded, dealing as they do with intersubjective discourse—and that they humanize time, making it memorable on the most basic level.

19. Ricoeur, *Oneself as Another*, 2–3.

20. Ricoeur, *Time and Narrative*, 3:246.

21. Ricoeur, *Oneself as Another*, 170.

22. Ricoeur, *Oneself as Another*, 114–15.

23. Ricoeur, *Time and Narrative*, 1:55.

24. Ricoeur, *Time and Narrative*, 1:58.

25. Ricoeur, *Time and Narrative*, 1:59.

26. Ricoeur, *Time and Narrative*, 1:65–66.

27. Ricoeur, *Time and Narrative*, 1:77.

28. Ricoeur, *Time and Narrative*, 1:71.

29. Kearney, *On Stories*, 25.

30. Kearney, *On Stories*, 25–26.

31. Jeffrey Meyers, *Hemingway: A Biography* (Cambridge, Mass.: De Capo Press, 1999), 138.

32. For problems related to "the spirit of abstraction," see my "Constellations: Gabriel Marcel's Philosophy of Relative Otherness," *American Catholic Philosophical Quarterly* 80, no. 3 (2006).

33. Kearney, *On Stories*, 134.

34. Kearney, *On Stories*, 19.

35. John Updike, *Self-Consciousness: Memoirs* (New York: Fawcett, 1989).

36. Mary Oliver, "Last Night the Rain Spoke to Me," in *What Do We Know: Poems and Prose Poems* (Cambridge, Mass: Da Capo Press, 2002), 36–37. For some significant challenges to this claim, however, see Marcia Eaton, "Fact and Fiction in the Aesthetic Appreciation of Nature," in "Environmental Aesthetics," ed. A. Berleant and A. Carlson, special issue, *Journal of Aesthetics and Art Criticism* 56 (1998): 149–56.

37. Jack Turner, *The Abstract Wild* (Tucson: University of Arizona Press, 1996), 66.

38. Ricoeur, *Time and Narrative*, 1:59.

39. See, for example, Rosalind Hursthouse, *On Virtue Ethics* (Oxford: Oxford University Press, 2002); David Wong, *Moral Relativity* (Berkeley: University of California Press, 1984); Martha Nussbaum, "Non-Relative Virtues: An Aristotelian Approach," in *The Quality of Life*, Martha Nussbaum and Amartya Sen, eds. (New York: Oxford University Press, 1993), 242–69; and Alisdair MacIntyre, *Whose Justice? Which Rationality?* (Notre Dame, Ind.: University of Notre Dame Press, 1998).

40. Aristotle, *Nicomachean Ethics;* Sandler, *Character and Environment;* Hursthouse, *On Virtue Ethics*.

41. Ricoeur, *Time and Narrative*, 1:59.

42. Ricoeur, *Time and Narrative*, 1:59.

43. In this vein, see Emmanuel Levinas, *Totality and Infinity: An Essay on Exteriority*, trans. Alphonso Lingis (Pittsburgh: Duquesne University Press, 1969).

44. "Once upon a time, in some out of the way corner of that universe which is dispersed into numberless twinkling solar systems, there was a star upon which clever beasts invented knowing. That was the most arrogant and mendacious minute of 'world history,' but nevertheless it was only a minute. After nature had drawn a few breaths, the star cooled and congealed, and the clever beasts had to die" (Friedrich Nietzsche, *Philosophy and Truth: Selections from Nietzsche's Notebooks of the Early 1870s*, ed. and trans. Daniel Breazeale [Atlantic Highlands, N.J.: Humanities Press, 1979], 79).

45. A narrative approach to virtue suggests that the *meta*ethical debate about the existence of absolute truth and/or our access to it will remain an abstract and theoretical one, because no one behaves, at the end of the day, as a relativist. Thus, even those who are inclined toward nihilism or exaggerated relativism of some stripe *act* as if there are some things that are true and as if there are criteria

for determining which account (of flourishing, virtue, etc.) is better. Truth might be pluralistic—perhaps 1) because of the fact that we never have unmediated access to truth, and 2) because of epistemic fallibilism—but it is not relativistic in the strong or exaggerated sense. I often use a humorous example from the Coen brothers' movie *The Big Lebowski* to illustrate to my students the untenable nature of nihilism and exaggerated relativism. In the movie, a trio of self-proclaimed nihilists—caricatures of German postmodernists who traipse around Los Angeles insisting, "We're nihilists! We believe in nothing!"—perpetrate a kidnapping hoax. In a climactic confrontation with the movie's protagonist, the "Dude," and his friends Walter and Donny, the nihilists demand payment. At one point, Walter screams, "There's no ransom if you don't have a f—king hostage! That's what ransom is. Those are the f—king rules!" To which the disappointed nihilists ultimately whine, "It's not fair!" Walter, justifiably indignant, shouts, "Fair?! Who's the f—king nihilist here?" The point, with apologies for the language, is that no one maintains his or her nihilism (or relativism) in the face of perceived injustice. Nihilism and relativism may be intellectual temptations, but they are not lived ethical standpoints.

46. Augustine, *Confessions*, trans. Henry Chadwick (Oxford: Oxford University Press, 1991), 139.

47. Ricoeur, *Time and Narrative*, 1:59.

48. Richard Kearney, *Paul Ricoeur: The Owl of Minerva* (London: Ashgate, 2004), 114.

49. Kearney, *Paul Ricoeur*, 114. See also Ricoeur's excellent "Life in Quest of Narrative," in *On Paul Ricoeur: Narrative and Interpretation,* ed. David Wood (London: Routledge, 1994).

50. See, for example, "The American Scholar," in *Ralph Waldo Emerson: Essays and Lectures* (New York: Library of America, 1983), 57.

51. See note 7 above. This is not an excuse for a lack of rigor, but an acknowledgment of the limitations of the subject matter.

52. I'm aware of the irony here, given that Ulysses did not in fact succeed in passing safely between the proverbial rock and the hard place; he lost six men to Scylla rather than risking all to Charybdis. This is, perhaps, an apt image, for avoiding both absolutism and relativism is no easy task. It is rather, a "ferocious tension," to use Merold Westphal's phrase. See James L. Marsh, John D. Caputo, and Merold Westphal, eds., *Modernity and Its Discontents* (New York: Fordham University Press, 1992), 160.

53. My colleague Dr. Brad Stone brought this pithy witticism to my attention. This assertion is no doubt the origin of the claim made by Arturo Pérez-Reverte's Diego Alatriste, fictional countryman of Unamuno, that one should "never trust a man who reads only one book."

Preserving the Eidetic Moment: Reflections on the Work of Paul Ricoeur
David Rasmussen

1. Concluding chapter in David Rasmussen, *Mythic-Symbolic Language and Philosophical Anthropology: A Constructive Interpretation of the Thought of Paul Ricoeur* (The Hague: Martinus Nijhoff, 1971).

2. Friedrich Nietzsche, *The Birth of Tragedy* (New York: Vintage Books, 1967), 52.

3. Paul Ricoeur, *Memory, History, Forgetting*, trans. Kathleen Blamey and David Pellauer (Chicago: University of Chicago Press, 2004), 3.

4. David Rasmussen, "Foreword to the New Edition," in *History and Truth*, by Paul Ricoeur, trans. Charles A. Kelbley (Evanston, Ill.: Northwestern University Press, 2006).

5. See my "Rethinking Subjectivity: Narrative Identity and the Self," *Philosophy and Social Criticism* 21, no. 5/6 (1995): 159–72. My essay reappeared in the book *Ricoeur as Another: The Ethics of Subjectivity*, ed. Richard Cohen and James Marsh (Albany: SUNY Press, 1998), 57–69.

6. See my "Justice and Interpretation," in *Between Suspicion and Sympathy: Paul Ricoeur's Unstable Equilibrium*, ed. Andrzej Wiercinski (Toronto: Hermeneutic Press, 2003), 531–38, and my "Justice, Interpretation and the Cosmopolitan Idea," *Distincktion: Scandinavian Journal of Social Theory*, no. 8 (2004): 37–45.

Contributors

Jeffrey Andrew Barash is Professor of Philosophy at the University of Amiens, France. His publications have focused on the themes of political philosophy, historicism, and modern German thought, and he is the author of three books: *Heidegger et son siècle. Temps de l'Être, temps de l'histoire* (Paris: Presses Universitaires de France, 1995), *Martin Heidegger and the Problem of Historical Meaning* (second, paperback edition, New York: Fordham University Press, 2003), and *Politiques de l'histoire. L'historicisme comme promesse et comme mythe* (Paris: Presses Universitaires de France, 2004). He has also recently edited *The Social Construction of Reality: The Legacy of Ernst Cassirer* (Chicago: University of Chicago Press, 2008). He is currently completing a book entitled *What Is a Political Myth?* and is also preparing a work on the theme of collective memory.

Boyd Blundell is Assistant Professor of Philosophical and Theological Ethics at Loyola University New Orleans. He is the author of several articles and the translator of papers by Paul Ricoeur, Jean Greisch, and Olivier Abel. Dr. Blundell has made numerous presentations in the United States, Canada, England, Poland, and Belgium. His book *Paul Ricoeur Between Philosophy and Theology* is forthcoming with Indiana University Press in 2010.

Gaëlle Fiasse is Associate Professor at McGill University. In terms of the history of philosophy and ethics, Professor Fiasse is a specialist in Aristotle and Paul Ricoeur. She is one of the Canadian correspondents in Canada for the Fonds Ricoeur in Paris and the author of *L'autre et l'amitié chez Aristote et Paul Ricoeur. Analyses éthiques et ontologiques* (Louvain: Peeters, 2006) and *Paul Ricœur. De* *l'homme faillible à l'homme capable* (Paris: Presses Universitaires de France, 2008) (a collective book). Her current research focuses on Fragility.

Jean Greisch, the former Dean of the Faculty of Philosophy of the Institut Catholique in Paris and a member of the Institut International de Philosophy, is currently teaching as the Romano Guardini-Chair at the Humboldt-Universität zu Berlin (Germany). His numerous publications include *Entendre d'une autre oreille. Les enjeux philosophiques de l'herméneutique biblique* (Paris: Ed. Bayard, 2006), *Qui sommes-nous? Chemins phénoménologiques vers l'homme* (Leuven: Peeters, 2009), and *Fehlbarkeit und Fähigkeit. Paul Ricoeurs philosophische Anthropologie* (Münster: LIT, 2009).

Ellen A. Herda, Professor of Anthropology, School of Education, University of San Francisco, teaches anthropology research, socioeconomic development, and policy analysis. Her publications on critical hermeneutic research reflect her own field work and project development in the areas of youth and adult education, community leadership, organic agriculture, and technology in Burma, Thailand, and Laos. Her book *Research Conversations and Narrative: A Critical Hermeneutic Orientation in Participatory Inquiry* was the first published work to serve as a guide to social science field researchers whose academic interests and personal praxes follow the interpretive tradition.

David M. Kaplan is Assistant Professor of Philosophy in the Department of Philosophy and Religion Studies at the University of North Texas. He is author of *Ricoeur's Critical Theory* (Albany: SUNY Press, 2003), editor of *Reading Ricoeur* (Albany: SUNY Press, 2008), and author of several articles on the hermeneutic and social-political theories of Paul Ricoeur. He also publishes in philosophy of technology, and food ethics/philosophy of food.

Richard Kearney holds the Charles H. Seelig Chair of Philosophy at Boston College and is visiting professor at University College Dublin. He is the author of two novels and a volume of poetry, and his most recent philosophical works include the "Philosophy at the Limits" trilogy: *Strangers, Gods, and Monsters: Ideas of Otherness*, *The God Who May Be: A Hermeneutics of Religion*, and *On Stories: Thinking in Action.*

David Pellauer is professor of Philosophy at DePaul University. He is the author of *Ricoeur: A Guide for the Perplexed* (London: Continuum, 2007) and has translated or co-translated many of Ricoeur's books and essays into English.

David Rasmussen is Professor of Philosophy at Boston College. He is the author of numerous books and articles, including *Mythic Symbolic Language and Philosophical Anthropology: A Constructive Interpretation of the Work of Paul Ricoeur*

(Leiden: Martinus Nijhoff, 1971) and *Symbol and Interpretation* (Leiden: Martinus Nijhoff, 1973). He is also the founding editor of the journals *Cultural Hermeneutics* and *Philosophy and Social Criticism,* on whose editorial boards Paul Ricoeur served.

Paul Ricoeur, who passed away in May 2005, was one of the most distinguished philosophers of his generation. During his long career he taught at the University of Strasbourg, the Sorbonne, University of Paris at Nanterre (Paris X), Louvain, and the University of Chicago. He was the recipient of many prestigious awards and honors, including giving the Gifford Lectures in 1986 and receiving the John W. Kluge Prize in the Human Sciences in 2004 (co-recipient with Jaroslav Pelikan). He worked on a wide range of issues, including identity, narrative, time, memory, ethics, and politics, and in the process engaged a remarkably diverse set of traditions, including phenomenology, structuralism, psychoanalysis, and analytic philosophy. Some of his major works include *Freedom and Nature, Freud and Philosophy, The Conflict of Interpretations, Time and Narrative* (three volumes), *Oneself as Another, Memory, History, Forgetting,* and *The Just.*

Brian Treanor is Associate Professor of Philosophy at Loyola Marymount University in Los Angeles. He has published widely in the areas of ethics, philosophy of religion, and environmental philosophy. His current work focuses on the role played by narrative in the cultivation of virtue. He is the author of *Aspects of Alterity: Levinas, Marcel, and the Contemporary Debate* (New York: Fordham University Press, 2006).

Henry Isaac Venema is Associate Professor of Philosophy at Brandon University, Brandon, Manitoba, Canada. He is the author of *Identifying Selfhood: Imagination, Narrative, and Hermeneutics in the Thought of Paul Ricoeur* (Albany: SUNY Press, 2000) and is co-editor and contributor to *The Hermeneutics of Charity: Interpretation, Selfhood, and Postmodern Faith* (Ada, Mich.: Brazos Press, 2004). His current areas of research are philosophy of religion, religion and violence, hermeneutics, and identity theory.

Index of Names

Perspectives in Continental Philosophy
John D. Caputo, series editor

John D. Caputo, ed., *Deconstruction in a Nutshell: A Conversation with Jacques Derrida.*

Michael Strawser, *Both/And: Reading Kierkegaard—From Irony to Edification.*

Michael D. Barber, *Ethical Hermeneutics: Rationality in Enrique Dussel's Philosophy of Liberation.*

James H. Olthuis, ed., *Knowing* Other-*wise: Philosophy at the Threshold of Spirituality.*

James Swindal, *Reflection Revisited: Jürgen Habermas's Discursive Theory of Truth.*

Richard Kearney, *Poetics of Imagining: Modern and Postmodern.* Second edition.

Thomas W. Busch, *Circulating Being: From Embodiment to Incorporation—Essays on Late Existentialism.*

Edith Wyschogrod, *Emmanuel Levinas: The Problem of Ethical Metaphysics.* Second edition.

Francis J. Ambrosio, ed., *The Question of Christian Philosophy Today.*

Jeffrey Bloechl, ed., *The Face of the Other and the Trace of God: Essays on the Philosophy of Emmanuel Levinas.*

Ilse N. Bulhof and Laurens ten Kate, eds., *Flight of the Gods: Philosophical Perspectives on Negative Theology.*

Trish Glazebrook, *Heidegger's Philosophy of Science.*

Kevin Hart, *The Trespass of the Sign: Deconstruction, Theology, and Philosophy.*

Mark C. Taylor, *Journeys to Selfhood: Hegel and Kierkegaard.* Second edition.

Dominique Janicaud, Jean-François Courtine, Jean-Louis Chrétien, Michel Henry, Jean-Luc Marion, and Paul Ricœur, *Phenomenology and the "Theological Turn": The French Debate.*

Karl Jaspers, *The Question of German Guilt.* Introduction by Joseph W. Koterski, S.J.

Jean-Luc Marion, *The Idol and Distance: Five Studies.* Translated with an introduction by Thomas A. Carlson.

Jeffrey Dudiak, *The Intrigue of Ethics: A Reading of the Idea of Discourse in the Thought of Emmanuel Levinas.*

Robyn Horner, *Rethinking God as Gift: Marion, Derrida, and the Limits of Phenomenology.*

Mark Dooley, *The Politics of Exodus: Søren Keirkegaard's Ethics of Responsibility.*

Merold Westphal, *Overcoming Onto-Theology: Toward a Postmodern Christian Faith.*

Edith Wyschogrod, Jean-Joseph Goux, and Eric Boynton, eds., *The Enigma of Gift and Sacrifice.*

Stanislas Breton, *The Word and the Cross.* Translated with an introduction by Jacquelyn Porter.

Jean-Luc Marion, *Prolegomena to Charity.* Translated by Stephen E. Lewis.

Peter H. Spader, *Scheler's Ethical Personalism: Its Logic, Development, and Promise.*

Jean-Louis Chrétien, *The Unforgettable and the Unhoped For.* Translated by Jeffrey Bloechl.

Don Cupitt, *Is Nothing Sacred? The Non-Realist Philosophy of Religion: Selected Essays.*

Jean-Luc Marion, *In Excess: Studies of Saturated Phenomena.* Translated by Robyn Horner and Vincent Berraud.

Phillip Goodchild, *Rethinking Philosophy of Religion: Approaches from Continental Philosophy.*

William J. Richardson, S.J., *Heidegger: Through Phenomenology to Thought.*

Jeffrey Andrew Barash, *Martin Heidegger and the Problem of Historical Meaning.*

Jean-Louis Chrétien, *Hand to Hand: Listening to the Work of Art.* Translated by Stephen E. Lewis.

Jean-Louis Chrétien, *The Call and the Response.* Translated with an introduction by Anne Davenport.

D. C. Schindler, *Han Urs von Balthasar and the Dramatic Structure of Truth: A Philosophical Investigation.*

Julian Wolfreys, ed., *Thinking Difference: Critics in Conversation.*

Allen Scult, *Being Jewish/Reading Heidegger: An Ontological Encounter.*

Richard Kearney, *Debates in Continental Philosophy: Conversations with Contemporary Thinkers.*

Jennifer Anna Gosetti-Ferencei, *Heidegger, Hölderlin, and the Subject of Poetic Language: Towards a New Poetics of Dasein.*

Jolita Pons, *Stealing a Gift: Kirkegaard's Pseudonyms and the Bible.*

Jean-Yves Lacoste, *Experience and the Absolute: Disputed Questions on the Humanity of Man.* Translated by Mark Raftery-Skehan.

Charles P. Bigger, *Between* Chora *and the Good: Metaphor's Metaphysical Neighborhood.*

Dominique Janicaud, *Phenomenology "Wide Open": After the French Debate.* Translated by Charles N. Cabral.

Ian Leask and Eoin Cassidy, eds., *Givenness and God: Questions of Jean-Luc Marion.*

Jacques Derrida, *Sovereignties in Question: The Poetics of Paul Celan.* Edited by Thomas Dutoit and Outi Pasanen.

William Desmond, *Is There a Sabbath for Thought? Between Religion and Philosophy.*

Bruce Ellis Benson and Norman Wirzba, eds., *The Phenomoenology of Prayer.*

S. Clark Buckner and Matthew Statler, eds., *Styles of Piety: Practicing Philosophy after the Death of God.*

Kevin Hart and Barbara Wall, eds., *The Experience of God: A Postmodern Response.*

John Panteleimon Manoussakis, *After God: Richard Kearney and the Religious Turn in Continental Philosophy.*

John Martis, *Philippe Lacoue-Labarthe: Representation and the Loss of the Subject.*

Jean-Luc Nancy, *The Ground of the Image.*

Edith Wyschogrod, *Crossover Queries: Dwelling with Negatives, Embodying Philosophy's Others.*

Gerald Bruns, *On the Anarchy of Poetry and Philosophy: A Guide for the Unruly.*

Brian Treanor, *Aspects of Alterity: Levinas, Marcel, and the Contemporary Debate.*

Simon Morgan Wortham, *Counter-Institutions: Jacques Derrida and the Question of the University.*

Leonard Lawlor, *The Implications of Immanence: Toward a New Concept of Life.*

Clayton Crockett, *Interstices of the Sublime: Theology and Psychoanalytic Theory.*

Bettina Bergo, Joseph Cohen, and Raphael Zagury-Orly, eds., *Judeities: Questions for Jacques Derrida.* Translated by Bettina Bergo and Michael B. Smith.

Jean-Luc Marion, *On the Ego and on God: Further Cartesian Questions.* Translated by Christina M. Gschwandtner.

Jean-Luc Nancy, *Philosophical Chronicles.* Translated by Franson Manjali.

Jean-Luc Nancy, *Dis-Enclosure: The Deconstruction of Christianity.* Translated by Bettina Bergo, Gabriel Malenfant, and Michael B. Smith.

Andrea Hurst, *Derrida Vis-à-vis Lacan: Interweaving Deconstruction and Psychoanalysis.*

Jean-Luc Nancy, *Noli me tangere: On the Raising of the Body.* Translated by Sarah Clift, Pascale-Anne Brault, and Michael Naas.

Jacques Derrida, *The Animal That Therefore I Am.* Edited by Marie-Louise Mallet, translated by David Wills.

Jean-Luc Marion, *The Visible and the Revealed.* Translated by Christina M. Gschwandtner and others.

Michel Henry, *Material Phenomenology.* Translated by Scott Davidson.

Jean-Luc Nancy, *Corpus.* Translated by Richard A. Rand.

Joshua Kates, *Fielding Derrida.*

Michael Naas, *Derrida From Now On.*

Shannon Sullivan and Dennis J. Schmidt, eds., *Difficulties of Ethical Life.*

Catherine Malabou, *What Should We Do with Our Brain?* Translated by Sebastian Rand, Introduction by Marc Jeannerod.

Claude Romano, *Event and World.* Translated by Shane Mackinlay.

Vanessa Lemm, *Nietzsche's Animal Philosophy: Culture, Politics, and the Animality of the Human Being.*

B. Keith Putt, ed., *Gazing Through a Prism Darkly: Reflections on Merold Westphal's Hermeneutical Epistemology.*

Eric Boynton and Martin Kavka, eds., *Saintly Influence: Edith Wyschogrod and the Possibilities of Philosophy of Religion.*

Shane Mackinlay, *Interpreting Excess: Jean-Luc Marion, Saturated Phenomena, and Hermeneutics.*

Kevin Hart and Michael A. Signer, eds., *The Exorbitant: Emmanuel Levinas Between Jews and Christians.*

Bruce Ellis Benson and Norman Wirzba, eds., *Words of Life: New Theological Turns in French Phenomenology.*

William Robert, *Trials: Of Antigone and Jesus.*